VIRAGO
MODERN CLASSICS
522

Madeleine Masson

Madeleine Masson was born in Johannesburg, South Africa. She studied History and Philosophy at the Sorbonne, Paris and gained a Ph.D. in Philosophy before going on to study Art and Humanities in Munich. She has published twenty-seven books and plays, both fiction and non-fiction, including *Edwina*, *Birds of Passage* and *I Never Kissed Paris Goodbye*. As a journalist, Madeleine has worked on the *Rand Daily Mail*, the *Cape Times* and as a freelance journalist in Paris. She has one married son, two grandsons, and lives in Bosham, West Sussex.

CHRISTINE
SOE agent and
Churchill's favourite spy

MADELEINE MASSON

With an Afterword by
FRANCIS CAMMAERTS
DSO, Légion d'Honneur, Croix de Guerre,
US Medal of Freedom

Virago

VIRAGO

First published in Great Britain in 1975 by Hamish Hamilton Ltd
This paperback edition published in October 2005 by Virago Press

Copyright © Madeleine Masson, 1975, 2005

The moral right of the author has been asserted.

A CIP catalogue record for this book
is available from the British Library

ISBN 1 84408 238 5

Typeset in Caslon by M Rules
Printed and bound in Great Britain
by Clays Ltd, St Ives plc

Virago Press
An imprint of
Time Warner Book Group UK
Brettenham House
Lancaster Place
London WC2E 7EN

www.virago.co.uk

For my family

'Poland, poor land, singing and weeping, my heart belongs with you.'

FREDERIC CHOPIN

'History is an argument without end.'

PETER GEYL

'There are only two aspects of war (or any other event) worth writing about: the war as it actually is before your eyes, and the actions and mental behaviour of the men controlling it.'

ALAN MOOREHEAD – *A Late Education*

CONTENTS

Introduction by the Author   ix

PART I: CHRISTINE IN THE SUNLIGHT

Chapter One   3
Chapter Two   17
Chapter Three   34
Chapter Four   73
Chapter Five   97
Chapter Six   120
Chapter Seven   147

PART II: CHRISTINE AND THE ARMY OF SHADOWS

Chapter Eight   171
Chapter Nine   196
Chapter Ten   219
Chapter Eleven   242

Author's Afterword   261
Afterword by Francis Cammaerts   276
Acknowledgements   280
Acknowledgements for the Author's Afterword   282
Notes   283
Bibliography   302
Index   306

INTRODUCTION

As the *Winchester Castle* steamed away from Capetown I had a presentiment that it would be a long time before I returned home. Yet the reason for my journey was a happy one. I was going to join the man I loved in England, and so deep was my joy at the thought of the coming reunion that it may well have blunted my faculties of observation and my powers of perception.

As a writer I am always on the search for material, and being of a curious disposition, I am interested in the actions and reactions of those about me. The human condition matters to me and if I have sometimes become involved in the lives of others it is simply because I believe that I *am* my brother's keeper.

On this particular afternoon in late May, 1952, my antennae were not working. For once I was not a spectator. I was the chief protagonist in the film of my life and this is why, cocooned in my emotional chrysalis, I was able to remain uninvolved in problems and emotions that were stronger, and certainly more important than mine.

As the liner steamed further from Capetown the tablecloth came down over Table Mountain. The distant city seemed to shrink back into a likeness of a watercolour of the tiny settlement – the Tavern of the Ocean, whose flat roofs and colour-washed houses and hospitable burghers had welcomed mariners for so many centuries.

I stood at the rail saying adieu to my thatched house perched high on the side of the rounded, herb-scented mountain; to the blue and tender circle of the bay, to the wood pigeons cooing among the oak trees planted by the early settlers, to my friends and familiar habits.

There had been many partings in my life. Leaving Paris the day the Germans arrived; saying goodbye to my brother, a beardless, round-faced little *Chasseur Alpin* who conceived it his duty to remain in occupied France until he could join General de Gaulle's forces while I made my way to the Spanish border to try and get back to South Africa. But this last farewell to my native land was terrible. It was the final sundering of the umbilical cord, for somewhere, back in the hinterland, my mother lay in the red earth, under the hot bright sun.

I went down to my cabin and began unpacking my suitcases. My main concern was the stowing of my writing materials and favourite books. I liked to have Pascal's *Pensées*, Rimbaud's poems and the Bible within reach of my hand. I had just taken out these books when there was a knock and my stewardess came in. I looked up and was aware immediately, though fleetingly, of some vital magnetic force emanating from the slender woman in her neat uniform. She offered me her services in a rather breathless, heavily accented voice. Wrapped in my homesickness, I said I needed no assistance and would ring for her later. When she went, I continued to unpack, but there was something about her which made me anxious to see her again. Even though the vibrations between us were faint and our communications poor, I was certain that this was no ordinary stewardess, and that the proud face, sad eyes and fine hands were those of a woman of character and breeding, with a past which on any other occasion but this would have presented me with the same kind of challenge that a safe offers to a crack burglar.

My stewardess was polite, efficient and distant. I used to lie in my bunk and watch her bringing in my tray and setting it down, and as she tidied the cabin, I marvelled at the grace and fluidity of her movements. I thought perhaps she was an ex-ballerina assoluta who had fallen on evil times. She did not invite questions and made certain that we talked only of the banal events of life at sea. Once or twice I noticed a great radiance in her; with her deep suntan she was glowing and golden; but at other times she looked tired, a slim, not-so-young woman with a shiny nose.

Only once did I see her laugh. This was when I told her the story of the horrified reactions of my four-year-old niece to the huge, robot-like walkie-talkie doll I had bought for her at Madeira. Then her face flashed into animation, her eyes sparkled and she looked young, vulnerable and beautiful. No warning bell rang in my mind to tell me that twenty years later, waking and sleeping, I should try to recall every word, every intonation and every gesture of this woman.

During the voyage I asked the captain about my stewardess's identity. He was guarded and non-committal, and when I told him my theories about her, he smiled and said that the writers he carried in his ships invariably tried to invest the most ordinary characters with interesting and romantic histories. 'It must be something to do with shipboard life,' he said, 'it produces a kind of euphoria. One writer . . .', and he went off into a long anecdote about a well-known novelist who, while travelling in this very ship, had had delusions about a member of the crew being a wanted criminal.

We landed at Southampton on a wet and windy day, but nothing could dampen my high-flying spirits. I went down to my cabin to lock my cases and tip my stewardess. I wanted to thank her for having looked after me so well. I rang the bell; but a gaunt, unknown woman answered my summons. 'Your stewardess is poorly,' she said, 'anything I can do?' I was disappointed. I wrote a little note of thanks and enclosed my tip in an envelope. 'What,' I asked the Purser, 'is the full name of my stewardess?' He checked down a list. 'You had Christine, full name Mrs Christine Granville.'

The ship docked on 13 June 1952. A few days later I was lying in bed, happy, relaxed and reading my morning paper, when I was shocked to read a small news-item which stated tersely that a Mrs Christine Granville, stewardess aboard a Union-Castle Mail ship, had been murdered in a London hotel

on the night of 15 June, by a kitchen porter from the Reform
Club. I was saddened by the sordid implications of the death of
my mysterious stewardess; but I was too busy arranging my
new life to give her shade more than a passing *vale*.

The following day, however, the humble news-item had
exploded into headlines. My stewardess was indeed no ordinary
woman. Born into a noble Polish family, she had been a British
secret agent in Poland, Hungary and France during the Second
World War. She was a heroine of the French Resistance, and for
her work in the field she had been awarded the George Medal,
the OBE and the Croix de Guerre with Silver star.

The newspapers were full of sensational stories of Christine
Granville's legendary exploits and bravery. I was angry with
myself at having missed the opportunity of getting first-hand
information to write a long-delayed book on the anatomy of
courage. I blamed myself for not having tried harder to get
through the barrier of reticence with which Christine Granville
protected herself from importunate questions. I thought a great
deal about Christine with her grace, her golden skin and her
shiny nose.

Then I married my sea-captain and we went away for our
honeymoon and everything else was temporarily forgotten. But
in the following years Christine was never far from my
thoughts, particularly when I returned to France, and saw those
of my friends and relations who had survived the German occupation and the concentration camps. Finally, during an illness,
I was nourished mainly on books about the Resistance and the
exploits of those who had worked for SOE, and I became
obsessed by the idea of writing a book about Christine
Granville, a book which should be a memorial to her and to
the small army of brave nameless women who had died for
freedom.

When I walked out of my flat in the Rue Jacob in Paris on 14
June 1940, as the Germans entered the city, I was ill-equipped
for an odyssey that lasted for four years, and which finally

brought me back to the place which for twenty-five years had been the core and centre of my intellectual being.

The day after I got back to Paris I began trying to contact my friends and relations. I knew that in the monstrous reshuffle of human beings that the German occupation had imposed on the French, many of my friends and colleagues had, as I had, gone abroad or gone to ground in the country. I could not believe that my circle had disintegrated forever.

Of a total of perhaps fifty people, many of whom were not Jewish and had no Jewish connections, sixty per cent had vanished. After a series of unsatisfactory, even sinister, telephone calls to the apartments of my friends, I made a house-to-house search all over Paris, knocking on familiar doors and ringing well-known bells.

Some of the concierges I had known in the past had gone, but those who remained told me stories of nocturnal knocks, of cries, scuffles and of my friends coming down the stairs, followed by their captors, looking, as one concierge put it, 'like sleepwalkers who had been brutally awoken'. Wherever I went it was the same shattering experience. I would knock at the door, wait expectantly and then it would open to frame an unknown who was either apologetic, frightened or downright rude.

It took me some time to complete my investigations. I found that all my Jewish relations, with the exception of one cousin, had been destroyed in the gas chambers of the death camps. My literary agent had perished in Ravensbruck. Three of the husbands of my closest friends were dead. One in the Maquis had died at the hands of the Germans; another, also a maquisard, had died of gangrene contracted from a piece of shrapnel from a hand-grenade. The third, an artist with a brilliant future, had succumbed from injuries inflicted on him during a series of interrogations by the SS.

Of a large number of 'café' acquaintances whom I had known over the years and among whom were poets, writers, journalists and actors, only a few had collaborated with the enemy, and these in the main belonged to the more decadent section of international society. I felt like a phantom walking in a ghost city, for wherever I went there were reminders of the pre-war days. The few of our group who were left huddled together in the Deux-Magots as unchanged as the church of St Germain-des-Prés opposite. Things had survived. Not people. Our usual toast was to 'absent friends'. We could not believe that we should never see them again. Finally, I could bear it no longer and, riddled with guilt at having been a survivor, I returned to my family in South Africa.

Years later when I began my researches into the life of Christine Granville and was warned off, I became obstinately determined to write this biography. The fact that I was told that a number of people were already engaged on a similar task failed to deter me. In fact it spurred me on and I pushed everything else aside and concentrated on getting my facts together.

I began by writing to Maurice Buckmaster, former head of Special Operations Executive's French Section, and a friend of Odette Hallowes, GC, who had introduced him to me, also to a member of his staff, the serene and intelligent Vera Atkins, without whose help anyone trying to write about people and events in this particular Section of SOE would undoubtedly fail.

Through my friend the distinguished writer Selwyn Jepson – Major Jepson who had been seconded from the Directorate of Military Intelligence to SOE (French Section) – and Professor M. R. D. Foot, whose excellent book on SOE in France must be the textbook of anyone trying to understand the work and protean ramifications of the Special Operations Executive, I was given much valuable information as well as a list of the names of some of the men and women who had known Christine in the field, and who had remained in contact with her after the war.

Searching out these people was a major task which I gladly undertook for I was determined to write as accurate a book as possible about a woman whose name had to be rescued from oblivion. Then began a strange series of coincidences which continued throughout the writing of this book. Strangers phoned me and encouraged me to persevere, my wanderings in the stacks of the London Library led me to a number of books which provided me with valuable clues. Fortuitously I met people who, it turned out, had known both Christine and Andrew Kennedy. A number of my friends had seemingly worked for SOE; but, since we had met long after the war, this part of their lives had never figured in our social conversations.

By this time I was immersed in reading everything I could about SOE. This was natural, not only because Christine's later activities had been directed by them from London and Algiers; but also because most of my information about her war years and work came from the people who had, in some way, been connected with the organization, which had recruited women of the calibre of Diana Rowden, Violette Szabo, Noor Inyat Khan, Odette Hallowes, Yolande Beekman and Eliane Plewman, all attractive gentlewomen whose only common denominator was their impeccable French and their desire to serve in the cause of freedom.

One of the strongest impressions I gained from listening to the talk of Christine's friends was that she hated any form of oppression, not only for patriotic reasons, but because she translated her own craving for freedom of thought and action into every human sphere. Anything that threatened her liberty or that of anyone else became a personal issue.

During the time I was writing to some of the people who had known Christine when she was working for SOE it struck me, as I addressed envelopes to distinguished generals and politicians, as well as a number of HM's ambassadors in far-away places, that the majority of men who had known Christine Granville well and who admired and respected her were themselves remarkable people who had made, or were still making, a valuable contribution to the welfare of their country. All these were picked to serve by SOE, and, though some bitter statements have been made about the Special Operations Executive, the fact remains that, almost without exception, the men they chose and trained made a success of their wartime work and of their future lives. There was nothing shoddy or second-rate about the people who cared for Christine.

But not all my letters were answered. I followed many false trails and suffered many setbacks and disappointments when my envelopes were returned with 'Gone Away' or 'Unknown' scrawled across them.

Everyone has his own image and interpretation of a famous personage, be they historical or contemporary, and this image, whether true or false, is the only one that a writer of integrity can put forward. Even those most closely involved with the personality about which they are writing can present only their own findings, their own conclusions and their own truth. A truth which must of necessity be coloured by their own experience and judgement; and a biographer must present his hero or heroine in the round with or without warts depending on his nature and capacity for hero-worship, white-washing or critical analysis.

Many have come forward with their interpretations of Christine Granville's character and motivations. There are those like myself who knew her fleetingly; those who came in contact with her in the line of duty; those who worked with her and became her friends. Those who knew her well and loved her. Each of these people cherishes the memory of the Christine he knew; but I believe that the truth about Christine lies not in the memories of her friends, but in her actions and in the total sacrifice she was prepared to make of her life.

To write this biography accurately it was necessary to place my subject against the background and events of her time. Because Christine was active in so many theatres of war this meant acquiring a detailed knowledge of the sequence and of some of the intricacies of the Second World War, which might have had some reaction or interaction on Christine's work and movements. Fortunately the Second World War is almost as well documented as the Napoleonic era. In the past decade the floodgates have opened and the presses and popular media pour out a constant flow of documentation on every aspect of those devastating years. In this great mass of literature and pictures, in all the accounts of betrayal, death, resistance, destruction and survival it has been an uneasy task to sift through memoirs and reminiscences. Nearly all those I met in my search for Christine had a different interpretation of the political climate and motivations of the time she and they had lived through together. It was obvious that one would have to take into account the national characteristics and partisan qualities of many of the writers on the war. Many post-war politics and policies had their roots in the Resistance, in the men of the Maquis planted there by their leaders; by those same men who have since walked the corridors of power in London, Paris, Washington, Berlin and Moscow. To some of these men power was more important than patriotism, and in some cases the reshaping of the world of tomorrow was the motivating force behind their actions; but to others, to men and women like Christine Granville who were prepared to die in the field, only freedom, and the dignity of man were important.

To most of the men who had worked with Christine she has become a symbol of their lost and shining youth; of a dashing and idealized era of their lives when the thought of capture, torture and the horrors of rotting in a concentration camp lay just below the surface of the day-to-day sharing of laughter, effort, fear and companionship. In that golden, adventurous age only the now was important. Past and future had no substance, and the emotions of these young men and women, unencumbered by the weighty baggage of the past, were stripped down to the bone.

Another factor I had to take into consideration when trying to decipher the bits of the puzzle of Christine's life was the fact that twenty years had passed since her death. She had died young; but those who had known her then had continued on into middle age and beyond. She had known them and reacted to them when they were young and at the peak of their powers. Their memories of Christine were hazed and embellished by the bright colours of time remembered – in the Proustian sense of nostalgia and what the Portuguese call *saudade*.

Christine had made friends in many spheres but her friends, like her life, were compartmented and she never committed the error of mixing them together. Nor did she ever talk of her own mysterious activities. She was a very private person. Vivid and animated when she was amused, she made a point of 'switching off' when she was bored, and she was easily bored. Yet meeting her was, for many people, an unforgettable experience and the men who had worked in the field with her found it difficult to talk about her courage, dedication and total abnegation of self without emotion; and these were her comrades and not the men whose lives she had saved or the men who had loved her. She had so strong, so magnetic a personality that it has transcended time and obscurity.

While it was comparatively simple to talk with men and women who had known Christine in her adult life during and after the war, it was far more complicated to find contemporaries who had known her in childhood and adolescence. Happily for me there is a large Polish community in England, many of whom have long memories and important connections.

Through the kind offices of Admiral Josef Bartosik, who acted as a liaison officer, I was put in touch with a member of the Skarbek family, Doctor Andrew Skarbek, the present head of the family. He was very helpful and gave me a number of important clues. I then met his brother John who worked hard to produce for me a brief memoir on the history of his distinguished family, as well as a reproduction of the family crest and a number of interesting photographs.

One of my most rewarding interviews was with one of Christine's first cousins; Mr Stanley Christopher was good enough to devote many hours to helping me. This courteous elderly gentleman has a prodigious memory and almost total recall, so that most of the facts he told me about Christine's background, parents, childhood and early adolescence are as authentic as human memory can make them.

Stanley Christopher had been a guest at Christine's first wedding. He said, 'It was a religious marriage held in Warsaw. There were not many people present. Christine looked very elegant in her white gown. She was a tall, slim girl, about five foot eight, I should say. Her husband was considerably shorter. The wedding luncheon took place in the private room of a leading hotel, I think it was the Bristol. Afterwards the young couple went off to Zakopane on their honeymoon.'

Yet, though most of Christine's contacts were kind and encouraging, writing me detailed letters and finding time to talk to me at length, I was uneasily aware that I was standing behind a glass wall through which I could dimly perceive figures and landscapes of vital importance to the development and authenticity of my story. Furthermore, at all times in letters and conversation coupled with the name of Christine was that of Andrew Kowerski-Kennedy, her closest friend, a Pole who had become a Major in the British Army and who had given Christine a permanent home in his heart.

For a long time I was unable to contact him. I knew that he lived abroad, but found it impossible to get his address. His friends, trying to protect him from being once again exploited and betrayed by sensation-mongers, stalled my efforts to reach him. Finally in despair I pressed the right button and was at last able to write my very important letter.

For some time there was no answer. I wrote again. By this time I had contacted Francis Cammaerts, another of the key figures in Christine's life. He too was a legendary personality.[1] He had written in answer to my letter to tell me he would stop off at my home in Sussex on his way from Southampton to London.

I had read a great deal about this man and seeing 'Shelley plain' standing in my drawing room was a strange experience. Cool and silent he radiated a great sweetness of spirit, and an aura of greatness. In the middle of his account of how Christine had liberated him from the prison at Digne, the telephone, plugged in at my elbow, rang. Impatiently, I answered it. A voice said, 'This is Andrew Kennedy.' I motioned Cammaerts to take over and without any preliminaries he said, 'Hello, Andrew, nice to hear you after a long time.' The two friends talked for a while until I was handed the phone. It was a situation that would certainly have amused Christine. The writer of her biography bringing together, long-distance, two of the most important men in her life in a cottage in the depths of the English countryside.

Andrew Kennedy said that he had finally received my second letter. The first had obviously gone astray. He said he hoped to be in London in the late spring and that he would contact me when he arrived. His voice was warm and friendly, and I felt a surge of hope that perhaps with his help I might get closer to unravelling some of the mysteries surrounding Christine.

The months passed while I continued my investigations. Vera Atkins and I had luncheon together. It was a long time since we had met; but I found her unchanged, youthful, still with her unlined, camelia-petal skin, and behind her clear blue eyes an immense baggage of secrets. As always, she was urbane and carefully helpful. She obviously knew a great deal about Christine, but she did not enlarge on any aspect of her life other than the times she had seen her in the line of duty. I gathered that on the rare occasions when they had met she found Christine 'prickly' and very much on the defensive. She said, 'Christine was a woman of quite unusual character. She was very brave, very attractive, but a loner and a law unto herself. She was utterly loyal and dedicated to the Allies, and nothing would have made her betray her trust. Andrew Kennedy was, I believe, her one lasting attachment.

'After the war she was quite unable to adapt herself to a boring day to day routine of work. She lived for action and adventure. Don't diminish her by white-washing her faults. She was no plaster saint. She was a vital, healthy, beautiful animal with a great appetite for love and laughter, and she had tremendous guts.'

The next person I saw was Tadeusz Horko, a Polish journalist and onetime editor of a paper called the *Polish Daily*. He and his pretty wife Sheila, whom I had known previously in South Africa, came to luncheon. Tadeusz was immensely helpful, giving me names and contacts abroad. He said, 'When I was twenty-four years old, and a budding newspaperman, I was sent to Teschen (Cieszyn) in 1938 to cover the Czech question. It was while I was on this assignment that I met a young woman reporter called Christine Skarbek. She was most attractive and I hoped to see her again. I asked her for her telephone number which, strangely enough, I found only the other day when I was going through some old diaries. But I did not phone her for a number of reasons, the main one being that I discovered that a great friend of mine, a fellow-journalist, Radziminski,[2] was madly in love with her. Even in those days Christine was supposed to be a "British agent". Though she was very quiet, there was something about her which put other women in the shade.'

Whilst everyone I questioned was agreed that Christine was a unique person, she appeared to have a chameleon-like quality of blending so perfectly with the climate of the moment, either political or spiritual, that she was able to preserve intact the core and private motivations of her being.

She revealed facets of her character only as and when she wished, and in so doing made up a kind of identikit of the Christine persona she wanted to put over. Vera Atkins had said she was a loner; others said she was a gregarious creature who liked being surrounded by people. One of her friends told me that if she were bored, and she became quickly bored at purely social functions, she became silent and colourless, like a radiantly hued shell which, picked from the ocean and brought away from its environment, soon becomes dry and drained of all its iridiscent beauty.

Following one of Vera's leads, I contacted a Mrs Nina Crawshaw, who had known Christine in Cairo and after the war. I telephoned Mrs Crawshaw, and she confirmed the fact

that she had known both Christine and Andrew well. She
added that she was just off to Italy, but would get in touch with
me on her return when we could meet; but that, in the meantime, she would send me a photocopy of a portrait Andrew had
given her after Christine's death. True to her word she sent the
portrait, an exquisite pencil sketch which she said closely
resembled the original.

A few weeks later Mrs Crawshaw, on her return, in the late
summer of 1974, came down to Bosham to spend the evening
with me. I had been told by her friends that she had been one
of the great beauties of her time, and, indeed, she still had
great style and the husky timbre of her voice was enchanting.

She was most helpful. She had known Christine and Andrew
in Cairo where she herself was working for SOE, as was her
husband, Colonel Guy Tamplin. It was Guy Tamplin, at one
time liaison officer for a Polish brigade, a most remarkable lin-
guist, who had introduced Christine to his wife.[3]

Nina was honest about her impressions of Christine. 'She
always seemed so cool and withdrawn that I was not particularly
attracted to her. I knew she was a special kind of person
because Guy had told me so without giving me any details of
her past achievements. He was devoted to her, as were so many
men. Those who were not in love with her had the same feeling as I imagine her officers had for Joan of Arc. It was an
emotion which transcended sex, and had its roots in admiration
of her heroic qualities.

'Christine was exceedingly reserved, and I never thought
her beautiful. Unusual looking perhaps, but certainly not beautiful, as were the two Tarnowski sisters-in-law, Sophie and
Chouquette. They, too, were Polish and were undoubtedly the
belles of Cairo society.

'Frankly, I don't know what Christine and Andrew were up
to in Cairo. I worked in the SOE Headquarters in Rustem
Buildings; but I never saw either of them there. This may, of
course, have been for security reasons.[4] I knew that Christine
was exceedingly unhappy and frustrated at this period of her

life. I've no idea why she was kept on ice for such a long time. It was the worst thing that could have happened to her.

'I suppose it sounds feminine and even catty to say that Christine, like many women in Cairo at that time, had a wide choice of admirers. There were so many more males than females around, and the British have always been attracted by the Slav type to whom they attribute mysterious qualities which do not seem to belong to their own blonde, fluffy or horsey womenfolk.

'After the death of my husband, I left Cairo and lost touch with Christine and Andrew. But after the war they used to pop up occasionally in my life. They never said what they were doing or where they had come from, or where they were going. Once, when I was PA to an important Allied general in Berlin, I got a phone call from Christine out of the blue. She was in Berlin without a permit. She asked me to use my good offices with my general to get her this very necessary document. Of course, I did what they wanted, and invited them to attend an international garden-party given by my boss. They turned up in a large, expensive car which Andrew said he had "organized". Christine looked gay and carefree. Three days later, they disappeared. Goodness knows where they went, or what their particular ploy was at that time.'

In fact, Christine was trying to get a divorce from George Gizycki, who refused even to communicate with her, so bitter was he after a fracas in Jerusalem when she told him she wanted a divorce.

Then Christine discovered that, according to the new Polish law, she could get a divorce in the Polish Consulate. She still had her old Polish diplomatic passport. Christine and Andrew applied to the British authorities in London, and then to Germany to give Christine a permit to come to Berlin and arrange her divorce. The British, who were quite happy to drop this girl all over France, refused her a normal permit to go to Germany as she was not a business woman buying steel or scrap, but wanting to do something for her private life. Andrew and Christine had tried to do things officially; but when they were refused, they took matters in their own hands and this is why they appeared in Berlin. She got her Polish divorce from George.[5]

'I used to see Christine from time to time when she was in London after the war,' Nina Crawshaw told me. 'She had become very bitter because she felt she had been badly let down by the British. She simply could not settle down to an ordinary job, and finally I heard she had become a stewardess in a liner. We never completely lost contact, but there was never anything spontaneous or warm about our meetings. I knew by then, of course, of her extraordinary exploits, and that she was a very brave woman. I respected her courage; but I never really did get through to her.'

On 20 July 1974, I was at Vassieux for the ceremonies attendant on the thirtieth anniversary of the Battle of the Vercors. This ceremony had been organized by the 'Association Nationale des Pionniers et Combattants Volontaires du Vercors', who, knowing my interest in Christine, known to them as 'Miss Pauline', had been kind enough to issue me with a special press pass and badge.

The village of Vassieux was rebuilt some distance away from where we stood on the great plain in the lee of a towering bastion of rock. The wall of the cemetery is backed by a semi-circular memorial. In the foreground are the rows of neat identical graves each with its cross. There were many people. This assembly, I thought, was the heart of the matter. This deep expression of national fervour is the final accolade.

The real France of the humble patriot was here represented in the wrinkled faces of the old men and women who had come to honour the memory of those they had lost. Although there were many young people, children and grandchildren and relations of the Vercors families, they could not, as did their elders, appreciate the full gravity of the occasion. Living in the comparative peace of the seventies they could not comprehend the magnitude of what had happened so long ago in their familiar and beloved villages.

They knew nothing of the sky darkened by enemy planes and gliders; of falling bombs or of the cries of the injured, the staring eyes of the dead, and of those days of terror when German soldiers had rampaged through the countryside, raping, torturing and murdering as they went from one burning village to the next. But the old ones, those who had seen it all and survived, remembered.

The ceremony began with speeches made by the distinguished guests who had come from all over France. The survivors of the families moved into the cemetery to stand beside the graves of their martyrs while the Roll Call of Honour was being read out.

At last there was total silence broken by the high, sweet voice of a little girl calling out the names of the civilian martyrs, whilst that of a boy intoned those of the soldiers who had died for France. 'Mort pour la France' echoed across the plain. It was a cold day and the wind whipped the flags into ribbons of colour. Then there was a slow roll of drums, followed by the 'Marseillaise' and the 'Chant des Pionniers'. I looked across the crowd at the tall figure of Francis Cammaerts – 'Roger' – standing there in his comfortable old tweed jacket, his wide shoulders blocking out the mountain. He was a calm and reassuring figure. He stood motionless, remembering, his pipe in his mouth, while those about me looked towards him with gratitude and affection. I thought of that time when Christine and Francis had stood here, perhaps on this very spot, scanning the skies for a sight of the long-awaited planes which were to bring men, arms and ammunition to the imperilled and beleaguered maquisards and defenders of the Vercors.

It was a stifling hot day in July when we packed into my car to visit Sir Frederick and Lady Deakin[6] in their home high above Toulon. It was the peak of the season, and the coast road was almost impassable, so jammed was it with cars and pedestrians all dashing, like lemmings, to fling themselves into the overcrowded waters of the Mediterranean seaside resorts.

My son, who had but recently passed his driving test, drove us first with extreme caution, and then with a wild brio and abandon which carried us triumphantly to the steep summit of the ancient hill village in which the Deakins live.

Their house, hidden behind high walls, has all the charm and atmosphere of an old French Provençal habitation converted into a comfortable home by a couple who, while scrupulously respecting the indigenous character of the house, have made the most of a dwelling with unparalleled views over a landscape which, but for its broad *autoroutes*, has remained unchanged since medieval times.

Cold drinks had been set out on the terrace in a kind of arbour bedecked with vines and flowers. 'Pussi' Deakin had expected me, but not my retinue of schoolboys and houseguests. The former were sent off by Mr (now Sir Frederick) Deakin to an excellent little restaurant nearby. Meanwhile, 'Pussi', without turning a hair, performed a small miracle in the kitchen and very soon we sat down to a splendid impromptu buffet which began with an admirable pâté accompanied by an ice-cold vin du pays.

The conversation during luncheon dealt with various aspects of resistance on which subject Sir Frederick is an expert, and in this quiet, cool dining-room I learned many interesting facts told with the authority of a scholar and of a man of action.

The names of Christine and Andrew drifted in and out of the conversation; but it was not until we were alone, Sir Frederick having kindly volunteered to escort my guests on a tour of the village, that 'Pussi' settled down to tell me what she remembered of her friendship with Christine.

'After Crete, the whole bunch of us left for Greece and Alexandria. I was working for SOE in Cairo, and I first met Christine Granville on the terrace of the old Shepheard's Hotel, which afterwards burned down. It must have been late in 1941. I saw a slim girl get up from her chair and walk over to me. She said, "You have the most lovely hands, they are like orchids. I see you are alone, why not come over and join us." Although

Christine was generally shy and undemonstrative, she was also very kind. She was not beautiful but she had the most extraordinary grace, and a casual sort of *chic*. She had exquisite hands and feet. She was thin, too thin, and this worried her at times. She was totally undomesticated. I never saw her sewing or mending; yet she always managed to look crisp and fresh. I don't think she could cook, but I'm not sure. Anyway, she never wanted to eat at home. She wasn't interested in material things and had few personal possessions. The only ring I ever saw her wear was a signet ring which had a thread of iron or steel embedded in what was certainly her family crest.

'I knew little about her background; but it was evident that she had breeding, and came from a good family. She was fantastically secretive and she was an embroiderer; not a liar ever, but she just had to cover her tracks. She was certainly mysterious in the nicest possible way. Though one did not ask questions in those days, I got the impression that Christine had travelled a good deal in the capitals of Europe. She knew Paris well and said something once about having sold cars on the Champs-Elysées, and she had visited East Africa.

'She had many admirers. I remember her arriving to see me one day accompanied by a splendid-looking Afghan major, Afterwards, she said, "He would die for me."'[7]

Faithful to his word, Andrew Kennedy arrived in England in the late spring. We spoke briefly on the phone. Next day he arrived at my house. Andrew is a tall, powerfully built man with a fresh, rosy complexion, wide pale green eyes and silvery hair. He looks like an Englishman, like a Scot, like a Pole, like a real man. His limp, for he has only one leg (the other was irretrievably damaged in a shooting accident), is unnoticeable except for a slightly rolling gait. His English, though accented, is fluent and idiomatic. It is obvious that he knows his way around. He exudes the charm of an international man of the world coupled with the courtesy and panache of the eighteenth-century buck.

From the beginning Christine was very much with us.

Andrew said, 'Christine was very highly strung and at times, specially when I was driving her somewhere and a dog or cat strayed near our wheels, she became almost hysterical. I always swerved in time; even so, my thigh was black and blue where she pinched me. She did not drive a car and did not understand the first thing about firearms. She hated bangs of any kind. Nor was she particularly mad about music, except for occasional bursts of Chopin. She was very positive about her likes and dislikes. She could be intolerant and did not suffer fools gladly. She had a brilliant brain and was always ice-cold in an emergency.'

I am certainly not the first writer to attempt a book about Christine Granville. Since her death in 1952, Andrew and their mutual friends have been approached by a number of would-be biographers. Some had excellent credentials, and the highest possible motives; but became discouraged when they found that there was, seemingly, so little material available. Others felt they were on to a good 'meaty' story with plenty of spy interest and distinct possibilities of plastering this tale together with great daubs of sex. These sensation seekers, who had obtained their information from the mass of lurid press-cuttings which had appeared after Christine's murder, found their way barred by a mysterious and powerful 'panel' formed by a number of Christine's friends, who had made a pact to try to prevent the wrong sort of book being written about her. Heading this panel was Andrew.

Throughout the years he had resisted all financial blandishments and refused to compromise with scenario-writers and authors and journalists with suspect motives; but conscious now that time was eroding his memory and that of his contemporaries, he was anxious for the book to be written.

Nearly all the facts in the mass of articles about Christine are inaccurate. Names, dates and events are muddled and often distorted. The most blatant of these inaccuracies is contained in a piece about Christine published in an *Encyclopedia of Espionage*. She, herself, had done a thorough job of 'covering her tracks'. It has been a laborious and difficult business to unravel the facts from a welter of maudlin fiction, and the curious thing is that, in Christine's case, fact is far, far stranger than fiction.

My next meeting with Andrew Kennedy took place in London. I wanted to visit Christine's grave with him. He asked me to luncheon at the Polish Club in Exhibition Road, which had replaced the 'White Eagle Club' in Albert Gate, Christine's favourite post-war haunt. A friend who had known her well in Algeria joined us. Havard Gunn was an SOE man whom I had known for years both as a brilliant PR man and artist of considerable talent.

We came out of the bright May sunshine into the cool, dark club. In the foyer a bookstall sold Polish newspapers, magazines and books, and there were showcases filled with pretty painted rustic handicrafts, dolls in costume and little bits of china and glass.

We went into the dining-room which gives on to a pleasant garden. The clientele of the club seemed to be mostly Polish, and though everything was sparklingly clean and neat there was, overall, an ambience of sadness, the nostalgia of the émigré in exile.

'The Polish emigration was a good thing,' said Andrew, studying the menu. 'The English-Polish combination produces fine children; solid British phlegm allied to Polish fantasy.'

Since I could not read Polish, I looked around to see what everyone else was eating. Plates were heaped high with appetizing food, which seemed more colourful than ordinary English fare. Andrew ordered borscht for himself, followed by some particular Polish delicacy which he hankered for, and described in detail. Havard's wife is Polish, so he was on familiar ground. As soon as the meal was ordered, Andrew went off to greet friends scattered round the room.

I got out my notebook to interrogate Havard. 'I saw Christine in a different light to most people,' he said, 'mainly, I suppose, because I knew so little about her or her background. I liked her because she was vital and full of fun. She had a marvellous sense of humour. Strangely, she did not appear to have any kinds of roots. She lived entirely for the moment, and seemed to look upon the future with some trepidation.

'I had had the idea of forming a certain type of Resistance party. I felt that those belonging to it should be trained, not only as saboteurs, but also in the political sense. I was given *carte blanche* by the War Office to select and form twelve parties, all of whom would be officers, who would be parachuted into the South of France, where things were building up to the final climax. I was, of course, in Algiers during the time all these people were being trained. Christine arrived. She was independent of my groups, and was to be parachuted into France on her own. For two months we were together a good deal. I saw her every day and we became friends. In fact, it was she who gave me my code name.

'We were walking in the countryside when we passed a large clump of bamboos which Christine stopped to admire. I was trying out a number of code names. I had to find something which would fit with "Chasuble" and "Roger". Not being very churchy, I did not care for the former, and I wanted something original. Christine came up with "Bambos", which was certainly unusual. She was living at Le Club des Pins, and we used to go to Algiers and have coffee in the Officers' Club. She was unusually tense and nervous for she did not know until the last minute when she was to be sent to France. I think she felt she had not been properly briefed. I tried to calm her down, and we talked about what we would do when we eventually found ourselves in France. We called it "playing Indians". One day she appeared with a teddy bear which she had just bought. She dared me to take it as a "passenger" when I took off for France. Teddy was with me when I jumped from the plane, but, alas, he was found to have been squashed flat on landing.'

It was just three o'clock when we left the Polish Club and said goodbye to Havard. I embarked in Andrew's Porsche car. He drives a car the way a cavalry officer rides his horses, with skill, control and intelligence. We roared off in the general direction of the Cromwell Road, in which was the hotel which Christine had made her home when she was in England.

I had already been to see the Shellbourne Hotel in Lexham Gardens. Its Polish owner, Mr L. Kozak, was out, but I was escorted round by a polite and venerable Polish clerk whom I had found at the reception desk. This is a modest residential hotel, more like a boarding-house than a bustling caravanserai. Everywhere was spotlessly clean.

I was shown one of the single bedrooms, such as Christine had occupied. It was a long, narrow, high-ceilinged room with draggy curtains at the large windows. The room had been divided into two, for half a huge ornate marble fireplace remained, a symbol of the departed grandeur of what had once been a large private mansion.

St Mary's Catholic Cemetery is in Kensal Green. Even on this golden day the English *campo santo* was as sinister as a drawing by Doré. Many of the graves were askew, as if wrenched asunder by an earthquake, or as if their occupants, unable to wait for the last Trump, had impatiently flung aside their blanket of earth; the plaster angels, open books, urns and crosses were also crazily tilted and grass and weeds rioted madly everywhere.

Typically, Andrew drove the car right up to the graveside. Everything about this tomb is a memorial of a deep and lasting love. Christine loved trees, so her grave is shaded by a great hawthorn tree whose pink rosettes made a welcome contrast to the whiteness of this pantheon of marble and plaster, whose pallid funeral ornaments are like bleached bones in the sun.

A simple headstone bears her name, date of birth and date of death and a list of her decorations. Beneath them is the 'Habdank', a sliver of serrated steel, part of the Skarbek crest and legend. Christine liked wood, so a kind of carved totem pole rises like a mast from this unlikely craft, and, in lieu of a sail, there is a shield bearing the White Eagle of Poland and a replica of the Black Virgin of Czestochowa.

We stood in silence. I knew that much of Andrew Kennedy's

soul was in that grave. Suddenly he looked tired and shrunken. I did not think that Christine would have cared much for the cemetery in which she lay. Andrew must have read my thoughts. He shrugged his shoulders and said, 'It's all one to her now for at last she is free.'

PART ONE

CHRISTINE IN THE SUNLIGHT

CHAPTER ONE

In the last days of December 1899, the handsome, extravagant and impoverished Count Jerzy Skarbek, a member of one of Poland's ancient and aristocratic families, married the daughter of a prominent Polish Jewish banker. Skarbek married Stephanie Goldfeder because he needed her considerable dowry to pay his debts and to allow him to continue living in the manner he thought befitting a *grand seigneur* with expensive tastes. Wine, women and hunting were important to Jerzy Skarbek. The Count felt no sacrifice was too great to ensure the welfare and comfort of his horses, and soon after he married Stephanie Goldfeder, they acquired the Mlodziesyn estate, some thirty miles from Warsaw.

The young Countess was plain, but she was well-educated, intelligent and had dignity. If she was temporarily beguiled by Jerzy's debonair manner and masculinity, she had few illusions about his reasons for marrying her. It had not always been fashionable for the members of old families to marry Jewish girls but at the time Count Jerzy began courting Stephanie, marriage between Polish aristocrats and assimilated Jewish families was looked upon with favour. Also, banker Goldfeder was very wealthy and for the Warsaw snobs the Goldfeders counted just a little beneath the immensely wealthy assimilated families such as the Natansons, Bersons, Kronenbergs and Rotwands. Although the Goldfeders were never in the same bracket as the Rothschilds, they were nonetheless allied to a consortium of rich merchant-bankers and industrialists,

among whom were the Wertheimers of Berlin and the André
Citroens of Paris.

The Goldfeders were a close-knit family and met often at
the home of the matriarch Roza Goldfeder. Stephanie had two
brothers, Josef and Bronislaw. Both had charming wives. At the
time of Stephanie's marriage her brother and his wife, who was
a sister of André Citroen, lived in considerable style in a house
in Warsaw. Bronislaw was for some time Honorary Consul for
Japan.

Stephanie Skarbek scrupulously carried out her role as châte-
laine of the estate and as brood mare for the Skarbek posterity.
But her pleasures lay in pursuits of the mind. She liked music,
poetry and French literature and, like most Polish women of
her class, she spoke excellent French.

Even though Count Jerzy was bored with his blue-stocking
of a wife, he respected her qualities of heart and in public
treated her always with courtesy. Soon after their marriage
Stephanie became disenchanted with her husband and his continual infidelities caused her great pain.[1]

The Goldfeder family were well aware that Stephanie's mar-
ital relations were not good. 'My mother's sister, Barbara,
married Augustus Goldfeder, a cousin of Josef and of his sister
Stephanie. In 1923 my mother took me to see Aunt Barbara,
and there we met Stephanie Skarbek and her husband, Count
Jerzy. He was very handsome, dark and Italian-looking with a
seductive little moustache. He was obviously bored with this
family gathering and left as soon as he decently could. The
moment he had gone his wife began to cry over her sad fate.
Skarbek, she said, neglected her and constantly ran after other
women.'[2]

Count Jerzy was extremely attractive to the female sex. One
of his nieces by marriage, Antonina ('Antolka'), remembers him
well. 'Skarbek was a very handsome man of patrician beauty.
He was not a family man, although he liked all of us, visiting us
from time to time, joking with us children (I had three brothers). He was very popular among his own friends. He was

always surrounded by women, spending with ease money by entertaining and being entertained.'[3]

Money, as such, meant little to him. It was a means to an end, but he did not care to handle it physically, and for this purpose employed a little groom whose duties included the care of his purse, which, in those days, was filled with gold coins.

Count Jerzy was proud of his ancestry. Even though his direct ancestors had dissipated their possessions, the Skarbek family had early entered recorded Polish history. Tradition, as well as ancient heraldic works, accepts Skarbimierz, a mighty and ruthless lord in the eleventh century, as founder of the family. Described as *comes* (earl) he took part in King Boleslaw's last expedition against Kiev, and was himself, according to a legend, a descendant of Skuba, the crafty tanner who destroyed the famous Krakow dragon. He stuffed a sheepskin so cleverly with phosphorus that even the cunning beast was fooled, devoured the bait and died in agony. The descendants of Skarbimierz started calling themselves Skarbek with the cognomen z-Gory, 'of the mountain'.

According to another legend, Jan z-Gory Skarbek was sent by Prince Boleslaw Krzywousty as plenipotentiary to the German Emperor, Henry II, who was at that time on the point of invading Poland. The vain monarch, wishing to impress the Polish envoy with his wealth and power, showed him coffers brimming with gold and precious stones and said, 'Look at my treasure, how can you think to oppose me?' In reply, Skarbek took off his own ring, threw it into the chest and said, 'Let gold go to gold, we Poles love iron.' Confused, the Emperor replied politely 'Habdank' (Thank you). Thus, 'Habdank' became the name of Skarbek's coat-of-arms representing a sliver of serrated steel on the shield.[4]

During the fifteenth century the Skarbek family became numerous, powerful and opulent. They formed and commanded their own regiment during the wars against the Teutonic Knights and in the Battle of Grunwald at Tannenberg in 1410 helped to win a decisive action against the most powerful and dangerous enemy of Poland and Lithuania. This victory had a great moral significance for, because of it, the supremacy of the Teutonic Knights in the Baltic countries was halted, and with it for a while the predominance of the German element in this part of Europe.

It appears likely that the Skarbeks suffered heavy losses in the wars of King John Albert in Moldavia, and it was not until the seventeenth century that members of the family were awarded high offices of palatins and castellans, which in the Polish Lithuanian Commonwealth indicated a family's importance and wealth.

Restricted to a few members only, two distinct branches of the family existed by the time of the Partition of Poland, one which settled in Galicia, then part of the Austrian Empire; the other, to which Count Jerzy belonged, lived in the Polish kingdom, a part of the Russian Empire. They were awarded the hereditary title of Count in Galicia in 1778, which title was confirmed in 1835, in Russia and Austria.

At the beginning of the nineteenth century, the Skarbeks produced an eminent economist and man of letters, Count Frederic Skarbek, great-great-grandfather of the present head of the family.

Count Frederic was the godfather of Chopin, whose father, Nicholas Chopin, had been his tutor, teaching him first in his home, the long, low annexe, or guest house, of the manor house of Zelazowa Wola, and later in his house in Warsaw. Chopin's wife, Justyna Krzyzanowska, a distant relation of the Skarbek family, helped Countess Ludwika Skarbek with the housekeeping and the care of her five children. The estate was administered mainly by the Countess, as the Count, her husband, a rake and a spendthrift, preferred to live abroad.

Young Frederic Florian Skarbek was ten years old when, calling with his mother on one of her friends, Madame Laczynska of Czerniejew, he first met his tutor. Mme Laczynska had two small daughters, one of whom, the beloved of Frederic Florian, was already of surpassing beauty. This child was later to become known to history as Maria Walewska, mother of Napoleon's son Alexander Walewski.

Friendly relations were always maintained by Count Skarbek and his family with his godson Frederic Chopin. The composer's first printed work, a Polonaise published in 1817 through the good offices of the local priest who had a printing-press in his parish, was dedicated to: 'Son Excellence Mademoiselle la Comtesse Victoire Skarbek par Frédéric Chopin âgé de 8 ans.'

The next Skarbek to figure in the public eye was Count Stanislas who belonged to the Galician branch. He started by losing almost all his possessions by gambling and high living in Vienna. When faced with bankruptcy and the refusal of his relatives to lend him further sums of money, he set to work and discovered that he had great ability as a businessman and administrator. Within a few years he had bought back his inherited estates and trebled his fortune. The secret of his success lay in his ability to accept progress in farming methods, in the industrialization of landed estates and also in his extraordinary luck at the gaming tables.

Then to the stupefaction of his friends and the chagrin of those relations who had hoped for legacies, Count Stanislas made a grand Tolstoyan gesture and offered his fortune and estates to the poor and dispossessed. Implicit in this gift was the stipulation that the donor should become the lifelong administrator of this charitable foundation.

Before the First World War, Alexander Skarbek, grandson of Frederic the economist, was a Deputy of the Imperial Parliament in Vienna, and after 1918 was one of the leaders of the National Democratic Party and a member of the Polish Diet.

The first child of Jerzy and Stephanie Skarbek was a son. He was christened Andrew. His father was pleased with his wife for producing an heir; but it was evident from the beginning that he was very much his mother's child. Physically, too, he took after the maternal side of the family, and Count Jerzy was relieved when his daughter Krystyna, Christine, born in 1915, seemed to have inherited his own good looks.

From the start there was a complete rapport between father and daughter. He called her his 'Happiness' and his 'Star'. Almost before she could walk he mounted her on a pony. Disregarding his wife's fears that Christine might learn rough manners and hear bad language if she spent too much time with him in the stables, he kept her with him as much as possible, teaching her to ride astride, instead of side-saddle.

Though small-boned and fragile, Christine did not need much encouragement to become a tomboy. She was utterly fearless and wanted only to follow her father whenever he rode out to inspect his farms, lands and woods. By the time Christine was five, Count Jerzy had sold Mlodziesyn and had bought another estate, Trzebnica, some forty miles from the provincial town of Piotrkow.

While the great Polish families such as the Radziwills, the Lubomirskis and the Czartoryskis owned magnificent town mansions and stately homes in the country, the *szlachta*, or gentry, farmed their lands from manor houses adapted to their simpler style of living.[5]

The Polish *dwor*, or manor-house, resembled the rambling French *maison de campagne*, which combined the attributes of the country house together with those of the farm. The long, low one-storeyed house was usually situated at the end of an avenue and benefited from the shade of tall trees primarily planted to act as a windbreak. The façade of the house was decorated by a porch.

Apart from the kitchen quarters, in which were the bakery, women's room, still-room and larders, most Polish country houses had one or two annexes set aside for guests, tutors or dependants of the family. These annexes were furnished in a cottagey manner being white-washed with beamed ceilings and with small windows with deep sills.

The main body of the house was generally furnished with a mixture of fine old pieces, together with new bits of furniture imported by successive generations of brides, whose tastes were conditioned by the vogue of the day. Family portraits and sabres and other souvenirs of a martial past adorned the walls, and here was preserved, like flies in amber, the *manes* of the old Polish nobility and gentry.

In the corners of the rooms stood tall, handsome tiled stoves, heated with pinewood, juniper and other fragrant woods. Most country houses were pervaded by the scent of resin mixed with that of the rose-leaves, lavender and rosemary, a legacy of the French émigrés of the eighteenth century, who, fleeing from the Terror and finding refuge in Poland, had brought with them their many intellectual talents and some quaint conceits adopted both in the kitchen and the salon.

Christine's early childhood was happy and secure. Count Jerzy was always pleased to see his two brothers, Martin and Charles, who were as dashing and thriftless as himself. He had only one sister, Christine's 'pretty, naughty Aunt Helena', who seldom visited her intellectual sister-in-law.

The Goldfeders liked to be together, and Christine was often taken to visit her grandmother Roza Goldfeder, who held court in her country house. One of the most amusing of her childhood memories was concerned with the estate of one of her uncles. His wife bred dachshunds, but could never bear to part with them, with the result that the whole house was over-run with small waddling animals. The uncle had a passion for topiary, and the great lawn fronting the house was laid out in the form of a steeplechase course with each obstacle carefully shaped in yew. To Christine's delight, when her uncle blew his whistle, dozens of dachshunds bounded from the house to take part in a crazy steeplechase race on the lawn.

Like most children Christine enjoyed her visits to the 'women's room', the particular domain of the housekeeper, ladies' maids and sewing-women, who came in from the nearest town to make-and-mend. This was the nerve centre of the house and from it emanated a continual stream of local gossip. Christine revelled in the familiar muddle of exciting and forbidden things heaped up on every available surface; dream-books, cheap, well-thumbed romantic novelettes, trays of scented flower petals and pots of jam. Christine knew that if the housekeeper was in a good mood, she would finally be allowed to choose a goody from one of the drawers in which were kept candied plums and gingerbread figures, as well as lumps of sugar used to cure fainting-fits by the addition of a few drops of ether. The lady of the house always kept her own bottle of smelling-salts by her in case of need.

But it was the countryside that held her heart. Riding on the endless melancholy plains under a sombre sky Christine identified herself with Poland, with her country which so often in its history had been invaded, and there entered into her young soul something of the Polish *zal*, the national *mélancolie*, of which Wodzinski said, 'Le zal Polonais colore la tristesse d'une teinte rose de poésie.' In Christine the *accidie* of the Polish temperament was enriched by the warm and lively Jewish blood from the maternal side, so that from her earliest childhood, she displayed the special qualities and character defects of the two races which would come to fruition in her adult life.

She was recalcitrant to any form of discipline and when her mind was set on some course, neither her mother's admonishments, threats of punishment from her nurse, nor the blandishments of her father prevented her from going straight to her objective. She was tender-hearted and full of compassion for the underdog, but she could be capricious with her friends, most of whom admired and copied her escapades, much to the irritation of their mothers who thought that Christine Skarbek was allowed far too much freedom for a little girl.

Her pranks amused her father and annoyed her mother. She never told anyone her plans; but slipped off quietly through the cordon of servants, most of whom loved the high-spirited child. She often went off alone to find her friends in field and village, according to the seasons.

Christine had always a close affinity with nature. From her babyhood, trees and flowers enchanted her. The living ornaments of nature meant far more to her than those made by man, and she preferred to look at and admire flowers rather than to pick them.

Christmas, observed in the traditional Polish manner, was always memorable. The Christmas table was spread with hay and covered with a cloth. Sheaves of unthreshed grain stood in the corners of the room. A star and a cradle were suspended from the ceiling. As the day closed in the youngest child was stationed at the window to watch for the first star. As it appeared in the frosty sky the ceremony would begin. On a plate were two consecrated wafers; the parents would break the wafers together and then it would be the turn of the children. The ritual words 'May we a year from now again break the wafer together' would be spoken, and then everyone would move off to the kitchen to give the servants their presents. In the evening the entire household attended midnight mass.

During the 'fat' years, the Goldfeder fortune provided Count and Countess Jerzy Skarbek and their children with a background of luxury, and before the First World War and the inflation curtailed their finances, Christine's parents travelled widely, visiting friends and relations and moving about the capitals of Europe with a retinue of servants.

Countess Stephanie bought her coats and dresses from Paul Poiret in the Rue Auber, and her pleated négligées from Mario Fortuny, who had opened his own *maison de couture* in Venice. Her perfumes came from Guerlain, her toilet water from Lubin. Some of her jewels were created for her by Bulgari in Rome, while Count Jerzy enjoyed using imported bay rum hair tonic, Pears' soap, riding boots from Bunting and the favours of ladies up and down the country.

During her childhood Christine took for granted a lifestyle that included living in a spacious house staffed by indoor and outdoor servants. She enjoyed the bustle that surrounded her father's departure for one of the annual or bi-annual shoots which took place on the estates of the great landowners. These were special occasions tied either to the shooting season or the carnival season when balls were held in the towns adjoining the magnate's estates. The morning shoots usually ended with a lunch in a neighbouring farmhouse, the main course consisting of *bigos*, a mixture of cooked sausage and cabbage. This humble peasant fare was washed down by unlimited draughts of vodka.

It was from her father that Christine acquired her deep pride of race and love of her country. The Count was far from being an intellectual, indeed his reading was light and limited; but he knew something of the history of Poland and this he imparted to his daughter. Polish history is as fanciful as a fairy tale. Fact and legend are closely interwoven, and the illuminated *Book of Hours* of Polish history is filled with tales of dragons, white eagles, symbolic mounds, miraculous images and the union of a half-savage young Lithuanian prince with a Christian princess, whose coming together founded a great dynasty.

Situated between the Carpathian Mountains and the Baltic Sea, Poland has always been sandwiched between greedy and predatory neighbours and in the course of ten centuries has come under the influence of the major migrations, conflicts and crucial economic changes experienced by Europe since the Middle Ages.

This country, which has so many times been attacked, savaged, occupied by enemy troops and even eradicated from the map of Europe, has nonetheless managed to survive and to retain always and intact its identity. For the Poles are fiercely nationalistic and never more so than when threatened or dominated by a foreign oppressor. Polish history records a series of patriotic uprisings under foreign rule, and whatever the price the Poles have always defended their country to the death. The Poles are a nation of survivors and no earthly power has throughout the centuries been able to crush their love of and pride in their native land.

Under her father's tuition Christine became an accomplished horsewoman, and at that time in her life the stables became her spiritual home and she was never happier than when she could sit in the tack-room listening to the chat of the stable-boys and grooms. A love of and instinct for good horseflesh was part of Christine, a genetic throwback to those long dead Skarbeks, her ancestors who had lived and died in the saddle.

There are people who still remember Christine's first race. She was in her early teens and as light as a feather. So light was she that the owner of the winning horse, Colonel Bobinski,[6] wondered how on earth she would stop her mount at the finishing-post. Seeing her well in the lead, he had a flash of inspiration and ordered the stable-mate of the horse Christine was riding to be brought to the race-course. As Christine's horse drew level with the winning post, it saw its stable-mate and, as Colonel Bobinski had intended, stopped dead.

It was at the stables that Christine's first meeting with young Andrew Kowerski took place. His father had brought him over from Labunie, the estate he managed, to play with the ten-year-old Christine, while he discussed agricultural matters with Count Skarbek.[7]

Andrew's recollections of this meeting are vague. He remembers very little about it except that it took place, and that he enjoyed looking over the Skarbek stud, for he, like Christine, was horse-mad and had ridden his own pony since the age of three. The casual encounter which mattered so little to Andrew or Christine must have amused the Fates, who were busily weaving together the threads of the destinies of these two children who were, one day, to become totally involved with one another and with the fate of their country.

The Kowerskis, like the Skarbeks, belonged to the landed gentry of Poland and were related to many well-known old families. Unlike Christine's family who tended towards politics and good works, the Kowerskis were more intellectually orientated and their passionate convictions and habit of implementing them by fighting any opposition did not endear them to their oppressors.

The Kowerskis had originated in Lithuania. In 1863 the January Rising took place and Andrew's grandfather flung himself wholeheartedly into the bloody struggle. He like many of his friends was exiled to Siberia. Here he met the Przewlocki family who were also in exile. The young man fell in love with Sophie Przewlocki and the young couple were married.

When they were finally allowed to return to Poland they found that, although the Kowerski estates had been confiscated, those of Sophie's family had not, so young Kowerski leased one of them, and set to work to manage it as successfully as possible.

His wife wanted her children to be able to read and write in Polish and since at that time Polish schoolbooks were virtually unobtainable, she tried her hand at writing her own textbooks. Her efforts were so successful that she boldly went from writing textbooks to the writing of novels and finally became well-known as a writer of romantic fiction.

The Kowerskis had several children. Two of the boys were strong, fine lads; but Stanislas, the youngest, was undersized. Having had polio as a child, he was afflicted with a permanent limp. These physical handicaps did not prevent him from having a brilliant academic career, for he became a Doctor both of Agriculture and of Chemistry, and was at one time Dean of the University of Cracow. His were unusual achievements for a member of the *szlachta*.

Stanislas Kowerski, Andrew's father, married twice. He chose, as his second bride, a girl who was fifteen years his junior. Her family owned a fine estate in the middle of Poland, near Sandomierz. Her father, like Kowerski, was an interesting character. He was handsome, well-read, a superb horseman, and something of an autocrat. His wife was not an easy woman to live with, mainly because she was obsessed by the fostering of the great musical talent of her elder daughter. She wanted this girl to have a brilliant career, and took her from one piano professor to another, thus tending to ignore the rest of her children.

Maria had two brothers, the younger of whom was her favourite. His death in the First World War was a great and unforgettable sorrow.

The musical prodigy finally became bored with the idea of a career and, to the fury of her mother, abandoned her piano studies to marry a wealthy landowner with whom she retired contentedly into anonymity.

Andrew was born in 1912. His mother was just twenty years old. With the exception of Christine, Maria Kowerska was the most important person in his life. His memory of her is of someone young, vital and gay. She played tennis and rode like a centaur. She had a fresh, clear complexion and even though her hair was white she was, with her young face and trim figure, often mistaken for Andrew's sister.

Andrew tells many stories of his mother's courage and endurance. One of them highlights her love for her husband. At the outbreak of First World War there was a positive epidemic of spy-mania. A Cossack regiment arrived at Labunie and accused Andrew's father of signalling to the approaching Austrian army. Since Poland was divided into three, her people were variously orientated. Some were pro-Austrian, some pro-German and others were pro-Russian.

Stanislas Kowerski was a Pole; but, if he had any bias at all, it tended to be towards Russia, which made the remarks of the Cossack officer even more ridiculous. The officer bundled Kowerski and his wife upstairs and insisted on ransacking the Labunie attics which were filled with the dusty debris of generations. These included some ancient lamps and lanterns stacked in a corner. The Cossack officer was triumphant. 'There you are,' he said, 'these are flagrant proof that you have been sending light signals to the enemy.' Upon which he arrested Kowerski and hurried him away.

Andrew was about two years old. Most of the male servants had been drafted into the army, but there were still a number of maids left. Maria Kowerska gave her baby son into the care of the maids, and, driving a gig harnessed to two horses, set off in search of her husband.

She set off at a fast clip in the direction of the retreating Russian Army. At the first halt she was met with the news that her husband had been shot that morning. She refused to believe this and pressed on. After three days she found her Stanislas unhurt; but so severe had been the strain of her ordeal that within the next few months her hair turned white. She was only twenty-three years old. Thenceforward, Maria Kowerska was known as the 'Silver Lady', and she emphasized her unusual silver hair by always driving a gig with two snow-white horses.

Andrew had two older stepbrothers. His sister was five years his junior. His was a happy and united family, and theirs was a hospitable home. Mr Kowerski and his wife took in an unusual selection of intellectual and scientific French, English and German magazines, as well as the papers and periodicals of the time read by the Polish intelligentsia. Though Maria Kowerska, who was deeply religious, took Communion every day, she never tried to foist her religious beliefs and habits on her children. But she supervised their early education herself and instilled in them her own high principles and moral precepts.

Mother and son shared a love of horses and of riding. Stanislas Kowerski had a large stud where he bred horses for the Army. From the age of three Andrew was taught to ride. One of his greatest pleasures when he was thirteen was to help with the training of a neighbour's racehorses. By the time he was sixteen, however, he was becoming too big and heavy to ride racehorses with ease. This was a tragedy. 'Riding for me,' he says, 'was like walking for somebody else.'

CHAPTER TWO

Christine Skarbek, skipping happily through her early childhood, never gave another thought to the boy Andrew who was growing up in the town of Zamosc. Her high spirits and determination to have her own way were causing concern to her mother, who found it impossible to make her husband realize that their daughter was growing up and needed discipline and the company of little girls of her own class, instead of that of stable-lads and village children.

Count Jerzy could not bear the idea of being separated from his 'Star', but finally Stephanie, with the backing of her own family and friends, won the day, and Christine was sent to the famous Sacré-Coeur Convent in the west of Poland; this school, whose mother house was in Paris, was famous throughout the world as a training academy for the daughters of the nobility and gentry.

Deeply unhappy at being sent away from home, Christine simply ignored all rules and regulations, and continued to conduct her life entirely to her own satisfaction. Her behaviour baffled the good nuns who could not tame the wild child who constantly thought up new pranks, some of which, like setting fire to the cassock of the priest while he was saying Mass, were downright dangerous.

Already Christine had a band of admiring followers who encouraged her in her defiance of authority. Eventually the Mother Superior, feeling that Christine's rebellious spirit might infect her flock, suggested to the girl's parents that they might find another institution more suitable to the young Countess's ebullient temperament.

Christine having achieved her objective now counted on being able to remain permanently at home where she could resume her pleasant, untrammelled existence with her father as her main companion. She was saddened and mortified to discover that, not only was she being sent to Jazlowiec, another and stricter convent school; but that, owing to serious financial reverses in the family fortunes, her parents were obliged to sell their estate, and move away from the country.

Count Jerzy had never been a realistic farmer though his unhappy financial position, like that of many landowners, particularly in ex-Russian Poland, was not due to losses on bank deposits, as few had deposits to lose. Farming was generally undercapitalized, labour intensive and unprofitable. Great damage in buildings and stock had been suffered in the First World War. In addition, the 'Achilles heel' of agriculture in this part of the country was still the unresolved problems resulting from the emancipation of peasants in 1864.

Under any other circumstances, a substantial injection of capital would have been forthcoming from Stephanie Skarbek's Goldfeder relations; but, owing to galloping inflation and to the world economic crisis, they themselves had suffered disastrous financial setbacks from which they were never to recover.

Christine knew little of her parents' difficulties; but the very fact of having to leave the country home which for so many years had sheltered, enveloped and protected her was a traumatic experience; and this first wrenching up of tender youthful roots was the beginning of the long exile of a soul.

Count and Countess Skarbek moved to Warsaw and Christine tried hard to adapt herself to her new school. She wanted to correct the unfavourable impressions the nuns might have had of her reports from the Mother Superior of the Sacré-Coeur Convent.

In a short while she was top of her class. She learned the French of Racine and Molière and to write in the graceful, distinguished hand which was the hallmark of the well-educated, convent-trained pupil. If the strict discipline to which she was now subjected irked her, she concealed her feelings, a process at which she was in time to become an adept. She was gay, vital and kind, and so popular was she that she did not arouse the jealousy of her classmates.

Much has been written about Christine becoming Beauty Queen of Poland. In fact, this is just another one of the legends which have grown up about her. The true version of the story is that Christine *was* elected Beauty Queen; but only by her friends at some social charity affair. However, her picture did appear in the newspaper, and it might have been this publicity which triggered off the suspicions of an old-fashioned section of Polish society that perhaps young Countess Christine Skarbek was a trifle 'fast'. Christine first attributed this censure to the loss of the Goldfeder fortune, for she soon realized that it was the Goldfeder gold that had provided the magical shield that protected and enriched her childhood. It was only later – and the realization came as a sickening shock – that she felt there might be some animus against her because she was half-Jewish.

Until that moment Christine had never had the slightest reason to think about or to examine the position of the Jews in Poland. Poland was her country and that was that. She had always accepted the fact that the Goldfeders were 'assimilated', and therefore on a par with families as ancient and as acceptable as that of her father and his friends and relations.

There had been Jews in Poland as early as 1100. German Jews, fleeing the marauding crusaders in the Rhineland, had found sanctuary in Poland. Here they prospered and were joined by other Jews fleeing from the Germans. The newcomers were welcomed by the nobility and King Boleslaw V the Chaste granted the Jews liberal charters of self-government in 1264. They lived in city or village, as they wished. Casimir the Great founded universities, encouraged trade and imported more and more Jews. Vitold, Grand Duke of Lithuania, opened wide his country to Jewish settlement.

In 1400 the evils which had fallen upon the Jews in the West caught up with them in the East, and a ritual murder charge against the Jews was whipped up by the clergy into a hysteria that spread throughout the country. In spite of efforts to restore confidence in the Jews, the first pogroms broke out in Poland around 1500.

In 1648, East Poland was ravaged by a horde of savage Greek Orthodox Cossacks, living on the border lands between Poland and Turkey. Their savagery knew no bounds; as many as 100,000 Jews perished in this holocaust. This pattern was repeated in the second half of the seventeenth century, which saw a still more terrible Cossack uprising, followed by two invasions by Sweden and a war with Turkey.[1]

The eighteenth century brought Poland no relief from bloodletting. She was invaded by Russia; an event followed by a civil war. Then Prussia, Russia and Austria partitioned the half moribund country three times until there was nothing left of Poland. The three successive partitions of Poland gave Catherine the Great an unwanted gift of 90,000 Jews. As she could not rid herself of them, they were ungraciously given permission to settle along Russia's Western border which became known as the 'Pale of Settlement'.

The destiny of nineteenth-century Europe and of the Jews was forged in eighteenth-century France after the murder of their King and Queen, the massacre of the 'aristos' and the rise to power of Napoleon Bonaparte. It was he who convoked the first Great Sanhedrin in eighteen hundred years; one had not been held since the destruction of the Temple by the Romans. The Great Sanhedrin proclaimed to World Jewry that Mosaic laws were religious, not secular, in nature, and that Jews owed allegiance to the State and that the jurisdiction of rabbis did not extend into civil and judicial affairs. This meant that the Jews no longer had a separate corporate state, but were part of whatever nation in which they had their home.

Superficially all the problems were thus smoothed out, but

in fact anti-semitism was never really buried; it was simply covered over with gold, and the higher the mounds of gold, the more 'assimilated' the Jews became. Once the money-bags were empty, the Jews, with Christine and her family among them, would in time be exposed to the full blast of the Nazi persecution.

It was soon after Christine's little triumph as a beauty queen that she went on a visit to her relations at Lwow. Her young cousin, John Skarbek, remembers her sitting on her bed in a cloud of long dark hair. 'My mother was very fond of her; but my father, being very much under the influence of *his* mother, had reservations about her reputation.'

Christine preferred the company of boys to that of girls, possibly because she enjoyed outdoor pursuits more than going to tea-parties and listening to feminine small-talk. She rode well, was a good skier, and was, above all, an indefatigable walker, a hobby which would stand her in good stead in her future activities.

By the time she was ready for the Polish equivalent of coming out, the family finances were decidedly shaky. Her father, having discovered that his 'love match' had turned into Dead Sea fruit, was inclined to be irritable to his wife and emotional with his daughter. This last was one of the manifestations of the tuberculosis which was undermining him. He was unhappy at not being able to give his 'Star' the dowry that should have been hers, had the Goldfeder fortunes not failed.

Count Jerzy's increasing fatigue and debility were sources of anxiety to his wife and to Christine. She could not bear to watch the decline of her handsome, debonair father, and to please him she accepted invitations which would reassure him as to the fact that his daughter was persona grata in the best salons in Warsaw. Although Christine never enjoyed purely social occasions she was young enough to enjoy the admiration of the young men who obviously found her extremely attractive.

In 1930 Christine was shattered by the death of her father. Count Jerzy finally succumbed to the illness that had threatened him for years, and Christine knew the first great grief of her life. At the same time the Goldfeder empire had almost completely collapsed, and there was barely enough money left to support the widowed Countess Stephanie.

Christine had no intention of being a burden to her mother. She went out job-hunting. Very soon she was working for the Fiat agents in their office over a busy garage. For eight hours a day Christine sat working at her desk, while fumes from the exhausts of the cars filled the little office. It was not long before Christine became gravely ill. The first doctor she saw, knowing of her father's history of illness, and seeing dark shadows on her lungs, diagnosed TB. A second opinion and a number of X-rays proved that she was not suffering from TB, but from the fumes of the car exhausts. Greatly relieved, Christine accepted compensation offered her by her employer's insurance company. She was not, at this point, to know that these same threatening shadows which remained on her lungs would later on save her life.

The doctors had advised Christine to give up sedentary work and to lead as much of an open-air life as she could. This suited her very well, and she began to spend a great deal of time walking and skiing in the High Tatras and in various mountain resorts. Her expeditions were not always entirely innocent, for she enjoyed pitting her wits against those of the frontier guards and customs officials and for 'kicks' she smuggled tobacco and cigarettes in and out of Poland, thus gaining experience which would be invaluable when she would smuggle human cargo out of the Nazi claws to safety.

During her skiing expeditions her headquarters were nearly always in the mountain resort of Zakopane which in those days, though still an unspoilt village, was a favourite meeting place of students and the younger members of Polish society. Christine had a great affection for this village whose streets were lined with old Gooral cottages. Always between Christine and the local mountain folk there was perfect communication. She was at her best with simple, uncomplicated people whom she trusted and who trusted her.

The little Countess was persona grata with the Goorals, a mountain people who still retained their traditional costume which, in the case of the men, consisted of a short jacket and trousers of pressed wool decorated down the seams with dark bands. Their jackets were gaily embroidered, usually in red, while the normal headgear was a round billy-cock hat. The women wore a white blouse with a full, flowered skirt of multitudinous frilly petticoats.

Their cottages were simple. There were only two rooms, the black and the white. The former took its name from a stove in the corner, smoke from which had blackened the entire room. The bed belonging to the mistress of the house occupied pride of place. Over it hung a cradle so she could rock her infant without having to move.

Farm implements were stored in the hall which gave on to the white room; this, with traditional mountain hospitality, was always reserved for guests, the whole family crowding into the black room to allow the honoured visitor to enjoy a large, comfortable bed and quantities of goose-down pillows in exquisitely embroidered pillow-cases.

Christine's open-air life soon restored her, and one of her contemporaries, remembering her in her late teens, said, 'She was a being of infinite grace. She was so *alive*. Everything about her shone, her white teeth, her skin and her glossy hair. She had a wide circle of friends and had the reputation of being a great flirt. When she found a young man who amused and stimulated her, she concentrated whole-heartedly on making him her slave; but she soon lost interest in anyone who was too possessive or clinging. Then she simply withdrew, retreating quietly into a no-man's land in which it was impossible to reach her.'

The news of Christine Skarbek's engagement to Charles Getlich was greeted with satisfaction by both their families. It was thought to be a good match. Charles was a pleasant, personable young man. Although his family came of German stock, they had for so long been rooted in Poland that they considered themselves to be unquestionably Polish. They were exceedingly wealthy.

At eighteen Christine was still naive and romantic enough to believe that when the honeymoon was over Charles would devote himself to his young wife. But Charles was first and foremost a business man and while he loved Christine, his work was his main interest. Furthermore, it soon became apparent that the young couple were totally incompatible. Quietly and without any bitterness the marriage was over, and Christine was free again.

It must have been at about this time that Christine made the first of her visits to Czestochowa, the Polish Lourdes, a famous place of pilgrimage and a town which had proud historic memories,[2] and whose greatest treasure was a miraculous Black Virgin housed in Jasna Gora, the Monastery of Light, abode of the Pauline monks.

While Christine was in no way deeply religious this particular painting meant a great deal to her, and while she attached little importance to personal possessions, a replica of this effigy accompanied her always and now, nailed upon the panel bearing the Polish eagle, hangs above her grave.

The original painting has had a long and varied history and is wreathed about with legends. Painted in the third century in Spain, the Miraculous Virgin in 1430 was once stolen by a band of marauding knights intent on pillaging the riches of the monastery. As one of the knights rode off with the precious Virgin, a great thunderstorm broke above him. Lightning flashed and thunder crashed. The knight's horse, feeling his rider accursed, refused to budge. The knight flung the picture to the ground and savagely slashed at it with his sword. Immediately the dry earth cracked open to reveal a bubbling well which to this day provides millions of pilgrims with bottles of holy water. Furthermore, the holy picture is still to be seen scarred across by the slash made by the knight's sword.

It was not long before Christine embarked on a major love

affair with a young, charming and eligible bachelor. It was a tempestuous romance while it lasted. Unfortunately the young man was penniless and his mother, a worldly and dominating matriarch, had other plans for her son's future. While she liked Christine and thought her an eminently suitable mistress for her boy, she had no hesitation in putting an end to the affair. She asked Christine to tea and over the silver *équipage* she made herself quite clear. Quite bluntly she told Christine that, had she been an heiress, she would have been the ideal daughter-in-law; but as a penniless divorcée, she could entertain no hopes of marriage with her son.

This was a blow from which Christine took some time to recover. Once again she had to take stock of her life. Nothing in her upbringing had conditioned her to earn her own living and her taste of servitude in the Fiat offices had confirmed her worst fears about a nine-to-five employment. Christine had inherited much of the Skarbek disdain for commercial activities and little of the Goldfeder financial acumen. Her endemic dislike of any sort of bondage allied to a total disinclination to observe any discipline except that of her own choosing was later to be her undoing, for, as she finally discovered, the world owes nobody a living, not even a courageous and much decorated member of the Skarbek line.

While considering what her future should be, Christine continued to visit Zakopane and to improve her skiing. One day, flying down one of the more dangerous ski slopes, she lost control. She was unable to stop and might have been in serious difficulties had not a giant of a man suddenly stepped in her path, and putting his arm around her, stopped her mad, downward descent. This encounter with a massive stranger was to have lasting repercussions in Christine's life. Her rescuer was called George (Jerzy) Gizycki. He was eccentric, a near-genius who, as someone remarked, 'looked like an eagle and had unsmiling chilly grey eyes'. George was prodigiously good-looking, he was also a moody and temperamental individual, given to violent fits of rage. He found it difficult to communicate, even with those he loved.

His rich family came from the Ukraine. At the age of fourteen George quarrelled with his father, ran away from home, shipped before the mast, went to America, became a cowboy and a gold prospector. Writing and painting came easily to him; but he became an author, travelling the world in search of material for his books and articles. After a sojourn in French West Africa he crystallized his impressions in a book entitled *The Whites and the Blacks*.[3] He knew Africa well, and hoped one day to return there.

George fell passionately in love with Christine and remained so all his life. On 2 November 1938, Jerzy Gizycki married her at the Evangelical Reform Church in Warsaw. It was not long before Christine discovered that she was married to a complicated character, but being both attracted to and dominated by her husband, she managed to sublimate the fear he inspired in her and which was finally to drive them apart. George Gizycki was never one of her stray dogs, and he was one of the few people to have come within her orbit whom she found it impossible to change, tame or subjugate. He was larger than life, and when he was in a bad mood his ire descended like a dark cloud on those around him.

Yet the Gizyckis were an interesting and picturesque couple. Those who met them in the early days of their marriage never forgot the impression made by Christine's glowing, fragile beauty that was offset by her powerfully built, good-looking and unpredictable husband. They made many friends, moving smoothly from one clique to another. George was good for Christine in that he widened her literary and artistic horizons and introduced her to the society of writers, painters and poets, all of whom interested her and stimulated her mind.

The Gizyckis were also on friendly terms with members of the Corps Diplomatique in Warsaw, for it was at this time that Christine met a number of diplomats, some of whom would reappear in her future life and help her in some of her activities.

It may or it may not have been Christine's meetings with diplomats that prompted her to dabble in journalism as a cover for what would later become her work as a secret agent. There is no doubt, however, that as early as 1938 when Tadeusz Horko first met her in Teschen (Cieszyn) word had already gone round that Christine was working for Britain.[4]

George was a restless man, and the Gizyckis travelled a great deal in Europe, spending long periods in France. Whenever George wanted to write in peace he retired to a mountain retreat where he worked, while Christine improved her skiing and her knowledge of the French language and of the French people.

In the meantime Fate had been keeping a watchful eye on the destinies of Christine's future *alter-ego*. It was no easy assignment, since Andrew Kowerski seemed hell-bent on breaking his neck, and vanishing from the scene as rapidly as possible.

The Kowerski estate was some sixty miles from the Pripet marshes. From it there was a clear view of the long plain which any invader coming from Russia was obliged to cross. It was obvious, therefore, that throughout history any estates in the way of the invaders would be damaged. But before the First World War, the Kowerski house was accidentally burnt down, and while it was being rebuilt, Stanislas Kowerski and his family moved to Labunie, where Andrew was born.

Later on when Mr Kowerski took up an important post in Warsaw[5] he decided that his original estate was too remote and difficult of access, and bought a second property near the provincial town of Zamosc. Andrew said, 'The towns in my part of Poland were rather scruffy, and built in a haphazard fashion, but Zamosc was unusual and beautiful.'

Architecturally, Zamosc was of particular interest. It was founded in 1580 by John Zamoyski, the Chancellor and Hetman of the country, a man of culture and wide attainments. Attracted by the Italian style of architecture, he planned to build his town in the Italian manner. He imported Italian architects and craftsmen from Padua, and the result of the initiative was a treasure of porticos, loggias and open staircases, while attics and gables, an inheritance from the Polish medieval period, were lavishly ornamented with the new motifs of decoration current in Italian and Renaissance art.

Andrew was sent to the local State school, where he made little progress owing to what he calls his 'incurable laziness'. Whatever the reasons his father decided to teach him mathematics and 'as he was very short tempered and impatient, I went through unlimited hell for two years or so'.

However, he finally managed to scrape through the necessary examinations, and at eighteen he was sent off to do his military service. His was a tough Army school for gunners, a cosy little place which allowed you two thin blankets in a temperature which was sometimes thirty below zero.

'After this exercise in mortification of the flesh,' Andrew recalls, 'I went to Cracow University to study agriculture. My parents had arranged for me to live with one of my grandmothers, a most imperious lady, who since the death of her husband, and in the fashion of her time, was draped in trailing garments and jetty black veils. Grandmother had her own ideas about nearly everything, and at first living with her was a real punishment. She was curious and asked endless questions. Finally, I got fed up and walked out. She asked me to come back, which I did on my terms. These were that she should sign a sort of fourteen-point pact. She finally did so and, as she had a great sense of humour, we got on very well from that time on. She was a profitable source of income; but I had to work quite hard for what she gave me. She loved gossip and social tittle-tattle, so, as a young man about town, I made it my business to pick up as many juicy little stories as I could.'

Andrew was fortunate in having such enlightened parents for he was anything but a model student. He was constantly in hot water of some kind or the other. He was a first-class sportsman; he rode, played tennis and skied for his university. One of the secrets he kept from his mother was his racing motor-cycle. Horses were accepted as a risk, but a motor-cycle was taboo.

When he was twenty-four, Andrew was involved in an accident that made headlines throughout the world. It was certainly unique, and he remembers clearly every detail of what took place the time he went skiing in Zakopane.

'I was not a gambling man. But I liked drinking. Vodka was my tipple. I never got drunk though. On this particular occasion I joined my friends who were travelling up to Zakopane on a special train named the "Dancing-Skiing Express". There was a whole bunch of us aboard, and during the four-hour journey a girl made a bet with me that I would not stop drinking for a month. Some of my friends joined with her in this challenge, and as it was a large bet and I was short of funds, I accepted the bet. I stopped drinking immediately which, as things turned out later, was just as well.

'The first person I ran into at Zakopane was my wealthy step-brother, George. He was ten years older than myself and had inherited a great deal of money from one of his grand-mothers, Countess Zamoyjska. George had had the good fortune to be educated at Oxford, and was able to splash out and spend money on a grand scale.

George was, as usual, living in the lap of luxury. Naturally he had a ski-teacher and every other convenience to make his hol-iday pleasant. He said that at dawn he and his party were going over the mountains to the Czech side, and he asked whether I would care to join them. I accepted with pleasure and, having arranged a rendezvous, went off to join my friends who were making merry in the town. Dancing went on all through the night. I danced, but I did not drink at all.

'Students were usually housed in a rough kind of hut which had rudimentary beds and boiling water, which you bought to make whatever beverages you fancied. You had to bring all your own supplies.

'At five o'clock I took my rucksack and set off to meet George. There were no ski-lifts in those days, and we stepped off briskly into the pure, clear mountain air. I felt a bit guilty at having refused to bring a friend of mine who had begged to come. I didn't think he was an experienced enough skier, and told him so. He was offended; but I think by refusing to take him with us I saved his life. It was this same man who, later, shot my leg off.

'Our party consisted of George, his ski-teacher Wladek Czech, whose wife, the reigning woman Polish ski-champion, was with us, two men and myself. Our plan was to go to the top of the mountain to the Czech border, whence we would ski down a really vertiginous descent. The mountain was shaped something like a kettle. George and the ski-teacher went ahead, behind them came the pretty wife and myself and two other men.

'It was cold, sunny and windy. The young woman decided her nose needed powdering. She opened her compact and her powder-puff, looking for all the world like an orange, rolled down the mountain-side. One of the party, thinking it *was* an orange, skied down after it, picked up the powder-puff and called up to us that the orange was not an orange after all. For quite some time I had felt very uneasy. Being country born and bred, I have an instinct for danger. Suddenly the guide said, "Stop!" "Why on earth is he stopping us like this?" I asked his wife. "He's frightened of an avalanche starting here." I was just about to say he should have thought of that an hour ago, when I noticed that George and the guide had reached a little ridge between two mountains. They stood there, and at that moment I heard what sounded like a hundred cannons being fired and a crevasse began to widen under our feet, the whole earth was moving and heaving.

'The avalanche immediately began to gather speed. My companions were all very experienced people and, though I was a good skier, I was not a man of the mountains. Yet I was the only one of our party to remove my skis, which one is always told to do if there is any threat of an avalanche.

'The next thing was I found myself sitting down. I could see the girl with her head down, screaming. Then I was covered with tons of wet spring snow; and snow is very heavy. I was still clutching my ski-sticks. I began scrabbling like mad with the two sticks. Finally, feeling that I was about to suffocate, I saw a chink of light. Then, owing to the fact that the avalanche had slipped into a kind of ravine, I suddenly shot up like a cork. This was the biggest avalanche ever recorded in Poland. It was going at eighty miles an hour and it was like being in a fast flowing river. A great rock ricocheted in my direction, smashing my sticks and practically stunning me. I remembered we were *en route* for a precipice just as the snow roller, with a great roar, hurled me, as if from a trampoline, over some sheer mountain peaks. Unwillingly I made a prodigious leap. I must have fallen two hundred metres. From that moment on I swore I would never tell anyone to commit suicide by jumping from a four-storey building. It was terrifying because it was like falling in a dream. Snow and stones were whirling past me and I past them; all this took seconds, although it seemed an age. I stretched out my arms like wings, and found myself up to the armpits in snow. Up till then I had been lucky because any stone I had encountered embedded in the snow would have sliced me in half.

'But my good fortune was of short duration. The rest of the avalanche came roaring down the precipice, and I was again covered with four metres of snow. It was an extraordinarily eerie feeling for, after the roar and noise, I now found myself in complete silence and darkness and there was precious little air.

'Luckily, my little rucksack had fallen over my head, and acted as a sort of canopy, protecting me from the snow and the stones, and also gave me a little air. The silence was unnerving, and I felt as if I were going mad. I tried to move my hands, but my muscles did not respond, which is not surprising, since one square metre of snow weighs nearly a ton. I don't know how long I remained conscious in my "concrete grave". I can't remember. I only know that I began to suffocate, then I panicked, screamed and screamed and finally fainted.

'In the meantime, a skier from down below, sitting outside the mountain hut and looking through field-glasses, had sighted the avalanche. He gave the alarm instantly, so even before George and the ski-teacher, who had escaped the avalanche by sheltering on a stony ridge, had rushed to our rescue, others were on their way.

'The ski-teacher, demented with worry about the fate of his young wife, was obliged to make a detour to avoid the precipice. When he finally reached the piled up masses of snow – in some places it was as tall as a ten-storey building – he found, almost at once, a piece of ski sticking up out of the snow. He began frenziedly to dig, and brought out his wife. She was dead.

'Alas, the poor beautiful young creature had not, like me, been thrown clear over the precipice; but had hurtled down, hitting rocks all the way down. By her death she had saved my life and that of my companions. After a little time the search party consisting of all the guests and ski-instructors from the hut began looking for us near where the body had been found.

'Looking for bodies in an avalanche is exactly like looking for a needle in a haystack. It is necessary to dig parallel trenches and then to probe, as delicately as possible, with long steel poles. The chances of finding a body are practically nil; but the chances of getting the *coup de grâce* through a steel pole are pretty good, particularly as the snow is so compact that two people have to work the steel rod up and down in the snow.

'After an hour or so of back-breaking toil, the search party came upon another of our companions. He was still breathing. It was beginning to be bitterly cold, and darkness was near. The search party decided it was time to give up and to start again afresh the next morning. They decided that nobody else could possibly have survived.

'Fortunately for me, my brother George and my great friend Andrew Tarnowski refused to give up the search. Andrew rushed back to the hut and fetched my rucksack, which was full of unused stores. He distributed brandy, vodka and food, saying reassuringly, "Come on, fellows, Kowerski is a strong chap, and I know he is still alive. We can't give up now. We must find him."

'Warmed by the alcohol, the search party set to with a will again. Then the miracle happened. One of the famous mountain guides, Krzeptowski, pushed his steel pole deep into the snow and shouted, "I've hit something!" "It's a stone," said another, but the first guide pushed harder and tore the skin off my shin. The excitement became tremendous, and everyone began digging like moles. Suddenly my leg came into view. It was an anxious moment, since there was no telling what had happened to my head!

'With shouts from Andrew, I was dragged from my icy tomb. I had been in it for about three and a half hours. The shock of the cold air was like a knife in my lungs. I regained consciousness for a moment before passing out again.

'My rescuers undressed me, and rubbed vigorously with snow as I was numbed through and through. I was told that, though I was seemingly unconscious, I began to curse everyone loudly for having stolen my shoes, and my vocabulary was extensive. I was carried down the mountain, and finally regained my senses to find myself being massaged by a crowd of girls, as all the men had returned to see if they could find the last member of our party. He was not found until two days later, a few yards from where I was buried. The avalanche had taken two victims.

'The story of my miraculous escape was duly reported to the local press and was picked up by newspapers all over the world. Photographs of me, grinning in the sun, appeared in all our papers, and my story was a nine days' wonder. It was then that I came to the conclusion that I was a born survivor.'

On one occasion Andrew Kowerski returned to Zakopane. He was buying a sweater in a local shop when Christine and George Gizycki came in. They were preparing to voyage to East Africa, and George wanted to sell his skis. For a moment the two men chatted, while Christine looked on, taking no part in the negotiations. Andrew bought the skis. This was Christine and Andrew's second meeting and, though he thought fleetingly that she was an unusually attractive young woman, this encounter, like the first, meant nothing to either of them.

CHAPTER THREE

George Gizycki was never completely content in Europe. Its ancient parapets confined his mind as much as living in small flats in crowded cities confined his large frame. He wanted to return to the wider horizons of Africa, and when the opportunity presented itself of his being able to represent his country as consul in Addis Ababa, he accepted at once. But George was a devious man, and, apart from his real interest in the country and its inhabitants, he had certain other private ploys to carry out, whose results would be embodied in confidential reports sent home to his Government.

Christine's mother was not very happy at the thought of her daughter going away for an unspecified period, but Christine herself was delighted at the thought of breaking new ground, and George's descriptions of the exotic country to which they were going had fired her imagination. After a final flurry of shopping and family farewell parties the Gizyckis embarked on their long voyage. As they had time in hand, George decided to take Christine first to Kenya, which he had explored as a young man. Air travel was still in its infancy and the only way to reach East Africa was by steamship.

The historic and cosmopolitan port of Mombasa was an exciting introduction to East Africa. For a thousand years its main export had been ivory and it still retained the Eastern atmosphere of an Arabian Nights' tale. This highly perfumed flavour was enhanced by the mixture of races that flowed through its streets, souks and bazaars. Swahilis swaggering in white kanzus with gay bolero and white-embroidered tarbush rubbed shoulders with Africans draped in the brightly patterned kikoi they wrapped around their slender waists and which reached half way down the leg. Hawk-nosed Arabs in blue embroidered cloth sauntered sedately by in couples, the young males with delicately linked fingers. The pagan women of the Giriama tribe, like a corps de ballet by Bakst, tripped past swinging their frothy multiple skirts of butter muslin. African Muslim women swathed from head to foot in black exposed only their eyes as they hurried home from market with bulging woven *kikapus*; while Indian women, bright as butterflies in their gauzy saris, flitted by, their delicate wrists a-tinkle with multifarious bracelets.

By the end of December or early in January, according to the wind, the European visitors would be treated to a memorable sight for it was then that, sailing before the north-east trade wind, the first vessels of a migration as traditional as that of the birds took place. Running down the *Kaskasi* came the great dhows, the ocean-going 'booms' and 'bangelas' thronging the harbour with noise and colour.

Curious travellers could avail themselves of the opportunity of visiting these dhows by being rowed from the old Customs' Landing Stage to the high-pooped ships whose *Nahodas* (captains) extended lavish hospitality to all who came to sit on their fine carpets and to sip the endless cups of sharp bitter coffee they dispensed from beak-spouted brass coffee-pots.

Mombasa had much to offer sun-worshippers like Christine. There was a string of quiet tamarisk-fringed strands with lilting names like Nyali, Twiga and Malindi. The latter in those days could only be reached after a hazardous journey on rutted tracks which petered inexplicably out into scrub or dongas. Transport was mainly limited to private cars and to a fleet of ramshackle buses held together by string and oaths. These were driven by odoriferous and extrovert Indian drivers who one and all drove hell-for-leather from stop to stop with a load of chattering, giggling Africans, Indians, babies, goats, fowls, bundles, baskets and clanking precious petrol tins whose uses in this country were legion.

All transport was obliged to cross creeks and rivers by ferry, a dreamlike experience intensified by the heat and by the rich resonant voices of the sweating, half-naked crew, whose mournful chant was punctuated at intervals by unearthly ululations from a conch shell blown by the ferryman.

Here under a sky which seemed more luminous than that of Europe, flora and fauna combined to form an exotic tapestry in which were interwoven bright birds – crested hoopoes, long-beaked honey-birds and sun-birds sitting on the telegraph poles or flying amidst the tangled wild roses by the roadside.

If Christine wanted to linger on the beaches of Mombasa, George was anxious to move on to Nairobi, and they left on the long hot journey by the Kenya–Uganda railway which, built at the turn of the century, ran from Mombasa to Lake Victoria. For the first time Christine looked out of the dust-crusted windows at a landscape that changed from the lush vegetation of the coast to lunar landscapes that were bone white under a sky palpitating with great stars. And when the train halted at a whistle stop to take on water Christine would lift her blind and see the lone corrugated iron shack that did duty as a station house and the African silence would be broken by the long-drawn-out call of a creature of the night.

The Nairobi that Christine discovered in 1939 was a mixture of old and new. The first settlers had put down their roots without paying much attention to the principles that govern town-planning. They built shops to trade in, offices in which the business of the day could be conducted, and bungalows in which to live. For decoration they planted eucalyptus trees which grew big and tall. In the course of time, some of the old offices were replaced by modern stone buildings.

There was nothing static about Nairobi and it produced a feeling of excitement, of elation even among those who visited it from up-country. One of these was the writer Karen Blixen: 'All the same, Nairobi was a town; here you could buy things, hear news, lunch or dine at the hotels and dance at the club, and it was a live place, in movement like running water, and in growth like a young thing it changed from year to year, and while you were away on a shooting safari, the new Government House was built, a stately cool house, with a fine ballroom and a pretty garden, big hotels grew up, impressive agricultural shows and fine flower shows were held, our quasi-smart set of the Colony from time to time enlivened the town with melo-dramatic rows.'[1]

The Gizyckis moved into the Salisbury Hotel. The owner of the hotel, Mrs Noon, like many people in the colony, had not had an easy life. She had been married to one of the men responsible for the building of the life-draining Kenya–Uganda railway. He had died suddenly, leaving her nearly destitute, with two small children. She opened a boarding-house for rail-way employees which prospered so well that Mrs Noon was, in time, able to build the Salisbury Hotel, a model of its kind, entirely furnished by Maples of London, and with its own swimming pool.

Christine, it seems, always preferred living in hotels or flats rather than in houses. She was not domesticated and household chores irked her. Fastidious in her person, she was not particu-larly interested in creating a decorative background for her personality.

George, since he was long familiar with this country, must have been aware of the pressures building up even then under the smooth surface of what appeared to be a model British colony. Here, as in South Africa, the dead hand of the British Raj conditioned the existence both of the European commu-nity and of the African and Indian population, lumped together, except by the discerning few, as 'the niggers'. The European community was made up mainly of pioneer farmers and their families, good, hard-working middle-class English folk; Government officials who were typical civil servants, with a sprinkling of shop-keepers, unassimilated foreigners and ticket-of-leave men, while at the top sat a bunch of amusing, decadent expatriates, many bearing famous names, who had brought their loose morals along with their polo ponies and crested silver, into a country big enough to contain and to filter their often unattractive habits and activities.

It was this particular 'quasi-smart set' which provided the scandals and gossip which kept envious middle-class wives in a permanent state of shocked titillation. Husband-and-wife swopping were the occupational hazards of belonging to the fast set. Orgies and jealous scenes culminating even in murder made up for no longer being able to participate in the excitements of the London season. But it was this small section of the population who really loved Africa and, unlike many of the more suburban-minded settlers, did not believe in the myth of their exile from 'home', that 'little old England' to which they returned so happily on leave, only to discover that 'home', in fact, had become their spacious African farms.

Africa was a place for legends and for larger-than-life characters. Such a one was the Danish writer Karen Blixen, who nine years before Christine's arrival had left her coffee-shamba at the foot of the Ngong Hills to return to her native land. More than any other writer before or since, she had been able to capture the essence of life in the Highlands of East Africa, and if anyone could have reconciled Christine to living in Nairobi, it would have been that great lady, whose farm had been the meeting place of so many foreigners and émigrés who liked good food, good wine and cultured talk. Karen Blixen had loved and understood the Africans, both those who worked on her farm and those who lived in the neighbourhood, but in general the European settlers tended to treat their Africans as the feudal landowners had treated their serfs; it did not enter their heads that they had taken over this vast land, its inhabitants and its multiple problems, or that they would, in the final analysis, themselves be overtaken by the march of events and be forced to give up what they considered was legitimately theirs and to return to a spent and overcrowded Europe that had no room for them and their pseudo-feudal ways.

But this Nemesis was in the distant future and the European population of South and Eastern Africa continued to live their spacious colonial lives. It was this spaciousness and timelessness that attracted Christine, and since she and George were not involved in the sometimes heartbreaking hazards to which the farming community were exposed, she was able to look, listen and absorb much of what Africa has to give to those who are silent and secret.

Christine already knew by this time that she had made an error in marrying George. Brilliant and entertaining as he sometimes was he gave her a feeling of claustrophobia; he loomed over her like a dark cloud and she began to wonder how she would ever escape from him. He on his side made it plain that he was satisfied with his marriage and that Christine would eventually settle down with him.

There was not, however, much time to settle into any kind of rhythm of living for the news from Europe was increasingly gloomy. Although war came to Poland on 1 September 1939, Hitler had begun taking the law into his own hands at a much earlier date. Austria was annexed in March 1938 and Czechoslovakia a year later and since the crisis which had begun in March 1939 the Polish people were aware of the danger of a military conflict with Germany. 'Up to March 1939 Poland's security had been based almost exclusively on the traditional alliance with France of 1921, and she now tried to consolidate it by negotiations for the final confirmation of the British alliance, and above all by the conclusion of a new Franco-British Military convention on 19 May; this convention obliged France to open an offensive against the German forces with the bulk of her troops not later than fifteen days after the mobilization of the French Army. The Warsaw Government also negotiated with London and Paris for the provision of immediate financial, technical and operational assistance, but did not succeed in obtaining any binding assurances since the Western Powers wanted to avoid any definition of their obligations to provide direct help because of their own military weakness and unfavourable geographical position.'[2]

But while their governments were discussing subscribing large sums for defence, the British and French ambassadors in Warsaw were recommending prudence and moderation. They were afraid that any action taken by Poland would provoke Hitler's ire. Even the Polish press were told to keep in step. Meantime the Germans were clamouring for Danzig and for an autobahn to be built across Pomorze into East Prussia and were inventing all manner of fabrications about the way the Poles were treating the German minority. Hitler was becoming more and more menacing but the Western democracies clung obstinately to their illusions. Though Poland was in no way militarily prepared for the massive German offensive, certain measures were already in existence to bolster up the nation's defence,[3] and from 1938 onwards a special section of the British General Staff known as GS/R under Colonel Holland was sent to investigate the European scene.[4]

According to F. W. D. Deakin, 'in the months preceding the German attack on Poland in 1939, a series of modest and brave efforts were made to establish communications in Poland, Czechoslovakia and France in such an event, on the pessimistic but realistic assumption that these countries would be overrun in the event of a major struggle. There had been discussions on sabotage of communications with the corresponding French services as early as June, 1939, and small dumps of arms and equipment were set up in France. The same special section of the War Office established what came to be known as No. 1 Military Mission to Poland for the same purpose.'[5]

On 30 August 1939 an incredulous Polish nation listened to Hitler's ultimatum. At 11.30 a.m. a news-flash announced that the Poles had violated the German frontier and had captured a radio station at Gleiwitz, killing all German personnel. It was subsequently proved that this operation was carried out by carefully primed German prisoners from a nearby jail, dressed in Polish uniforms to carry out their *coup*. Once their role was over they were shot out of hand.

At 5.30 a.m. on 1 September, Germany invaded Poland.

Shortly afterwards the United Kingdom which had guaranteed Poland's territorial integrity declared war on Germany. The Polish armies fought a gallant defensive action.

Although both George and Christine knew that the tides of war would not immediately engulf East Africa, their decision to return to Europe was simultaneous. George was not certain of what he would do when he got back but Christine already had a plan. It was not cut and dried simply because it was dependent on so many extraneous factors. She was quite determined to make use of her many contacts, her knowledge of languages and her flashing intelligence in the service of her country. There were no heroics about her decision. She was a Pole, a Skarbek and a patriot.

There was never any doubt that Christine would always achieve her objective. Once she had made up her mind her powers of concentration were such that she simply ignored all obstacles. Furthermore she appeared, at times, to possess mesmeric powers and if her methods were sometimes unorthodox, she unquestionably got results.

It is not easy to analyse the motives which prompted Christine to choose England as the springboard and background for her career as a secret agent. Her own background and culture were European; her French was flawless and her appreciation of Gallic *mores* and logic was great. Yet in the beginning she felt that there was something solid about Britain and the British which gave reassurance to her wild spirit. Though she was brave, patriotic and passionate about her own country as are all Poles, she admired the British phlegm and was prepared to go along with a people who took their sports so seriously but such grave matters as honour and death with nonchalance, almost frivolously.

The development of Christine's love affair with England is important in the light of her subsequent bitter disillusionment in the codes of conduct of a country which, generous and magnanimous in time of war, could, so easily in time of peace, turn against the greatest of its servants. The rejection of Winston

Churchill, repeated in a minor key in the rejection of herself, was a blow from which she never recovered.

By the time Christine and George reached London, a Polish Government had been set up in France under President Raczkiewicz, nominated successor by the former President who had remained in Rumania. General Ladislas Sikorski was appointed Commander-in-Chief and at once started to rebuild the Polish Army. News from Poland was salt on an open wound and Christine had only one thought: to return home and get her mother to safety. George was like a bear with a sore head, for he had tried to join the Army and had been rejected as being too old. Nothing daunted he determined to go to the aid of Finland. Even the most carping of his critics had to admit that George was an exceptionally brave man.

The Gizyckis found temporary accommodation in London with two middle-aged ladies who fell instantly under Christine's spell and who introduced her to their friends, many of whom were influential in the world of politics. It is impossible today to untangle all the threads which led Christine from one contact to the other; there was Sokolov,[6] son of one of the founders of Israel; there was a Polish general, and there was the brilliant editor of the review *Nineteenth Century and After*, Freddy Voigt. Described by Julian Amery as a liberal who was also a realist,[7] he held court most evenings in the Majorca restaurant, and it was with Voigt that Christine met a business man called George Taylor.

There was an instant rapport between Christine and George Taylor who almost certainly brought her to Sir Robert Vansittart at the Foreign Office.[8] The Foreign and Commonwealth Office have provided the following account of Christine's visit: 'The officer who first interviewed her reported very favourably on this intelligent, smart-looking ardent Polish patriot. She submitted a well-thought plan to proceed to Budapest where she intended producing propaganda leaflets to maintain the spirit of resistance of the people of Poland. She was prepared to go to Poland via Zakopane in the Tatra mountains. She was also planning to organize the exfiltration of POW's to Allied territory and to collect Intelligence. Being an experienced skier and well known to the local guides at Zakopane, she was confident of their willingness to assist her. The plan was approved.' Christine was 'in'.

At the instigation of George Taylor, Freddy Voigt fixed Christine's cover and it was as a British journalist collecting data for articles that Christine left England on 21st December 1939. Christine arrived in Budapest aflame with the intention of making straight for Poland. Her mission, a touchingly naive one, was to explain to the Poles that England should not be blamed for the disaster that had overtaken them. She soon discovered that getting to Poland was not as simple as she had imagined; but with her characteristic verve and energy she began making contact with the Poles in Budapest who were already linked with the Polish Government in exile.

As soon as the Germans invaded Poland, thousands of Poles slipped into Hungary. Officers and soldiers alike were interned and segregated in camps; the Hungarians were passionately pro-Polish, for they had never forgotten the age-old debt they owed to Poland for liberating them from the Turkish yoke; and nearly all Hungarians, from the humblest peasant to the greatest landowner, were prepared to perjure their soul to protect the Poles in their midst.

Civilians as well as the military found their way from Poland to Hungary and, owing to the fact that Poland still had diplomatic relations with all countries including Italy, the Germans could do nothing against the civilians. The Hungarians treated the exiles with respect and generosity. They were offered food, clothing and accommodation. Even hotels were put at their disposal.

Under these circumstances it was easy for the newly formed Polish Government in exile in France to form organizations in Hungary and Rumania, and these organizations were not underground cells, they were official. As such they found ways of helping the refugees with money and petrol. The Polish Ambassador was still in full control of his official functions, as was the Military Attaché, much to the fury of the Germans, who tried to find a Polish Quisling to head a puppet government. This useless exercise, which cost them a great deal of time and money, expired in a flurry of mortification, memoranda and barbed jokes, which infuriated the Germans even more against the Poles.

Christine was not a refugee. Her husband was a diplomat, she was a journalist, and she had a healthy bank account. She soon found a pleasant furnished service flatlet in a private house and lost no time in contacting those she thought might help her get to Poland as quickly as possible.

One of these was the Polish Consul whom she had known in the past. He kept open house for the émigrés and Christine often called there in the late afternoon, as much to collect information as to steep herself in the entirely Polish ambience of her compatriots.

Usually the moment she arrived she was surrounded by friends. On one particular occasion, on a day which was to be one of the most important of her life, she came into the smoke-filled room to find that the centre of attention was a tall, fair, rosy, one-legged lieutenant who was holding forth about the collapse of Poland. Because of the press of people, Christine stood in the doorway listening, while Andrew Kowerski continued his tale with greater and even more sensational embellishments.

Andrew said, 'Ten minutes after I had begun talking, the door opened and a girl walked in. I stopped and stared at her. She was slim, sunburnt with brown hair and eyes. A kind of crackling vitality seemed to emanate from her. She was introduced as Christine Gizycki. After a moment or so I realized that we had met before, and as we shook hands, she said, "We met at Zakopane the time you were caught up in the famous avalanche; you bought my husband's skis. Do please go on with your story. It's not often one has a chance to talk with someone who fought with the Black Brigade." So I went on with the tale of our adventures, and I saw that Christine's eyes were shining with tears.

'Later we talked together. When she said she had recently

arrived from London I asked her why the British had abandoned us after guaranteeing us their help. She smiled and said it was too long and complicated a subject to discuss in public, and why didn't we dine together the following night. "I'm inviting you to dinner," she said.'

Andrew was glad of that as he could not have invited her. Every penny he had went into buying petrol for his 'work'. At the outbreak of the war Andrew Kowerski had joined Poland's only motorized brigade. It was called the 'Black Brigade', because everyone in it wore black leather jackets. Under the command of a fine soldier, Maczek, who was afterwards to fight in the Normandy invasion, this suicidally brave and gallant brigade fought the Germans, were captured, escaped, reformed and attacked again and finally crossed into Hungary.

According to international law, the officers and soldiers of the Polish Army were immediately interned. Andrew Kowerski was among those detained. After forty-eight hours Lieutenant Kowerski, who already had the Virtuti Militari[9] for his exploits in the field, escaped. He had no money and no clothes to replace his uniform. This did not prevent him from starting up a one-man escape organization. He became a sort of Polish Scarlet Pimpernel. The main object of the undertaking was to help Polish soldiers to escape from the internment camps, and set them on their way to France whence they could rejoin the Polish Army.

In the early days before Christine's arrival Andrew had had great difficulties in finding suitable accommodation. He and his assistant, his cousin, Baron Adam Konopka, who was in charge of obtaining, preparing and forging (when necessary) all the vital documents needed by the escapees, stayed in an hotel with the Hungarian Committee who had taken over the problem of housing the Polish refugees. This was the Metropole. It was not the Gelert, the smartest hotel in Budapest, but a decent enough place.

One night when Andrew returned from an exhausting trip he found two Hungarian policemen waiting to question him. He knew at once that the hotel porter had alerted them. All over the Austro-Hungarian Empire the same system was operated; by informers working through hotel porters, waiters and taxi drivers, tittle-tattle of every kind was carried to the police. In this case, the hotel porter had obviously told them that Andrew Kowerski often came back late at night stone-cold sober, but utterly exhausted and with his clothes in a filthy condition.

Andrew was arrested and taken to the police station where he was questioned and accused of having escaped from an internment camp. The police knew he was an officer. Andrew pointed out that, in being an officer, it was unthinkable that he could have an artificial leg; and with that he put his wooden leg on the table.

He had made his point. He was released.

He returned to the hotel Metropole a very worried man. The room he shared with Konopka was a haven for the escapees – there were never less than ten of them sleeping on the floor – but it offered him little opportunity for rest, and, now that he had had one brush with the police, he was anxious about the security of them all. He told Konopka to look for a flat which would afford them more privacy. Within two days, Konopka had found a room in a very quiet street; it was spacious, on the second floor, and belonged to an amiable old music teacher who had two remarkably pretty nieces. Andrew was jubilant and congratulated his cousin on having found a room which was both inexpensive and well placed. He was particularly impressed at there being ample parking space outside. That night he drove to the Yugoslav border – not one of his favourite drives as it meant driving up to the axles in thick sludgy mud. Invariably his black car was plastered with the stuff which turned a whiteish blue and was very difficult to remove.

Andrew drove back to Budapest in a relaxed mood. He was looking forward to a long sleep in his new peaceful quarters. It was four a.m. and he was dropping with fatigue.

He made straight for the new street. To his horror it was ablaze with lights; there was music blaring and people walking up and down. The whole place was humming with activity. Andrew looked at the name of the street, 'Vic ucca' (Street of Joy), and the truth hit him. He was in a street lined with brothels, which explained its silence in the daytime. All his neighbours were recovering from their nocturnal activities.

In a fury, Andrew raced upstairs and found cousin Adam Konopka fast asleep in bed. Andrew shook him violently. 'You bloody fool,' he said, 'come to the window and see what you've let us in for.' Konopka looked down into the busy Street of Joy. 'We'll move tomorrow,' he said apologetically, climbing back into bed. Andrew remained at the window. He was looking at his car which was caked with clay. Behind it was another car similarly muddied, and in front of that a long line of cars which had come in from the country, all like his own, plastered with mud. 'We won't move,' he said. 'Unwittingly you've found the best street for our needs. Nobody would ever think of looking for us here in a red light district in which muddy cars are the norm. Congratulations, Cousin, on a fine piece of planning.'

Much of Andrew's success in helping a record number of prisoners to escape was due to the fact that, in the early days before the Germans began to apply pressure on them, the Hungarians did everything they could to help the Poles with whom they had, since time immemorial, been in sympathy.

Whenever possible the Hungarian officials turned a blind eye to Andrew's activities, but he was well aware that if he was caught with escaping prisoners they would be obliged to put him in jail. His work was no sinecure. The winter was terrible. It was one of the worst in living memory; the temperature was sometimes twenty below zero and there was an unusual amount of snow. Andrew's car was unheated and his was one of the few to take to the road. The going was tough, for often the car would stick in a snowdrift and Andrew had to put blankets under the wheels to get moving again. Sometimes he was obliged to get the help of villagers who brought a pair of horses to drag the car out of a snowdrift.

*

On the day Andrew first met Christine in Budapest he was not looking his best. He was wearing his only suit which had been given him by a very stout man. Christine however seemed unaware of this, and before she slipped away, reminded him of their dinner date.

The next day, Andrew had to organize an escape and was unable to keep his date with Christine. He asked Adam Konopka to telephone, make his apologies and take her out in his stead. Christine politely refused this invitation. Next morning, Andrew having successfully completed his escape operation was drearily wondering where he could obtain a meal. The telephone rang. To his joy it was Christine. Once again she invited him to dinner. They arranged to meet on the embankment of the Danube, near the Landshut chain bridge.

'It was windy and cold,' Andrew said, 'I decided to be there in good time not to keep her waiting. I stopped my car and from far away I saw Christine walking as she did when she was in a good mood. She walked in a dancing way, full of grace. She had pretty legs and on that evening had on a kind of duffle coat with a hood pulled over her hair.'

Andrew drove Christine to a little restaurant she knew. They had an excellent meal. Both were aware that this was a momentous occasion. 'There was a great spark between us,' Andrew said. He found her extremely attractive. He drank a great deal of wine but noticed that Christine hardly drank at all. Occasionally she would pour some water into her wineglass. Andrew asked her why she was not drinking with him. 'Why should I? I can do everything that other people do under the influence of drink, but I don't need it.'

As the evening progressed Andrew aired his views about life and politics. Encouraged by her interest he launched into an attack against the British Government: 'I was terribly bitter.'

When Christine had an opportunity to talk about her own activities she mentioned vaguely that she had been sent by an organization to counteract German propaganda in Poland. In those days the walls of nearly every Polish town were splashed with giant posters showing a mother with a dead child in her arms and in the background, a burning town. The wording was simple. 'England, this was your work.'

Christine intimated that her role was to restore the credibility of England in Poland. She defended England and France, saying they would never allow Poland to perish. They would go on fighting to the end. 'France will not fail,' she said, for she still believed that France was the France of Napoleon.

Andrew said, 'Well, we know that the morale of the Poles is fantastic, but they need help. They need arms, ammunition, money, clothes and food.' 'I know,' replied Christine, 'that is why I intend going to Poland to see exactly what is wanted.'

He stared at her. 'My dear girl, you must be joking. You, a girl, trying to get to Poland in this weather? You'll have to wait for the summer, and even then I doubt whether you will make it.'

Christine said, 'I cannot wait for the summer. I've made up my mind, and once I do that I never change it. Also, I am a very good skier. Will you help me find someone to get me into Poland soon?' He said he would do his best to find someone but he wasn't very hopeful. She looked so frail.

Andrew and Christine sat talking about their childhood, their families and significant events in their lives. Christine was warm and sympathetic. She wanted to know all about the accident that had resulted in the loss of his leg. He told her how it had happened.

He had just finished at Cracow University in 1934 and, in accordance with the custom in Poland at that time, was about, as his father's eldest son, to be given the family estate. This was at Dub in south-eastern Poland. Andrew was sitting in his flat preparing a list of guests to be invited to the traditional three-day shoot which followed handing over the estate; the custom was that only the son's friends should accept the invitation, the father's should refuse.

Andrew had decided on the twelve people he wanted, when in came the young man whose life he had saved by refusing to take him on the perilous 'Avalanche' party. He wanted to know why he had not been invited to shoot. Andrew told him that his twelve guns were already chosen but he was so persistent that finally Andrew gave in and asked him to join the party. He was the thirteenth guest.

At the end of the third day, when the sleighs were already coming to pick everyone up, the thirteenth guest, standing less than a yard away from him, inadvertently shot Andrew through the foot.

In those days there were no roads and only one train came through every twenty-four hours. Andrew was taken to the nearest town, four hours' ride away. At that time, in 1935, no penicillin was available. By now extremely ill, he was transferred to Lwow, where a famous surgeon, a friend of the Kowerski family, used all his skill to keep him alive. For six months Andrew was on the danger list; several amputations were performed on his leg, and at one stage he developed blood poisoning.

A whole year of his life was spent in the University Hospital before he was allowed to leave.[10] In 1937 he went to England and was fitted with an artificial leg before returning to Poland. He still attributes his survival to the love and prayers of his mother.

Christine was deeply moved by this story. Andrew drove her home to where she lived in Dereck Ucca in Buda, behind the old town in a new part in the hills which had not been completely built over. Christine directed Andrew through a maze of tiny twisting streets which curved higher and higher. At Dereck Ucca he stopped the car, and the two of them sat in silence, conscious of the mutual attraction which was making it difficult for them to part. Finally, Christine invited Andrew to come in for a cup of coffee.

'I walked to her flat. It had a little front garden and its own separate entrance. There was a tiny little hall in which we hung our coats, and then I went in to a very pleasant room with two large windows. The walls were plain and the curtains and covers were of chintz, which was unusual in this part of Europe.

'It was a one-room flatlet with a good bathroom, and in a

corner was a tiny kitchenette. There was a big sofa which at night became a bed. Though Christine had only a few photographs and lamps, the whole place was amazingly warm and cosy. I was very impressed, particularly as the room I was then sharing with my cousin Adam was small and uncomfortable.

'While Christine was preparing the coffee, I sat and watched her, marvelling at her extraordinary grace. Then she gave me a cup of coffee and suddenly, we were in one another's arms. I stayed the night but we both knew that this was no casual affair but was the beginning of an important and unique relationship. Everything was magical and wonderful and funny. When the little maid came in with Christine's breakfast tray, she found her sitting up in bed as usual, while I was hiding in the wardrobe. The girl must have been puzzled by the fluctuations of Christine's appetite. When I was there I was always hungry and did not leave a scrap of butter or crumb on the tray.

'We decided that we must keep our affair as secret as possible. I was doing my work and Christine was busy with her various activities. She was in touch with British journalists and passport officials and I met a number of them with her. She always worried about the possibility of my being caught when I was driving my escapees. At the same time she did not lose sight of her mission, and she kept on pressing me to find someone to escort her to Poland.

'Some time in February I met Jan Marusarz, one of the ski-teachers from Zakopane, where I had spent a great deal of time skiing. Both Jan and his brother Stach were famous skiers and members of the Polish Olympic Team. Jan, the older, was a large, sensible sort of chap with masses of black hair and a sharp face. He was strong and reliable. He knew Christine, and when I told him that she was in Budapest he was delighted and said he would like to see her. I said, "Janek, she wants to go to Poland. Will you take her?"

'His reaction was exactly like mine. "You must be joking. Don't you realize what conditions are like in the mountains? The snow is over four metres deep in some places. There's no ski-piste or any other kind of road. The only way to get over these mountains is to take a zig-zag course and even for an experienced mountaineer like myself the journey is almost unendurable. How do you think a girl would survive such a trip? Christine must be crazy."

'"I agree," I said, "but all the same you'd better come and talk to her."

'I drove him to her flat and such were her powers of persuasion that after an hour or so he said, "Very well, I'll take you. I'm a courier for the Polish Military Attaché, and I have absolutely no right to take anyone with me, but I'll do it for you."'

Immediately preparations were begun for Christine's journey. As the roads were blocked by snow Andrew could not drive them and the only possibility was to take a train to the Slovakian border. Jan explained that he had a safe house in Koszyce on the Hungarian side and that his usual procedure was to cross the mountains into Slovakia. He then took a train to the Polish border. From there he went over the Tatra mountains to Zakopane. It sounded simple but in fact it involved an awe-inspiring journey under abominable weather conditions over the Tatras up to the pass which was over two thousand metres and then down again to Zakopane. The temperature was thirty degrees below zero, and the snow was generally four to five metres deep.

Both Andrew and Janek pointed out the hazards to Christine but she declined to discuss them, saying quietly, 'If Janek goes, I go with him.'

On the day she left – it was the middle of February – the weather was still appalling. Andrew packed Christine's rucksack, putting in a number of small items which he knew from experience might be vital. Christine seemed unimpressed by all the precautions taken for her wellbeing, and could not understand why he thought it so important to make her take extra mittens, vitamins, aspirins and other pills. Andrew did not repeat to her the stories he heard every day from refugees from Poland who had crossed via the mountains. Some had lost their companions in the snow; others were dangerously ill with frostbite. Each time Andrew looked at the frail, thin young girl who was planning this suicidal journey he determined to stop her, but already he realized that there was no stopping Christine once her mind was made up.

On an icy day in February Andrew drove Christine and her companion to Budapest Station and, with a heavy heart, said goodbye to them. He knew that until they came back he would have no news of them.

In those days the Germans were less highly organized than they became later on. Since they believed that in the prevailing weather conditions nobody would be mad enough to try and cross the Tatra mountains, their security was not proof against experienced and determined travellers.

From Koszyce, where Christine and Janek stayed in the 'safe house', they crossed next day to Slovakia in good time to get the early train going to the Polish border. Janek had arranged for the tickets to be bought for him, and the Slovak guards did not interfere when two late travellers flung themselves into the train at the last moment.

The journey across Slovakia and to the Polish border went without a hitch. Just before the train reached the station, Christine and Janek jumped out and made for another 'safe house' on the Slovakian side where they waited before crossing the mountains into Poland.

It was then that the really gruelling journey began. They started to climb on skis and the going was rough. Janek led the way making tracks for Christine to follow. It was a slow and desperate climb upwards in the deep snow. Their bodies were burning hot while their hands and feet were frozen.

They had reached the 'Quiet Valley', Cicha Dolina, when a blizzard got up. This could have been a disaster, since once the snow was blown in every direction it was impossible to move. Fortunately Janek, the experienced mountaineer, found the way to a hut, though by the time they reached it, even he could hardly drag himself through the door. Christine, who had kept up with him all the way, collapsed in a corner. In a short while Janek made tea while Christine dosed them both with some of the remedies Andrew had packed into her knapsack. Having drunk the hot, sweet tea they drifted into a half sleep. Outside the wind was raging. Suddenly Christine woke Janek. 'I can hear people shouting for help.' Janek listened and heard only the howling of the wind. 'You're dreaming, girl,' he said, 'let's get some sleep.' But Christine became agitated and went to the door. 'I can hear voices. We must go and help them.' Janek put his head out of the hut. Through the swirling snow he could hear distant voices crying out, but it was impossible to know from which direction they came. He closed the door firmly. 'I'm sorry, Christine, we have important work to do and I cannot jeopardize our lives by going out into that raging snow. Forget it and get some rest.' But Christine, listening only as the distant voices grew fainter and fainter, kept repeating, 'We must help them.' Janek had almost to use force to prevent her from going out.

In the morning the wind had died down. The snow was piled higher than ever. Christine could not forget the voices in the night. Half an hour after they started they came across the frozen bodies of a man and a girl. They searched their rucksacks for some kind of identification but found none. Later they heard that thirty people had perished in the blizzard that night on the Tatra mountains. Finally they reached the home of Janek's parents where Christine, whom they remembered from her skiing days, was given a heroine's welcome. Janek was completely exhausted; but after twenty-four hours' rest, Christine was as bright as ever, and longing to get away. As Andrew had seen to it that she was equipped with all the necessary false papers provided by the Polish underground organization, Janek felt she was as safe as a Pole could be in German-occupied Poland.

On arrival in Warsaw Christine went straight to her mother. Countess Skarbek appeared to be supremely unconscious of the danger she ran by remaining in Warsaw, and though

Christine pointed out that being Jewish she would inevitably be kept under constant surveillance, she refused to contemplate moving. Feeling that her mother would be compromised if it ever transpired that she was in Warsaw, Christine stayed for only two days, then found a 'safe house' from which she could make contact with a number of her friends, engaged in work similar to her own.

Christine soon discovered that war-torn Warsaw was totally unlike the prosperous bustling city of her youth. While the Germans had not yet unleashed the full flood of their oppressive measures, they had concentrated on draining Poland of most of her resources, so that the majority of people had to go without fuel, food or leather. The Poles were driven to wearing wooden clogs as a protection against frost and snow, and their garments soon showed signs of wear since they had no replacements, having bartered their few 'good' clothes for flour and potatoes.

This was the thin end of the wedge. The Government of the Reich's plan was simple: to exterminate the greater proportion of the Polish nation. Indeed, as the war progressed, they began enthusiastically to realize this project. Nonetheless the country as a whole was determined from the moment they were invaded to continue the struggle. At the beginning of the Occupation organizers of the Polish Resistance came forward to lead the struggle against the enemy. 'Until the springtime of 1940, a few groups, the remains of the regular army of 1939, were active. Parallel to their guerilla activities a host of clandestine organizations both political and military came into being and this in spite of the most severe repressions (the death penalty) on the part of the Germans. All those who could assembled and hid arms and ammunition. At the same time the development of political life in a clandestine ambience and the maturing of the concepts of the struggle resulted in the regrouping and polarization of the forces of the Polish Resistance.'[11]

It did not take Christine long to discover that the Home

Army had set up, supplied and was successfully running a whole series of minor industries in Warsaw, of which the Underground Press was a shining example. Only a month after the final defeat of the Polish Army, at the beginning of 1940, two weekly papers began to circulate in Warsaw. The Germans immediately took over all printing presses, made the purchase of paper in bulk illegal and said they would shoot anyone caught distributing uncensored literature. Nobody paid the slightest attention to these efforts at intimidation, and in the following twelve months half a dozen new periodicals and one daily paper were launched.

The first and main weekly, *The Information Bulletin*, appeared faithfully on the same day each week for the next five years and its circulation was over 50,000 copies. With it was printed a news-sheet containing a transcript of the BBC and Reuters broadcasts.

Other aspects of the Home Army's creative output were centred on the main industrial complex of the underground: the Quartermastership or IVth Department. This had two basic tasks – to satisfy the current needs of the sabotage unit and to build up stocks for an eventual general uprising, scheduled to break out in the final stages of the war in conjunction with Allied action on Poland. The Quartermastership had inherited a number of caches laid up by various units in the last days of the 1939 campaign; it also had a small amount of equipment from British air drops and could capture or buy off arms from individual German or other sources. But this was not sufficient; overcoming all difficulties the Home Army set to and manufactured the most urgent items of equipment.

Besides weapons and explosives, the Quartermastership produced a wide range of ancillary material such as medical supplies, maps and forged papers of every kind.[12]

Christine soon discovered that some of her friends belonged to an underground organization called 'The Musketeers'. It was under the leadership of an unusual man called Witkowski whom Christine had known in her Paris days. He was an engineer and a great eccentric. He had arrived on the Gizyckis' doorstep one day with plans for some kind of revolutionary invention. Witkowski was at his best in a crisis. A war or a revolution was the breath of life to him. A first-class organizer, he was daring enough to risk everything, but never took stupid risks. He and Christine got on well and he promised to assist her in every way possible. She was still able to move freely in Warsaw, making contacts and collecting information. The Germans at that time were too busy deporting important people to bother with tracking down workers in the underground movement.[13]

On this, her first trip, Christine spent five weeks in Poland. After a silence of three weeks Andrew received a postcard, a typical card of the period saying, 'I am well, everything is all right. We are here, trying to leave. Everything is fine. I hope you will soon have some news from my cousins in Paris.' This meant that she would be returning as soon as possible.

She came back the same way as she had gone, via Zakopane with the faithful Janek. It was not an easy journey as it was well into March and the snow was vanishing fast. Also the Germans had had time to organize themselves and their first repressive action was to confiscate all skis and skiing equipment, to prevent people escaping over the mountains.

There was only one frightening episode. 'Christine hadn't been in the Polish War,' said Andrew. 'But on one occasion I was walking through an open field to my observation post with my soldiers, when a Messerschmidt spotted us and started chasing me, playing with me as a cat plays with a mouse. It went to and fro trying to machine-gun me. I lay flat on the ground but the sound of the machine-gun was confoundedly close. Christine told me that they had just reached the mountain top when a German reconnaissance plane arrived. They were certain he had spotted them and was circling them, when they took cover in the lee of a big rock. There was no snow, only a patch of grass, and it was maybe thanks to this that they escaped the plane's attentions.'

One cold and miserable day in mid-March the phone rang

and Christine's voice said 'Andrew, I am back. Come immediately or even quicker' – a typical Christine phrase. Andrew jumped into his car and in a few minutes was holding her in his arms. She looked tired and thin but was full of life, sparkle and enthusiasm. She couldn't wait to tell him of what she had found in Poland, of the fighting of the people, of the miseries inflicted on them by the Germans and of her plans for the future.

There was so much to tell. It took all day and half the night to give him a detailed report of all she had said and done and whom she had met. When he could get a word in edgeways Andrew told her what he had been doing.

His organization had grown considerably from its days as a one-man, one-car band, taking only five escapees out at a time. Andrew wanted a lorry. He found a very rich man who had transported all his furniture and pictures out of Hungary in a fleet of eight lorries. 'I'd like one of your lorries,' said Andrew. 'I could lose the lorry,' answered the millionaire. 'Yes you could, but I could lose my life, and at this moment we are all risking our lives.' The rich man shrugged his shoulders but would not part with the lorry.

Some days later Andrew went to the Polish Consulate whose six rooms were jam-packed with a milling throng of never less than two hundred persons all trying to get passports, information or visas. Outside, the Hungarian police kept benevolent watch. Andrew was standing there when an enormously tall man came over to him. 'I hear you need a lorry?' 'Yes.' 'I have a lorry. It belongs to me and I have all the necessary papers. I escaped from a place near Wieliczka[14] in my lorry with Polish soldiers and other people, and if you need it, the lorry is at your disposal.' Andrew said, 'Man, the lorry is the only thing you have. By giving it to me you could lose it tomorrow if we were caught and arrested.' The big man said, 'Lieutenant, you are talking to a Pole.'

The name of the benefactor was Michalek, a true patriot, a man without nerves, and of incredible courage.

More and more helpers joined Andrew's organization. As it

grew, so did his troubles. He was arrested and put into prison by the Hungarians. On this occasion he had the opportunity of talking with a charming man, a Major, whom he soon discovered was an Intelligence officer in the Second Bureau.

The Major interrogated Andrew who denied all allegations. The Major said, 'Look, Lieutenant, I know what you are up to. If I had been a Hungarian officer in your position I would act the same way, but you must understand that I have to do my duty, so don't put me in the embarrassing position of having to deal severely with you. You can go this time but next time you will have to take the consequences.' 'Major,' said Andrew, 'I am most grateful.'

Christine was back at work in Budapest. She was putting the finishing touches to her reports and making more and more contacts specially with the people in the Polish Socialist Party in Budapest.[15] It was of vital importance to keep the flow of information going, and in this, with new couriers constantly arriving, she succeeded brilliantly.

Some of the people whom Christine and Andrew recruited were 'characters' in their own right, whose qualities of resourcefulness, perception and concentration made them the successful agents they were. Such a one was Michael L.

He had met Christine at a cocktail party in Poland before the war, when his wife pointed her out, and told him that they had both been expelled from the same convent. They had scandalized the good nuns by climbing a tree. This prank was not in itself a serious matter but the fact that the young ladies involved were not wearing knickers made it a very heinous offence indeed.

Michael L. became a devoted friend of Christine and Andrew, and worked with their organization after their departure from Hungary. He had some interesting adventures to relate to them when they met later. After the German occupation of Yugoslavia, Hungary and Bulgaria, though still theoretically neutral, gave the Germans many facilities, including the use of airports. There were rumours that the Germans were preparing to take Turkey, and there was a concentration of German troops in Yugoslavia. The British Intelligence Service were badly in need of reliable information on this subject, so Michael L. was chosen to undertake the trip to Istanbul with all available information, including a microfilm.

Michael L. first set off for the Yugoslav border. Almost immediately he was arrested for carrying false papers, handcuffed and put under guard on a train bound for Budapest.

Michael L. had no intention of giving up his freedom without a fight. He asked permission to go to the lavatory, and, accompanied by his guard, made his way down the corridor of the train. At the end of the corridor there was a little open platform. Michael L. made for it and dived onto an embankment. He then rolled over into a field of standing corn. When he tried to get up, a searing pain in his right knee told him that he had damaged his knee-cap. He spent a whole day in hiding and then, during three nights, walked north, guided by the Pole star. His only food was a small bread roll which he broke into four. He walked about fifteen miles each night, and finally made his way to a village where he found sanctuary in a church. The local priest was a kind and compassionate man. He took Michael L. into his house, put him to bed and called a doctor and a blacksmith to remove the handcuffs. Conversation between Michael L. and the priest was difficult, since the priest spoke no Polish while Michael L. was unable to speak Hungarian. They compromised by talking to each other in Latin.

It was a month before Michael was able to return to Budapest; but he still had the precious microfilm intact. Almost at once he made arrangements to fly to Istanbul.

He first obtained an Estonian passport in the name of Baron A. H. Ostrog, as well as a forged letter purporting to be signed by Goebbels, appointing the Baron to organize Baltic émigrés (who had fled from the Baltic countries after the Russians occupied them in the summer of 1940) in a resistance and liberation movement which was to have active German cooperation. Michael, through sources of his own, made contact with the

German Commandant of Budapest Airport, a heavy drinker, who, after a number of sessions with the 'Baron', became quite friendly. During a party, Michael showed the Commandant the famous Goebbels letter, and said he thought he might have difficulties in getting in touch with émigrés in Sofia. The Commandant, deeply impressed by Michael's letter, thenceforth treated him as a VIP, and offered him air transport. After a delay of a few days, the Commandant personally escorted Michael to a plane flying direct to Sofia. On board were the pilot, co-pilot and three officers, one of them a member of the Gestapo. A bottle was provided by one officer, and there was much hilarity as toasts were drunk to Hitler and to victory for Germany.

The plane landed at Belgrade, and Michael remained in the plane with the pilot. Ten minutes later an SS officer arrived and shouted through the open door, 'Mr Ostrog, please get out with your luggage.' Michael objected that he was going on to Sofia. 'We've received a telegram from Budapest,' continued the officer.

Michael, who by now had got his 'L' tablet ready, was certain that this was the end of the road, and was crawling over the bags in the plane, when he heard the SS officer finishing his interrupted sentence by saying, 'Yes, we have received a telegram from Budapest to reserve you a seat on a more comfortable plane.'

On arriving at Istanbul, Michael rushed to the British Embassy, where he was received by A. G. G. de Chastelain[16] in his pyjamas. The information which Michael had brought proved to be of vital importance, and Michael and de Chastelain left immediately for Ankara.

Later Michael L. was incorporated into SOE, was parachuted into Albania and Italy, and in 1944 was awarded the MC.

During their early days together in Budapest, Christine and Andrew were getting to know one another. Though they were deeply in love and hated being separated, they had agreed not to let their rapidly growing need for one another influence their work. The extreme tension under which they lived, though it heightened certain aspects of their intimate life together also took its toll of their nerves, and there were times when frayed tempers would erupt into rows which were over almost as soon as they had begun. Both Christine and Andrew had a well-developed sense of humour, and their laughter and sense of the ridiculous saved them from introspection and from too close an examination of the sometimes desperate situations in which they found themselves.

One of the greatest problems the Polish soldiers faced during the war was the German tanks. In comparison with the Germans, the Poles were badly equipped. Just before the war every regiment received an issue of sealed boxes with instructions that they were to be opened only on the order of the Commanding General. He in his turn was empowered to transmit this order only if given leave to do so by the Commander-in-Chief of the Polish Army. So rapidly did the Germans invade Poland that half these boxes were never opened. Their contents were important for they contained a Polish invention, a rifle with an unusually long barrel and a bottle-shaped cartridge. This rifle had so high a velocity that it could pierce the armour of a German tank, so that a good shot equipped with this particular rifle could stop an advancing tank in its tracks.

In all the military textbooks in England, France and Poland it was generally laid down that tanks cannot operate at night. The Germans proved this was not so by attacking by night and finding nothing to halt them.

'One day in Budapest,' says Andrew, 'my friends and I were discussing the new Polish high-velocity rifles which had never been used. Our friend the Polish Consul suggested that I go and talk to the French Military Attaché about this remarkable weapon.

'France was for me, as for every Pole, an invincible country, the home of freedom and of culture. I prepared myself very carefully for this visit. I was full of the horrors of the war in

Poland and of the courage of my soldiers. I talked for some time to the French Military Attaché, a Colonel, telling him that France and England must be prepared for a complete change in war tactics, as the old methods were useless. After half an hour the impeccably turned out Colonel stroked his moustache and said, "Vous oubliez, Lieutenant, que la France n'est pas la Pologne!"

'The only thing I said which brought a glint to his fishy eyes was when I mentioned the famous rifle. Then he brightened. "I'd like a sample of one of those guns. The French Government would even finance an expedition into Poland to retrieve one." I said I would do my best to arrange this and went off to contact my cousin, Ludwig Popiel. I knew that when he and his cavalry regiment were dismounted, they had buried their uniforms, arms and some boxes of the anti-tank rifle on his estate. We decided that since Ludwig had buried the rifle, he should be the one to bring it back. The French Colonel was enthusiastic about this expedition and promised us all French decorations.

'Ludwig and a commercially experienced friend accompanied him. They had an unbelievably difficult and dangerous journey. But they returned triumphantly with one of the guns which they had cleverly dismantled. The moment Ludwig got back to Budapest he rushed round to tell me that he had the rifle hidden under his bed in the boarding-house where he lived. He said that his travelling companion was insisting that Ludwig was not the owner of the gun which he himself now intended to sell to the French for a very high price.

'While Ludwig and his mercenary friend were having a furious row, Christine slipped quietly away, went to Ludwig's room, collected the gun and hid it under *her* bed. This was the first proof I had of her astonishing intuition, for half an hour later, Ludwig's boarding-house was raided by the Hungarian police. The gun was never used because France collapsed. Nor did we even collect the promised French decoration.'

Andrew was to see many other facets of Christine's personality:

'There never was such a woman for collecting stray dogs. She was always kind and patient with anyone she suspected of having an inferiority complex with the result that the most unlikely men fell violently in love with her imagining *she* needed their protection. Such a one was Radziminski, a Polish journalist who had long been an admirer of Christine. He never stopped asking her to marry him. Finally she told him that he had absolutely no hope of being anything more to her than a friend. Broken-hearted he rushed off to the nearest bridge, jumped off it straight on to the frozen Danube and broke his collar bone.'

As soon as he was patched up he reappeared at Christine's flat which at that moment was packed solid with guns and ammunition. Andrew listened fascinated while the poor man alternately pleaded with Christine to marry him or threatened to kill himself if she refused him again.

Exhausted by one of his long and tiring journeys, Andrew dropped off to sleep to the drone of Radziminski's voice. He was brusquely awakened by the sound of a shot – the rejected lover had shot himself in the thigh. Once Christine and Andrew had bandaged him up and made certain that it was no more than a slight flesh wound, Andrew drove him to a Polish doctor.

Tension began to mount as Andrew and Christine continued their clandestine activities, which included collecting more guns and ammunition. Apart from a full working schedule, the couple led a full life, divided between their clandestine work, visiting friends and sitting in Christine's favourite café where among those she entertained were a number of English journalists, some working for the same organization as herself.

Christine, being a true European, enjoyed café life, which left her free to get up and go whenever she felt so inclined, unlike the social conventions in a private house. Another of her favourite ways to relax was to visit a movie-theatre where, in the stuffy, anonymous dark, her tired and jangled nerves could unwind a little.

Christine and Andrew were always welcome at the British

Legation, the large eighteenth-century house set in a courtyard high above Buda and the Danube. Sir Owen O'Malley, the British Minister, his wife Ann Bridge, the distinguished traveller and novelist, and their young daughter Kate were soon warmly attached to the unusual young couple to whom they gave much friendly hospitality. Sir Owen was well aware of their activities, and had the greatest admiration for Christine of whom he said, 'She was the bravest person I ever knew, the only woman who had a positive nostalgia for danger. She could do anything with dynamite except eat it. I loved her dearly – God rest her soul.'[17]

The O'Malleys were an interesting family unit. Sir Owen concealed a shrewd mind behind the bland façade of a career diplomat. His clothes gave his valet an inferiority complex, for Sir Owen was nearly always dressed in 'an incredibly creased and worn tweed suit in a russet grey pattern.' Eighteen-year-old Kate was an incurable romantic, and the handsome, dashing one-legged Andrew became her 'beau idéal' from the moment they met. Like her father, she admired Christine's great qualities, but it was Andrew's presence that stimulated her and quickened her pulse. Passionately in love with Christine as he was, Andrew was not completely immune to the adulation of an intelligent and extremely pretty young girl. Kate was dedicated to the Polish cause, and was always ready to help Andrew and Christine. She became so attached to her new friends that Sir Owen had to remonstrate with her for being seen with them so often. But her father's admonitions had little effect, and Kate O'Malley continued to phone Christine each day and to meet her and Andrew as often as possible.

It was about this time that Sir Owen and Christine began to concoct plans for a regular escape route for British POWs from Polish camps. The general plan was that Christine and Andrew should maintain liaison with the Polish Underground association with which they were already in contact to facilitate the escape of POWs to Athens, and thence to England. Sir Owen made these plans known to the Foreign Office in London, and, having applied for a large sum of money to implement this enterprise, was staggered when, for the first and last time in his life, he got a telegram saying that the sky was the limit.

One day, one of Andrew and Christine's British contacts arrived with the news that a very important man in the French Underground was arriving in Budapest. His name was de Lorme and, since he had first-class contacts in Slovakia, his help in assisting Czech pilots to escape would be invaluable.

Andrew was surprised that a Frenchman should have such important contacts in Slovakia; but his fears were allayed when he was told that de Lorme had lived for many years in Slovakia, and was also well-known in Budapest. Andrew and Christine were to take charge of him and to make sure that the Frenchman never went anywhere public, or showed himself outside.

Andrew was used to such requests from London, but, all the same, he was anxious for a little more background information on Monsieur de Lorme. He got little satisfaction, and was simply told that the new arrival was important. M. de Lorme arrived. He was rather plump, charming, with a slightly upturned nose, laughing blue eyes hidden by enormous dark glasses and, squashed down on his bald head, a large soft hat which all but covered his face. He looked exactly like the popular conception of a spy. He arrived at Christine's flat and enchanted everyone. He spoke French without an accent. His German was flawless, but he neither looked nor behaved like a Frenchman.

After some time Christine started to tease the newcomer, calling him *Masque de Fer*. He seemed amused at this, and having talked at length about Czechoslovakia, the three young people began talking about their families and family connections. By that evening, he, Christine and Andrew were on Christian name terms. His name was Eddie.

After a day or so, Andrew said, 'Come on Eddie. What is this masquerade? We can see that you have to keep up a front for the rest of the world, but we, who are your guardian angels and have to take care of you, should know who you really are.'

'How stupid,' he said. 'I travel on a French passport and my cover name is de Lorme, but in fact I thought you knew who I was.'

Masque de Fer was Prince Eddie Lobkowitz, whose family owned vast estates on the Czechoslovakian and Austrian border. During a sojourn in the United States, Eddie had married an American heiress. He was a gregarious, amusing, easygoing fellow; but the moment his own country went to war, Eddie left the security of the USA and hurried across the Atlantic to fight the Nazis. It took a certain amount of cool courage for a Lobkowitz to arrive in Budapest on a false passport.

The moment Christine and Andrew found out who their 'prisoner' was, they groaned at the stupidity of those who had had the mad idea of sending him straight into the lions' den. Eddie was well known in international society, with so many friends in Budapest that it was inconceivable that he would not be recognized there.

Andrew and Christine did all they could to amuse him, but he became increasingly bored with nothing to do all day. Little seemed to be happening from the Czechoslovakian side, so Christine prepared herself to go to Poland and to get through to his Czechoslovakian contacts from there.

One day Andrew and Christine were sitting deep in conversation at Hagli's on the banks of the Danube. Hagli's had a great reputation, and catered for a mixed clientele who liked to sit in the sun, drinking coffee and talking war and politics. It was a gay, stimulating and dangerous place which attracted many Germans and their stooges.

To Andrew's and Christine's horror, *Masque de Fer* sauntered in. His hat was jammed down over his face, his huge glasses obscured his eyes, and he was fanning himself with a newspaper. Andrew was furious, and said, 'Eddie, you're a bum. You're not only risking your own life, but you will drag us down with you.' Eddie got very upset, and, spreading the newspaper in front of his face, made a little peephole in it with his cigarette, through which to look round at all the pretty girls.

Andrew and Christine saw the funny side of the incident, and could only laugh.

But soon Eddie got completely out of control and insisted on joining them at luncheon at Florisch's, a restaurant almost as well known as Gerbeaux, whose admirable patisserie was one of the wonders of Budapest. Florisch's was not very large. Downstairs there was an oval room, and above it a sort of gallery which was the chic rendezvous for those who liked to be seen in the right places.

Andrew had told Eddie not to come to the restaurant. 'Look,' he said, 'I'm certain that dozens of people, including the police, are well aware that you are in Budapest, masquerading under the name of Monsieur de Lorme; but so long as you keep quiet, the Hungarians won't make a move. They are trying to be neutral and, with your family connections, they don't want to make an example of you. But they are under pressure from the Germans, and the moment you are officially recognized, you'll be in serious trouble.'

Andrew and Christine were sitting on the first floor at Florisch's when Andrew whispered, 'Masque de Fer.' Just as Eddie came bumbling in through the door, a famous character in Budapest, a giant of a man called Count Pali Palfi, was walking out. He spotted Eddie and, opening wide his arms, trumpeted in German, 'Eddie Lobkowitz, um Gottes Willen, was machst du in Budapest?' For God's sake, Eddie, what are you doing in Budapest? 'Shut up, shut up,' begged Eddie, kicking his friend in the stomach. 'What on earth is the matter with you?' gasped the astonished Palfi, releasing his hold. The watchers in the gallery held their breath, but nobody came forward to tap Eddie on the shoulder. Breathing a sigh of relief, they rushed downstairs and hustled him out of the restaurant.[18]

There was so much work to do that there was little time for personal grievances of any kind. The British asked Andrew and Christine to arrange for some kind of watch to be kept on navigation on the Danube. Six of Andrew's men were put on day and night observation duty. Every single craft coming or going was checked and noted. Finally, all the disparate bits and pieces had to be put together to form an intelligible pattern.

Andrew was finding his own transport work more and more difficult, as he was once again driving the cars himself. He had sent his invaluable Michalek to the Polish Army, which by now was in the Middle East.

'About this time,' says Andrew, 'we met a Pole who seemed very keen to make our acquaintance. He was effusively friendly, and seemed very interested in what we were doing and kept offering us his services. After a while I began to worry about him. His questions were intelligent and highly "sensitive". He said he had come to Budapest via the Carpathians, which was plausible, since hundreds of people were using this route. He said his intention was to join the Polish Army; but as he had bad frostbite he hoped that, until he was healed, we would employ him in our escape organization. Or, better still, we might detail him to help Christine, who he had heard would soon be going to Poland. I said, "What utter rubbish, how could a frail girl like Christine go to Poland? She can't ski, she couldn't possibly attempt such a journey." But I didn't like the feel of this character at all.

'There was a big German minority in Poland. They were completely dominated by the Nazis, who used them to infiltrate the Polish Army in France, in the Middle East, and in any clandestine organizations such as ours. It was difficult to spot these traitors, for they spoke fluent Polish, having attended Polish schools and, sometimes, even a Polish University. Since I had no proof of the man's intentions, there was not much I could do; but I told one of my men to follow him, watch him and report his reactions. If they were satisfactory I felt it would be all right to employ him.

'The report I got was anything but reassuring. My volunteer was seen with a member of the German Embassy. I knew then that he was a rotten apple and must not be allowed in our barrel. We fed him a stream of wrong information, telling him that we were not really keen on the work we were doing;

particularly as we knew that France could not possibly win. But he was clever, and went on insisting that he wanted to work with us. I thought it was time to act. I went to my "thieves"[19] and told them that I was worried about being infiltrated by a traitor. They reacted exactly as I had hoped.

'"Why don't you bring him to visit us? The temperature is about twenty below zero. Tomorrow night would be ideal."

'I had absolutely no scruples about taking my inquisitive friend to this rendezvous. I told him we were going to see some very important underground contacts, and he was, of course, anxious to meet them. When we arrived we were warmly greeted; and then we started on the biggest drinking spree I've ever known. At least my guest was drinking. I drank only water, as did the hosts. The thieves pressed endless glasses of slivovitz on my friend. We drank to the health of Hungary, to that of the Hungarian President, to the Hungarian flag, to anyone we could think of to toast. The man occasionally made a feeble effort to refuse a fresh glass; but in the end he was paralytically drunk.

'"Now," said my friends, "we must take this fellow on the embankment for a little walk." They dragged him to the nearest bench where he flopped out in a stupor. "Let us now go and have a little refreshment," said the Hungarians. "We won't wake your friend. He needs rest, so we'll let him sleep." The next morning my songbird was found stiff and dead on his bench.'

Christine's brother had joined the Polish Army (Armia Krajowa), the Resistance Movement. She was depressed by her inability to convince her mother of the danger in which she was living,[20] and in the spring she began planning her second trip into Poland. The information collected by the Musketeers and relayed to her was far from reassuring. They suspected that Russia would be attacked by Germany; but, as the campaign against France was in full swing, all attention was focused on that theatre of war. In fact, the situation there was disastrous for France was collapsing like a sandcastle in the tide, and it was dramatically evident that the much-vaunted Maginot Line was as useless as a paper screen.

Andrew was having difficulties getting his people out because the Germans had begun to put pressure on the Hungarians, and clearly it was only a matter of time before Andrew and his assistants would be in serious trouble. Christine's unlucky suitor Radziminski, knowing that he would soon have to leave Budapest, asked Andrew to take him along on one of his dangerous missions, and though Andrew was loath to involve the little chap, he did take him on a particularly arduous mission.[21]

In May Christine endeavoured to return to London for consultations and to make further plans for the exploitation of the contacts she had made. But she failed to obtain an Italian transit visa, and soon afterwards Italy entered the war.

Early in June 1940, Christine made her second trip to Poland. By this time there were very few loopholes. The simplest way to catch people was at the station, where tired, exhausted and hungry refugees tried to board trains. All the couriers had different systems; some went as far as the second or third station; but this meant a long stiff walk, and there was always the danger of being spotted in the empty countryside. Others had contacts with the Slovaks, and paid large sums for tickets bought in advance. Christine's very expert companion always carried a vast suitcase, elegant, shiny and chic. It was empty save for a natty outfit consisting of a suit, shoes and a Homburg hat, all of the best quality.

This particular courier's method was to arrive at the end of his journey, dirty, sweaty in his thick skiing trousers, anorak and woollen stockings, ski boots and cap. In a forest clearing, where he would be temporarily safe since the Slovaks were not at that time working with dogs, he would strip off his dirty travelling clothes and change into his city gent's outfit. Then, immaculate and carrying his suitcase, he would make for the station. Christine followed his example and changed in the forest from her trousers and anorak to a smart town suit.

Christine had foolproof Polish papers, and her companion was fully armed. He had a pistol and hand grenades, and was not prepared to surrender to anyone. At the Polish border the Gestapo, armed, highly trained and dangerous, sat waiting for their victims. At the last station in Slovakia, Christine and her courier left the train and changed back into their dirty mountaineering clothes. They did so with the complicity of the pro-Polish Slovaks about them. Then, all through the night Christine and her courier walked to get to the Polish frontier before dawn. It was a long night, and dark, with no moon and no stars, and suddenly the dawn wind was in her nostrils, and Christine knew she was back home, back in German-occupied Poland.

Christine remained in Poland long enough to collect much military and economic information which, on her return to Budapest, was sent to London where it proved of considerable interest. At this time she wanted desperately to get her mother out of Poland to safety, but Stephanie Skarbek was obstinate, and could not understand why Christine was making such a fuss. Though she was well aware of what was happening all about her to her Jewish friends, she simply refused to abandon her home in Warsaw, or to leave her work – teaching French in a clandestine school for young children.

Christine's first cousin, Stanley Christopher, was sworn to secrecy by his mother, who, when she went to visit Countess Skarbek, found her niece Christine trying to impress on her mother the danger of her situation. Some time after Christine returned to Budapest, the dawn knock on the door aroused Countess Stephanie Skarbek. Two men with swastikas on their armbands dragged her out to a waiting car. Nothing more was ever heard of her; and, since it was Christine's habit to bury the things that mattered most in the silence of her own being, she rarely mentioned her mother.[22]

CHAPTER FOUR

On her return journey to Budapest, Christine decided to take another route. Instead of going over the Tatra mountains she went via the Carpathians. The voyage was tiring, but uneventful, until she took a train heading for Nowy Sacz, a little town not far from the border. The compartment was packed. Christine sat quietly pretending to doze but keeping a close watch on the reactions of her companions. By a gleam of light which came from a signal box she noticed a young man in a dirty trench coat who was, seemingly, fast asleep. Yet her intuition told her that he was feigning sleep, just as she was, and that he was engaged on the same work as herself.

Christine made straight for the safe house where she was to lie up and wait for the next leg of the journey. She had not been there long when her fellow traveller in the dirty trench coat arrived. Her instinct had not failed her. 'Jan Grodzicki' was indeed a secret agent, and he was making his way back to Budapest. His real name was Count Wladyslaw Ledochowski, and his background was similar to Christine's; highly intelligent, he had done exceptionally well at University and was a skilled engineer. His interest was immediately aroused by the young woman, whose cover name on this occasion was Andrzejewska,[1] and who was to be his companion on the return journey to Budapest.

In the late afternoon Jan and Christine made another journey by train to the foothills outside the town, where they were to pick up a guide to take them over the mountains. Jan knew every move in this game, and when he told her to follow him, no matter what he did, she did so unquestioningly. They crossed into Slovakia without any trouble, leaving the train before it reached the Slovakian border. Unfortunately, they were spotted running into the woods, and a hue and cry started after them. There was a great deal of shouting and firing of rifles; but fortunately their pursuers never caught up with them, and they were able to get to the Hungarian frontier without further incident.

Jan was deeply impressed with the tireless and courageous 'Andrzejewska', whom he found an ideal and undemanding travelling companion. She, in her turn, was stimulated by his undisguised admiration. At dawn they came to another valley, and to another safe house, where they rested until late afternoon when they started out for Koszyce.

They walked for a long time, and then Jan realized they still had a long way to go. He was tired and so was Christine. They decided to spend the night in the woods, and to go on again at first light. It was cold. Jan did all he could to make Christine comfortable. Both young people were tense and over-stimulated by the exertions and excitements of the past days. That night, spent in the woods with Christine, was one that Jan would remember for the rest of his life.

As for Christine, her meeting with Wladyslaw Ledochowski marked a watershed in her life. From this time onwards she divided her emotions into a number of watertight compartments, into which were slotted her feelings as a patriot, her duty as a secret agent and her love for her family and for Andrew. These last three were to be the only constants in a mind so well disciplined that the valves of each compartment could be sealed at will, cutting off everything that mattered, except the matter in hand.

Christine enjoyed every facet of her life. But danger was her main stimulus. Challenge and danger and a duel of wits had their roots in a subconscious nourished on tales of chivalry and of the ancestors who had fought and died for Poland. Danger heightened her emotions, and sharpened her faculties so that many of her relationships, begun in a casual manner, assumed for the time of their duration an importance which faded once the emergency was over. Christine could dissociate her physical needs from her spiritual requirements; but it was by physical contact that she found release from pressure and tensions of imminent danger.

When Christine and Jan reached Budapest, they were like people who have escaped some great disaster together, and are loath to part. Finally, Christine took Jan back to her flat. Early the following morning Andrew phoned her. Hearing his voice suddenly shocked her into a realization of how much he meant to her. By this time Jan was utterly fascinated by this extraor-dinary creature, who was so unlike any woman he had ever met. Though she had told him all about her relationship with Andrew, who happened to be a friend of his, Jan felt that, in view of their recent intimacy and the fact that she had brought him back to her flat, she must have resolved all her doubts about their relationship, and had made a choice – in his favour.

They arranged to meet that evening at Hagli's restaurant. All day, while Jan was working, the thought of Christine was upper-most in his mind. He could not wait to be with her again. He hurried to the restaurant at the appointed time, but she did not appear. Thinking there might have been some mix-up, he dashed over to her flat. He was relieved to see that she was in, as all the lights seemed to be on. As he stood below on the pavement, craning his neck upwards, he saw Andrew Kowerski at the window, closing the shutters.

Christine told Andrew what had happened with Jan. He was very distressed; but so deep was his love for Christine that he accepted her rather lame explanation that she thought he had left Budapest, and gone to join the Polish Army. His handling of Jan was masterly. He says, 'We saw a lot of Wladyslaw. He wanted to talk to me about his involvement with Christine; but I did not want to go into any explanations. I merely said, "We're in the middle of a war, and who knows whether any of us will be alive when it ends, so let us forget what happened." To which he surprisingly replied, "All right, but should you know when and if Christine plans to go back to Poland, please let me know, as I would like to go with her."

'I looked at him, and said, "I'll let you know. Not because I trust you not to make love to Christine; but I do trust you to protect her, and to do your best for her."

The unusual situation did not prevent Andrew and Christine from seeing a great deal of Ledochowski at this particular time. Christine enjoyed having her admirer around and, though he was far from happy at the way things had developed, he found he could not bear to be away from her. Furthermore, she was starting to prepare her third expedition into Poland, and Andrew had given his permission for Ledochowski to go with her.

Andrew refused to allow jealousy to cloud his judgement, or to diminish his sense of responsibility where Christine's work was concerned. It was of vital importance that Christine should get safely to Poland, and he had no doubt that Ledochowski was the right person to escort her. Christine was impatient to be off; but as the Polish Military Attaché did not manage to get Jan's papers ready in time, she decided to go off on her own. But she was held up at Koszyce, and returned to her flat exhausted and frustrated. Andrew came home very late. He was depressed and sad, thinking Christine had gone; and when he saw her shoes and rucksack, and realized that she was still there he was wild with joy.

A week later Jan was ready to accompany her and they decided to set off again. As always, Andrew prepared Christine's rucksack and as he opened it he found a large envelope containing photographs given to Christine by a Pole in the Consulate. Andrew gazed at them with dismay; they showed General Sikorski in a variety of poses, decorating Poles in Paris, shaking hands with Churchill and similar activities. Andrew was furious. 'The man who gave you that must be crazy. If you're caught with these photos, what explanation can you possibly give? That you're bored with life abroad and are coming home to decorate your home with photographs of Churchill and Sikorski?'

Christine promised to leave the envelope behind. But when his back was turned, she slipped it back into her rucksack. It was a foolish thing to do, but she felt that it would give a big boost to the morale of her friends in Poland if she could produce the photographs and have them copied for general distribution.

Christine and Jan started off from Koszyce. Then they crossed to Slovakia. Since they could not go by train or by road, they went through the forest, finally emerging in a place where they found a rickety old taxi which took them all the way to the Polish border. Taxis often crossed Slovakia to the border; but it was risky, not only for the passengers but for the drivers, who insisted on being paid in dollars, in their view the only stable currency.

Unwisely, Christine and Jan then made for a station on the Slovakian border, where they were arrested by the Slovaks who knew at once that they were couriers. In spite of their glib stories about being unhappy in a foreign country and wanting to go home to their families, the frontier guards marched them off without searching them to a nearby frontier post.

As they were crossing a bridge over a river, Christine suddenly started to limp. 'I can't walk any more,' she said. 'You must let me stop for a moment to bandage my foot.' The frontier guard agreed, and Christine sat down with her back to him. Jan took advantage of the guard's inattention and whipped the envelope containing the photographs from Christine's rucksack.

As soon as Christine's foot was bandaged they started off again, Jan hiding the envelope under his windcheater. Then, very courageously, he lay down and flung the envelope into the river. The guards immediately panicked and rushed about trying to fish the envelope out with long sticks. They were unsuccessful, and it floated away out of sight. The guards were furious, and asked Jan what it contained. He said only a few family photographs and that it had slipped out of his hands.

Christine tried to turn her charm on to the guards; but they refused to talk to her and searched her rucksack. In it they found something like a thousand dollars in different currencies. This was a vast sum of money. Christine guessed what was in their minds, and said, 'If you turn us in, you'll have to hand the money over as well. Furthermore, you'll be in big trouble because you weren't quick enough to stop my friend getting rid of that envelope, which might or might not contain incriminating documents. Why don't you let us go? You keep the money, and nobody will be any the wiser.' After some deliberation the frontier guards agreed. Once they had allowed their prisoners to go a certain distance, they began firing into the air. The only disagreeable part of the incident was that they had retained some of Christine and Jan's papers.

When Christine and Jan returned unharmed to Budapest and told Andrew what had happened he was very worried in case the frontier guards had passed the incriminating papers with photographs of both Jan and Christine to the Gestapo. Jan, to this day, is inclined to think that this did happen; but Andrew is not so sure. What was certain was that both Christine and Jan were finished as couriers in this particular context. Jan was sent back to the Polish Army via Syria and Palestine. Though Andrew was sad to see Jan go, he was relieved that Christine could no longer leave Budapest, and was adamant when she said she wanted to try once more to get into Poland. This was not a good time for them. The news of the fall of France shook them to the foundations, for they would not believe the stories of the deplorable morale of the French army and of their refusal to continue the war.

From the moment Churchill made the first of his fighting speeches, a wave of enthusiasm and hope fired Christine, Andrew and their helpers. They knew then that England would continue the struggle to the end. The O'Malleys – Sir Owen, Lady O'Malley and Kate – boosted their morale enormously, assuring them that the power of England and of the Commonwealth would finally defeat Hitler, and that most certainly America would come in and tip the scales in favour of the Allies.

Nevertheless, the pressure was on, and the Germans became even more arrogant. Hordes of them came to Budapest in enormous charabancs, wearing mufti and pretending to be tourists. Hungary was completely dominated by the Germans. This was a situation over which the Hungarians themselves had no control and which often riled them as much as it did those who had taken refuge there.

Andrew's team, on watch on the banks of the Danube, were equally depressed. Seeing supplies being ferried to the enemy exasperated them, and Andrew and Christine decided to put limpet mines under some of the barges going to Austria laden with Rumanian petrol. They drove to a place on the Danube where Andrew had often gone swimming.

The plan was that Andrew and a friend would swim out to the barges and there append the only two limpet mines they had. The mines were timed to explode twelve hours later, so it was hoped that the barges would blow up in an Austrian port.

Christine and the friend who was driving sat waiting while the two saboteurs slipped quietly into the anything but blue waters of the Danube. Andrew had left his artificial leg in the car, and warned Christine to keep a sharp lookout and see where they surfaced once their work was done. Unfortunately they were carried much further than they wished, and by the time Christine caught up with them, Andrew was sitting shivering and blue in the biting air. They heard later, with considerable pleasure, that a barge *had* exploded in an Austrian port and, as a result, all barges sailing down the Danube thereafter were equipped with searchlights.

After Dunkirk and the bad news that followed, Christine and Andrew received orders to concentrate all their efforts on getting hold of pilots. Polish pilots were to have top priority, but it was imperative to try and get pilots of other nationalities as well. Into their net came all manner of people, including an Austrian pilot who had managed to escape from the Nazis.

Andrew's team now consisted mainly of people who could not go into the army or were too important to be sent away; things were becoming more and more difficult.

Andrew was again caught and put into a jail near Budapest. As before, he was released by the Hungarians, but this time with a very clear warning to watch his step. Andrew was grateful for their interest in his welfare and survival, but had to carry out his orders. England needed more and more pilots, and he was determined that he would do all he could to see she got them. He drove his pilots variously from the Czech frontier or the Polish border occupied by the Germans; and saw to it that they got safely across the Yugoslav border. It was exhausting work. Often he left Budapest at four in the afternoon and drove to the frontier. The same night he would drive all the way back to the Yugoslav border.

'It was a hell of a journey,' said Andrew, 'stopping on the Yugoslav border and helping those escapees to cross with the help of my organization of smugglers. Quite often I was forced to walk long distances with them before we made contact with the smugglers. My leg was in a frightful state because after the Polish war it had not had any kind of medical attention. Poor Christine used to suffer more than I when she saw me getting up in the morning, and watched me trying to get over the pain of the first few steps.

'The most difficult part of my work was collecting the people from the Hungarian-Russian border, as representatives of both countries were extremely vigilant. The Hungarians loathed the Russians. The three frontier zones were so zealously watched and patrolled that there was no chance of crossing by car, for which you needed a special pass. This border was the entry to the Carpathian mountains, the most beautiful mountains in Europe with their gentle slopes and thick forests. When escapees came by train, they were always caught, and I spent a great deal of time racking my brain for a way to get to this border without too much risk.

'Then help came from a most unexpected quarter. I had a

phone call from my great friend Colonel Schell, whose sister was married to a Pole. He invited me to dine with him and I went with pleasure. We had an excellent dinner. Schell said, "If England survives for the next few months and the Germans don't attack her immediately, they will be in trouble. But I am afraid England will be taken in the next few weeks." He poured me another glass of wine, and continued, "I know what you're doing and I want to ask you a special favour. I am sure you are aware that the Germans know all about you and Christine, and if you get caught nobody will be able to do anything to help you. Having said this I must tell you that I am in a bit of a spot myself.

'"When the war broke out my sister was in Poland. She left immediately; but her children were evacuated to the south of Poland which she thought would be safe. In fact, it was overrun by the Russians. We have tried through all the diplomatic channels to get the children back, but without success. Do you think you can help?"

'I said, "I think I can help because I can call on the assistance of my friends the smugglers. But even so, I can't go personally because I must go by car, and I haven't got a pass."

'"That's one difficulty I can overcome," said Schell. "I'll drive with you and arrange to get a special pass for you and the car from the War Ministry."

'I was delighted because this was a chance, at last, to get back and see how everything was working and how I could help. I was in a state of total exhaustion, mainly because I had never really caught up on sleep since the twenty-two days of the Polish war, during which I must have had about two hours' sleep a day. I fell asleep when I was walking, and once I dozed off standing on one leg. By the time I got to Hungary I was suffering from permanent nervous fatigue; I kept falling asleep at parties and, what was even worse, when I was driving along the long Hungarian roads. In those days no Benzedrine or pep pills were available, and all I could do was to warn whoever was next to me not to let me fall asleep, or we would all end in a ditch.

'When Schell and I set off together I told him that he must keep me awake. He did not believe that I was serious; but I had not driven very far before I nodded off for a split second. Schell shouted at me, and I came to with a jerk. Apparently I had nearly killed a cyclist by knocking him off his bike. I had absolutely no recollection of the incident. In fact, the man was quite all right; but from that moment on Schell never stopped talking to me. He told me the story of his life, the story of the First World War, the story of everything he could remember, and from time to time he shook me.

'Having the War Ministry pass was a wonderful "open sesame", and we sailed through with no trouble at all. At the frontier, I believe it was Munkacs, I asked Schell to let me go off on my own because I knew that with a Hungarian officer in tow I would have no chance of making contact with the smugglers in the Carpathian mountains. I was optimistic. I had the address and the password. So I drove into the Carpathian mountains, going first by road, and then following the winding tracks.

'I was familiar with the territory, where my parents had long owned a stretch of forest. The mountain people were Ruthenians, and were pro-Polish. After sleeping in the car, I started at five o'clock next morning to walk to a gamekeeper's cottage where I was supposed to be told how to reach my contacts. I was walking uphill with a stick; after two hours I felt quite ill with exhaustion. My leg was paining me terribly, and running with pus. At last I found the cottage and staggered up to its door.

'The password was "Can I have a glass of milk with honey here?" The gamekeeper, a smart, erect-looking fellow with a gun over his shoulder, came out with the ritual greeting, "God bless you." "And God bless you," I answered. "I've walked a long long way and I should be glad if I could get a glass of milk with honey here."

'"I can get you a glass of milk, but we haven't any honey."

'I repeated the password a couple of times; but he simply looked blank and went off and fetched me a glass of milk. He was pleasant, but obviously had no interest in me. He sat quietly smoking his pipe.

'Finally I said, "I'm not here for my health. I'm here on a special mission. I want to ask you whether you can do me a favour." He sucked on his pipe, exhaled a plume of smoke and then said, "Yes?"

'"A friend has two children in Lwow on the Polish side occupied by the Russians. I understand that you might be able to help get them out. Money is no object."

'The gamekeeper did not turn his head. He sat musing for a moment and then said, "We used to do such things but we don't do them any longer. It's too risky."

'"But they told me in Budapest that you would know someone who might still help in a good cause."

'"There is a woman up in the mountains, she might be able to help."

'"How far is it?"

'"Not far, you can see it from here."

'I squinted up at a speck on the distant skyline, and my heart sank. "Not far" to the mountain people meant two hours of solid walking. I tried to explain that my artificial leg hindered my walking; but he did not seem at all impressed. He said, "I'll give you a guide, my little nephew. He'll take you to the woman."

'The sun was already high when we began our upward climb. I was a mass of sweat and my leg felt as if it were on fire. Finally we came to a dirty little hut. An old woman emerged. The boy said, "Her name is Grandmother Kirilowa." The old crone said kindly, "Sit down. I can see you are tired. Would you like a glass of milk?" I nodded, and she brought out a glass of sour milk which was cold and delicious. I went through the same routine as with the gamekeeper and she, like him, said that she no longer did any "arranging" on the other side. I controlled my temper with some difficulty and reiterated my question, but she was obdurate. It was too risky, and she was not "arranging" things for anyone any more. I asked if she knew of anyone who might help. She said that there was a man who might help. He lived practically next door.

'An hour and a half later I found a peasant. I put my question to him, got yet another glass of sour milk and the same reply I had had from the two others. He no longer did any "arranging", it was too risky.

'Tottering with fatigue, I stumbled down the mountain back to the gamekeeper's cottage. It was long past noon, and I had walked nearly all day with only three glasses of sour milk to keep me going. I was in pretty poor shape when I reached the cottage. To my utter surprise, the gamekeeper came towards me with outstretched hand. "Now," he said, "you can have some milk *and* honey!" I didn't know whether to hit him or thank him. I said, "For God's sake, man, why on earth did you make me go through such hell?"

'He said, "We're not very keen on encouraging spies. We've had people sent by the police before, and we're taking no chances. We were all watching you through our binoculars while you were doing your walking tour. Now we know you are all right, so we'll do all we can to help." The extraordinary thing was that his attic was full of Polish escapees who had just come over the border, among them a friend of mine.

'When I got back to the Colonel I was more dead than alive. He was delighted to see me because he was sure that something dreadful had happened, I had been away so long. I told him that everything was fixed and that the children would be got out. In due course they arrived; but my bonus in this affair was my pass from the Ministry of War, which permitted me to drive unmolested in the frontier zone. Furthermore, our team included a well-known Lwow artist, known as Mikus, who was brilliant at forging passes similar to my original whenever they were required.

'While we were driving back to Budapest, Schell said, "Andrew, you and Christine must get out of Hungary as fast as you can. It is already extremely dangerous for you to be here, so take a tip and don't ask me any more questions. Get out, and get out quickly."

'I said I was grateful for the warning, but we still had a bit of unfinished business to do before leaving. "I know all about your unfinished business," he said, "smuggling pilots to the Middle East for service in England. Well, the Germans know about it, too, and are quite aware that each pilot you smuggle out is another nail in their coffin." He added, "I hope you're not smuggling Czechs, because, if you are, I couldn't possibly help you." This was typical of the long-standing animosity between the Czechs and Hungarians; as much as Hungarians love the Poles, so do they hate the Czechs. I said, "Come off it, Zoltan, why should I have anything to do with the Czechs? I don't like them any more than you do."'

'By now my affair with Christine was a *secret de Polichinelle*. Too many people knew where her flat was, and even the landlady was getting suspicious of her lodger's ever increasing appetite. So we looked and found another, a very pleasant one not far away. The first-floor windows overlooked a courtyard; there were two rooms, a little hall and a bathroom, and we moved in without any fuss or bother from anyone.

'Strangely enough, even at this time, once you had a foreigner's permit, you were not required to report changes of address to the police. It was only after the war that new rules and regulations for foreigners were enforced.'

The new flat had numerous advantages. So many more cars were parked in this street that nobody paid attention to odd comings and goings. Furthermore, the courtyard, which was completely enclosed and resembled a prison exercise-yard, contained a little greenhouse which, because of the shortage of fuel, was no longer used. Andrew at once appropriated it as a garage for his beloved Opel Olympia, the gutsy little machine which was to be the heroine in their final escape and long journey from Budapest to Cairo.

This was Andrew's own personal property. The car he used for his work, a large roomy sedan, belonged to the Military Attaché. The Opel was small, compact and the ideal get-away vehicle; Andrew kept her always filled with enough petrol to take her at least a thousand kilometres.

Though Christine and Andrew were completely happy at being together, they were deeply concerned by the news of France's collapse and by the lack of information about the movements of those of the Polish Army who had not been able to get to England. They knew that some of them were interned in Switzerland, and that the strict and neutral Swiss would never let them go, whereas the Hungarians proved their affection for the Poles by tacitly conniving at the clandestine work they were doing.[2]

Christine and Andrew were collecting, sifting and passing on a great deal of information to the British. They had a splendid and dedicated team of helpers, one of whom was a Jesuit priest called Father Laski. This small, lean man with a Goya-like face hardly ever raised his eyes; but when he did, they were black, brilliant, intelligent and as penetrating as a laser beam. He was thought to be working for the Vatican. He went back and forth to Poland several times. He was finally arrested by the Germans in Budapest, sent to Mauthausen concentration camp and was torn to pieces by Alsatian dogs set on him by his captors.

Another willing helper was Prince Marcin Lubomirski, whose delicate health had prevented him from joining the army, but whose iron spirit never flinched at the exacting tasks set him in Andrew's organization. The Musketeers were providing Christine and Andrew with regular information through the couriers they sent from Poland, including news of German troop movements. Christine was somewhat shaken by the casual way in which the British authorities received this information. Even the collapse of France did not seem to have shaken them out of their complacency.

Escapers from Poland continued to arrive, and Andrew was still ferrying them to safety. His work was now mainly concerned with these people, and less with getting soldiers out of the internment camps. He was again arrested and taken to prison in Budapest, where he met his old friend, the charming Major from the Deuxième Bureau. The Major was still courteous, but, this time, he did not mince his words. 'Lieutenant, you're lucky to be here in the Maria-Theresa Barracks, which is still completely controlled by Hungarians. I hope you take my meaning? Please leave Hungary as quickly as you can.'

No sooner were they settled in the new flat, than Christine told Andrew she was going to make another effort to go to Poland. Andrew pointed out that her photograph and papers, as well as Ledochowski's, might well by now be in the hands of the Gestapo, but she paid little attention to the argument. At first she had wanted to set out in October; but she reluctantly agreed to wait until the first snows in November, when the frontier guards would be less anxious to sit in the icy woods waiting to trap people. Another reason was Andrew's anxiety that she should wait until Janek Marusarz, who had escorted her so successfully on her first trip, was free.

In mid-October, a courier arrived to report to Christine that sixteen British soldiers, who had escaped from POW camps in Germany, were hidden in a deaf-and-dumb asylum in Warsaw. They were in great danger since it was rumoured that Hitler was about to implement his plan for the 'mercy killing' of the mentally and physically handicapped.[3]

Christine realized that the discovery of the soldiers was only a matter of time, and began packing her rucksack. This time Andrew checked her packing very carefully, making sure that she took no additional photographs or documents. She was issued with a new identity, fresh papers, and a new photograph in which she wore a completely different hair-style.

Christine left Budapest on 13 November, reaching Warsaw on the 18th. She went straight to the deaf-and-dumb asylum, only to find that the British soldiers had already left. The leader of the group had insisted on being evacuated by the Polish Underground, and had requested their assistance to cross into the Russian-occupied zone. Christine then asked to help get two other British soldiers out of Poland into Hungary. When they reached Warsaw their condition was so poor that the doctors pronounced them unfit to undertake a long and arduous journey without having at least three weeks' rest. The information which Christine had to deliver in Budapest could not wait for their recovery, so she handed her charges over to her friends the Musketeers, who helped them escape from Poland. Later, they had a cheerful reunion with Christine in Belgrade.

Every moment Christine spent in Poland was dangerous. The Germans were now operating street arrests. This meant that they closed a number of streets, and simply arrested everyone walking in or living in these particular streets. The victims were herded into a barracks and searched, and if they could not produce a bona-fide permit to prove that they were working with the Germans, they were sent to hard labour or to concentration camps.

Christine came back to Budapest at the end of November, in poor physical condition; she had a bad attack of influenza and was completely exhausted. During her absence, it was work as usual, but Andrew was uneasily aware of being continually watched and often followed. It was no easy job to shake a persistent car off his tail, and the moment Christine got home he told her that it was high time for them to get out.

She was not prepared to listen, saying she could not leave Budapest until various matters she had set in train and which must await the arrival of couriers from Poland, were clarified. Then she retired to bed for two weeks to nurse her flu and, to Andrew's horror, began coughing blood. Their Christmas celebrations that year were anything but merry.

'By the time February arrived,' said Andrew, 'I was as jumpy as a cat. I kept telling Christine that we must not be arrested together. If two people belonging to the same network are arrested simultaneously, there is no possibility of letting anyone know where you are incarcerated, so it is difficult to get help. There is always the risk of the prisoners saying different things during interrogation.

'I had naturally warned my boys and organized them as well as I could. I was pretty certain that if we were arrested we should be taken to the famous prison of the Hungarian Second Bureau, which had been taken over by the Germans.'

True to the German custom of using ordinary houses as their infamous prisons, this place of detention was in Hortemiklos Ucca. Behind the normal façade was a courtyard, beneath which the prison proper, built underground, housed Jews, political prisoners and others. Andrew's team were told that if he or Christine disappeared they were to keep close watch on this house.

'All over the world police choose four o'clock in the morning to arrest their victims,' said Andrew, 'who at that unearthly hour are usually fast asleep and, being taken by surprise, are less likely to put up any kind of resistance. I was dreading the four o'clock knock which was beginning to prey on my mind, and I insisted that Christine get up and leave our flat at three a.m. as a practice run. She utterly refused to move. I insisted, but she refused.

'"You go tonight," she said, "and I promise I'll go tomorrow."'

Andrew left the house, looked right and left; but the street was empty. It was freezingly cold. He got into his car, released his brakes and rolled downhill. At that hour the city was dead. There was nowhere to go. He was cold, tired, miserable and irritable. He went and sat in the station, but after half an hour was tempted to go back home to his warm bed. However, he resisted the temptation because he was going to insist on Christine following his example to the letter. When he finally got back at five a.m., he found Christine happily curled up and fast asleep.

'"You see," she said, "you're a silly old Cat sometimes."

'"That may be," I said, "but you did promise and tomorrow out you go as arranged."'

The following night they dined with Kate O'Malley and some friends in a restaurant. They had a pleasantly relaxed evening and got home late.

At four in the morning the doorbell rang. Andrew and Christine knew at once that the long-dreaded moment was upon them. Christine flung on a dressing gown, while Andrew strapped on his leg. The bell pealed again and the banging on the door became louder.

Andrew opened the door to four members of the Hungarian police. Two were in uniform, and two in plain clothes. Silently they pushed past him into the flat. Switching on all the lights, they began a systematic search of each room. Apart from ordering Christine and Andrew to dress, they said nothing. Naturally any incriminating papers had long since vanished; all that remained was a number of harmless letters, a quantity of brightly coloured tourist folders and maps advertising hotels and restaurants. All these the policemen neatly packed away in suitcases.

Christine said to one of the men, 'I'm going to the lavatory.' For a moment, the policeman said nothing, but then, when he heard the cistern flushing, he dashed after her and said furiously, 'Why did you pull the chain?' Christine smiled, and said in her normal voice, 'Isn't it usual to flush the loo after use?' When Andrew followed her to the lavatory, he was accompanied by a policeman, who stood watching him unblinkingly throughout the whole performance. He was desperately trying to think how to get rid of a notebook filled with telephone numbers. Though the numbers were in code, sooner or later he would have to explain why none of the telephone numbers seemed to be attached to a subscriber. He said in Polish to Christine, 'What the hell do I do with my notebook?' 'You are not to talk to each other,' said one policeman, 'but if you have anything to say, you will say it in German.' 'Madame does not speak German,' Andrew said. 'In that case, there will be no talking at all.'

The flat was searched for an hour. At five o'clock in the morning Andrew and Christine were bundled into a big police car. Christine was as peaceful and relaxed as if she were going for a drive with Andrew. As they drove away, she managed to whisper, 'Give me your notebook.' Andrew shook his head. He had no intention of involving her any further in what was already a very dangerous situation.

The car drew up outside the pleasant house in Hortemiklos

Ucca. One of the policemen rang the doorbell; the door was opened, and the little group went in. Facing them was an iron door guarded by another policeman. After an exchange of papers, two more men joined the policeman on duty. The iron door was opened and Christine and Andrew were herded upstairs to a large room. Almost immediately Christine was taken away.

Andrew immediately recognized two of the occupants of the room as Germans from the Jägerhof Hotel. One was a slim, attractive young man, the other was a great hulking brute. The Hungarians were also present, but in a completely subservient role.

'Take your coat off, and come here,' barked the Brute. Andrew removed his overcoat and one of the Hungarians began meticulously searching the garment, pricking each seam and pocket with a long needle. There was nothing in the coat, but the notebook was burning a hole in Andrew's pocket.

'Hang your jacket up,' snapped the Brute. As Andrew did so, he managed to slip the notebook into a pocket. Then his captors took him apart. He was stripped down to his underpants, and his artificial leg was practically taken to bits to see whether it had been used as a hiding place for microfilms. When they were satisfied that there was nothing concealed on Andrew's person, he was seated on a hard upright chair, and the interrogation proper began.

The two Germans began by stating that they knew everything about Christine and Andrew's activities. Andrew parried their questions with sarcasm. This worked well, but only because, at that stage, the Germans were not prepared to use physical violence under the eyes of the Hungarians.

Even so the ordeal lasted from five in the morning until ten o'clock at night, during which time Andrew was given nothing to eat. When he asked if he might relieve himself, he was told to sit still. Amiably, he said he would have to make a puddle on the floor, so he was escorted to the lavatory. In the meantime, one of the policemen was going through all the papers and documents and folders that had been taken from the flat. The interrogators kept asking if he had found anything incriminating, but the man could only shake his head sadly.

At midday another team arrived to relieve the Germans. By this time Andrew was exhausted, and was beginning to feel faint. He had to concentrate not to contradict himself. At one moment he gave a sarcastic answer to a question, and the German hit him. His lip started to bleed and he tried to hit back.

There was such a commotion that the door opened and in came a Hungarian officer. It was Andrew's courteous Major from the Second Bureau.

He stared at the prisoner without a flicker of recognition. Andrew cried out, 'We are in the Royal country of Hungary, and I am a Polish officer. Will you permit this brute to hit me?'

'So you admit to being a Polish officer?' said the German triumphantly. Andrew laughed. 'Once an officer, always an officer. But an officer without a leg is not much use.'

The Hungarian Major signalled the German to follow him, and they left the room. When the German returned he was furious. 'Wait till we get you over the border, you bastard,' he said, 'we'll show you a thing or two then.'

By seven o'clock at night Andrew was so worn out that he was hardly conscious. The good-looking German with the gentle voice came over and began to walk him round the room, saying soothingly, 'It will be much better for you if you confess now as we have an agreement with Hungary, and have no need to get an extradition order to get you over the border.'

The large room had two doors, the one through which Andrew had come in, and another which was closed at the other end of the room. The German interrogator propelled Andrew towards this door which suddenly opened to reveal the battered remains of a man who was being held up by two policemen. Andrew stared at the swollen, livid face of the stranger. 'You know this man?' asked the German. Andrew shook his head. It was fortunate that the man was unknown to him for he felt that, had this been a friend, he would not have been able to control his facial muscles.

Then the interrogation began again, and the questions became more difficult to parry. The Germans kept on asking why Christine and Andrew spent so much time in the British Embassy, to which he replied that he did not think that the German Ambassador would have welcomed them. Andrew soon realized that, unless the Germans could prove that he and Christine were working directly against the Third Reich, the Hungarians would refuse to extradite them. The main danger lay in them finding out that Christine had been to Poland several times, which would have meant that she was, as they suspected, a British secret agent.

At ten o'clock, the Germans had got absolutely nowhere with their interrogation. They were furious and finally decided to send Andrew to cool his heels in prison, while they thought out a new method of approach for the next day. A Hungarian guard took him to the bunker prison where a Hungarian corporal took down Andrew's name, rank and other personal details. The Hungarian left, and Andrew was made to hand over all his possessions to an obviously sympathetic little soldier, who locked them all up, including the notebook, in a locker.

Andrew was then shown into a cell which was already occupied by two men lying on the only two bunks. The corporal shouted at one of the men to give Andrew his bed. The little man slid out of the bottom bunk, looking daggers at Andrew, and climbed into the upper bunk with his friend. The corporal banged the door behind him.

Andrew apologized profusely for having taken one of the bunks, but the two men made it clear that they did not want to talk to him. A little later there was the sound of tapping on the wall of the cell.

'That bloody fellow,' said one of the little men. 'He's at it again. He never stops sending out Morse signals.' Andrew was particularly upset that he did not know the Morse code, because he thought the signals might be coming from one of his boys who had disappeared mysteriously and who, it was suspected, had been brought to this very prison for interrogation.

At five a.m. the prisoners were woken, told to dress and taken to the lavatory and washroom. After some time Andrew was brought back to his cell to find his cell-mates lying uncomfortably on the top bunk with their legs spread wide apart. Once again, Andrew tried to talk to them, and this time the response was less chilly. One of them said, 'We thought you were a stool pigeon, but now we know you are not.'

'How do you know?'

'We got a message in the lavatory through the grapevine. One of the chaps recognized you.'

'It must be my boy,' said Andrew. 'Anyway, what are you in here for?'

'Because we are Jews. We were interrogated. We're very lucky. We were sentenced yesterday. I got fifteen years and my mate got twelve.'

'What's so bloody lucky about that?' Andrew asked.

Both men laughed, and one of them said, 'Before we finish our sentence the Russian army will be in Budapest, and we're both Communists.'

The Russian army finally did arrive, but long before that the two Jews were dead, gassed in one of the death camps. Andrew discovered that there was a good reason for the awkward way in which they lay or sat with their legs wide apart. For seven months they had been continually interrogated. The method used to get them to confess was to invite them to lay their testicles on a table and then to beat them with a pencil. Over this period of time their genitalia had become as black and as swollen as if they had had elephantiasis.

At noon Andrew was taken upstairs again, to find the original reception committee, looking extremely glum. Also present was the friendly Hungarian Major, still very spruce and elegant. As Andrew came in it was evident that there had been a fierce argument between the Major and the Germans. They stopped talking immediately, and one of the Germans began shouting at Andrew, telling him to confess that he had been instrumental in helping Countess Skarbek to go to Poland by driving her to the border, and also that he was involved in getting escapers out of Hungary to fight with the enemies of the Reich.

Suddenly Andrew lost his temper and roared back at them. At this moment, to his complete surprise, the Germans walked out, and Christine walked in. She was as pale as paper. Andrew grabbed her in his arms, kissed her on both cheeks and said, 'Are you all right, my darling?' 'Yes, I think so,' she answered, 'though the doctor says I am not at all well,' and she squeezed his hand meaningfully. He understood that a doctor had something to do with her being brought back to him. The Hungarian Major, meanwhile, stood looking benevolently at this reunion. Then he said, 'You are being temporarily released owing to the illness of Countess Skarbek; but you are not to use any form of transport save a tram. You can return to your flat, but you may not leave it without our permission.'

They thanked the Major warmly and got out as quickly as they could. They were accompanied by two policemen in plain clothes, who ordered them to go to their usual rendezvous, the Café Hagli.

This was, of course, another trap, since they knew that if two members of an underground team vanished and reappeared, all the others, despite warnings never to make this mistake, were liable to cluster round asking questions, which would allow the police to pick up one member of the team after the other.

As Christine and Andrew walked down the street on their way to Hagli's, he spied one of his boys standing on the opposite pavement. He made a discreet, but unmistakable, sign and the young man understood that Christine and his boss were being followed. He took to his heels, ran like the wind, and by the time Christine and Andrew and their escorts arrived at the café, nobody greeted them and they sat by themselves at a

table and ordered a much-needed cup of hot coffee and a
sandwich. Only when they got a signal that it was safe to go, did
they move. Then they went home, and Christine told Andrew
her story.

CHAPTER FIVE

The moment they were alone in their flat, Andrew took Christine in his arms. She looked strained and pale, and he was seriously concerned about her. She said that at first her interrogation had been conducted in a quiet and orderly fashion. The Gestapo men sat her down in a fairly comfortable chair. There were three teams who took turns in questioning her. They accused her of going on spying missions to Poland, but, as they were unable to prove this, they changed their tactics and asked why she and Andrew went so constantly to the British Embassy.

Though Andrew and Christine had rehearsed the story they would tell when, and if, they were arrested, there might well have been divergences in the detail of their stories; as it happened, both the prisoners told exactly the same tale. Like Andrew, Christine said ironically that she did not think that the German Ambassador had any wish to see her. She added that Andrew's reason for being such a constant visitor at the Embassy might have had something to do with the Ambassador's attractive daughter.

After three or four hours of exhausting, non-stop interrogation, Christine decided she would create a diversion. There was a Hungarian sitting in on the act, and from time to time, he gave her what she thought and hoped was a sympathetic glance. Summoning up all her powers of concentration and will-power she bit her tongue so hard that blood flowed from her mouth and down her chin. The Hungarian looked startled and said, 'How long have you been spitting blood?'

Christine did her best to look like the 'Dame aux Camélias' in the last stages of her illness. Since she was a consummate actress, she succeeded very well. The Hungarian said, 'Have you been to a doctor?'

'No,' said Christine, putting her handkerchief to her mouth and coughing, 'I did not want to alarm my friend, but I was a bit worried as I was spitting blood more and more often. I was just about to see a specialist when you arrested me.'

She then managed in the most subtle fashion to convey to her interrogators that she had enlisted the help of her aunt to find her a lung specialist. The moment the Hungarian realized that Christine's aunt was related to the Regent, Admiral Horthy, he became even more anxious to help her. The Germans, however, were unimpressed, and continued to grill their prisoner.

Towards midday Christine began to look so ill that she was taken back to the prison and a Hungarian doctor was called. Christine told him she was feeling desperately sick and produced the racking cough left over from her recent attack of influenza, as well as a stained handkerchief which she pressed to her mouth. The doctor was visibly shaken and decided to take an immediate X-ray.

Christine was then taken out of the Gestapo prison building, and was transferred by car to a Hungarian prison which had all the necessary medical facilities.

She was duly X-rayed, and some time later the Hungarian doctor returned with the plates in his hand. He looked at Christine with great compassion. 'Did you know how ill you are? Your lungs are in a terrible state, and you must get immediate treatment.' Christine realized at once that the doctor had attributed the shadows on her lungs from her former poisoning by exhaust gas, to tuberculosis. She said sadly, 'I thought there must be something very wrong.'

The Hungarian doctor looked at her reflectively. It was quite obvious to her that he sympathized with the Poles. He said, 'Leave this to me.' He went back to the Gestapo with Christine's X-rays. When he returned he looked relieved. He did not tell her what he had said to them, but putting his hand over hers, he said, 'Stop worrying. Everything will be all right. But you have got to begin a cure.'

Christine knew then that she was safe. She said, 'Thank you, doctor. Of course, I will do whatever you suggest. But what about my boyfriend, Andrew Kowerski? What is going to happen to him?' 'Everything is going to be all right for you both,' said the doctor.[1]

Both Christine and Andrew knew that they were out 'on parole' as it were. They knew that the Gestapo intended pulling them in again as soon as they possibly could. It was imperative that they should start making plans to get out of Hungary as soon as possible. While they were debating ways and means, the telephone rang. It was a mutual friend called Antek, who had been involved with Ludwig Popiel in the famous anti-tank high velocity rifle episode. Antek was a jolly, bibulous character who refused to take life seriously.

'Thank God you're back,' he cried, on hearing Andrew's voice.

'Thank you for your good wishes,' replied Andrew in Polish, trying to warn him. 'But do be careful. The phones today are far from safe.'

There was a click, a silence and then a reproving voice said, 'If you say things like that you will be sent straight back to prison. You are to answer the phone in a normal way, and you are *not* to try to warn your friends that your calls are monitored.'

This admonition gave Christine and Andrew a nasty jolt, for, though Antek was nothing to do with their team, the fact of their being under such close surveillance meant that they must take immediate action. They began packing surreptitiously, because they did not know whether the owner of the house might not see what they were doing and warn the police. While they were sorting out their things, the doorbell pealed, and in came Antek looking quite unconcerned.

'You idiot,' said Andrew, 'don't you realize that we're being watched and that everyone who comes in and out is being scrutinized?'

'So what?' said Antek, 'I don't give a damn and I've brought you a bottle of slivovitz.'

Andrew filled two glasses and even Christine took a sip for good luck. Though there were not as many listening devices as there are today, Andrew made certain that their conversation could not be heard by playing records very loudly. Under cover of this noise, he asked, 'Did you see anyone sitting outside, watching the house?'

'I believe I did see two men sitting in a car, but I'm not certain. What are you going to do?'

'Finish our packing, and then drop the suitcases out of the window.'

Though the Hungarians had ransacked the flat they had never examined the greenhouse in which Andrew garaged his little sandy-brown, two-door Opel. Antek, who did not seem to have an anxious nerve in his body, helped to dispose of the suitcases. Then, whistling nonchalantly, he went out to see if Andrew's big car, which was parked near the house, was in good order. He came back triumphantly, having seen nobody outside. Andrew's big Chevrolet was still there.

It was now getting late, and both Christine and Andrew were dropping with fatigue from their ordeal of the previous days. However, they packed up the Opel with suitcases and parcels. Antek, considerably cheered by constant nips at the slivovitz bottle, suggested that they celebrate their release from prison by dining with him. They refused as gracefully as possible, and as soon as Antek had gone, fell into bed. They slept peacefully, knowing there was little likelihood of another four o'clock alarm so soon after the first one. Early next morning Antek came round to tell Christine and Andrew that once again a private car was waiting outside the house with two men in it.

'You,' said Andrew to Antek, 'will go out into the street. You

will get into my big Chevvy and drive her right into our courtyard. If anyone asks what you are doing in my car, you will
simply say that I asked you to bring the car in for me. In the
meantime, Christine and I will be waiting in the Opel. The
moment you drive in, leaving the gate wide open, we will drive
out hell for leather. Do you understand?'

Antek nodded and went out. Christine and Andrew left the
flat looking tidy and lived-in, so that anyone coming in would
think they had only gone out for the day.

Antek drove the Chevrolet into the courtyard and waited,
honking his horn. Almost immediately Andrew revved up the
Opel and drove at full speed out into the icy road. There was a
terrible moment when the car went into a spin; but he managed
to pull her round, and, pressing his foot hard on the accelerator,
he tore down the steep hill into the city proper. At one point
Christine informed him that they were being followed. This
spurred him on and he drove faster and faster until he was certain that he had thrown his pursuers off the scent. As the police
had the number of the Chevrolet, but not of the Opel, he knew
it was unlikely that they would catch up once they got under
way.

Their first move was to phone their British contact, who
invited them to his house; but when Andrew used the code
word which told him that they were on the run – this was
'We're on a one or two day cure' – he was less pleased at the
idea of seeing them. He was a phlegmatic sort of man and did
not seem to realize the urgency of the situation, even when
Andrew made it crystal clear that, in his view, they had
exactly three days' grace before the chase would be on again.
Christine pointed out that there were plenty of places where
they could go to ground in Budapest, but only for a very limited period. He did not seem convinced, and Andrew began
to get angry. Christine said calmly, 'Forget it. We'll find a
way.'

Leaving a perplexed man behind them, they drove straight
to the British Embassy. It was a cold and sunny day and

Andrew, glancing at Christine's pinched little face, suddenly felt desperately anxious. He parked the car at a reasonable distance from the Embassy and phoned Kate O'Malley. Andrew told her briefly that they were in trouble and she sprang into immediate action, telling them that if they made for the little door let into the heavy *porte cochère*, a feature of the older and grander town houses, they would find it open. Christine and Andrew walked there separately and passed through the little door unchallenged by the policeman on duty.

Kate, her face shining with excitement, took them to her quarters. They told her their story and she said, 'You must see Daddy immediately.' Sir Owen heard them out without comment. Three anxious pairs of eyes scrutinized Sir Owen's. He stared back, his face giving away nothing of his thoughts. It was the bland visage of the accomplished diplomat used to assessing human beings and situations.

'How long do you think you can stay safely in Budapest?' he asked.

'Three days, sir,' replied Andrew, 'three days at the most.'

'And then what do you intend doing?'

'There are two options open to us. One is hellishly risky as Christine is in such bad shape. But, knowing the frontier passes as I do, I thought we might have a chance of crossing via the Green Frontier.[2] I'm not sure that Christine could stand up to it, because it means crossing at night in appalling weather conditions and with little protective covering.'

'What is the alternative?'

'If I had the right passport, I could do my usual trick.'

'What's that?'

'When I get to a frontier, I can usually sense the "climate" because I know the soldiers so well. If the soldiers rush out and try to stop us, I'll risk driving straight through to the other side. They won't be able to shoot because the Yugoslav border is so close. But the point is, we can't get into Yugoslavia without visas, and we cannot get visas with the Polish passports we now hold.'

Sir Owen thoughtfully stroked his chin. 'And what would happen if you had other passports with the right visas?'

'That would be completely different. I'd pretend to push the car over the border as I've done many times. The guards would check the visas on our passports, then I should produce the other passports with their correct visas and we should then be safe in Yugoslavia.'

Sir Owen considered this plan for a minute, and said, 'I think it may be feasible for you; but I doubt very much whether the guards will let two people push the car over the border. When do you propose leaving Budapest?'

'In three days at the latest.'

'I don't think so,' said Sir Owen, and Andrew's heart missed a beat. He thought, that's it, he's not going to be able to help us.

Sir Owen was looking at Christine. 'I think you should get out of Budapest immediately, now, this minute.'

Andrew and Christine could not believe their ears. They knew from his tone that he was going to help. Christine jumped up and warmly embraced the Minister. He patted her hand. He was devoted to her.

'Take them upstairs,' said Sir Owen to his daughter, 'and leave me to work this one out.' Turning to Andrew, he said, 'I don't think it is a good idea for Christine to drive with you. If you want to risk your neck, that's OK, but I think we have to make other arrangements for her. She's a sick girl and we've got to make things as uncomplicated as possible for her.'

Upstairs Christine and Andrew congratulated Kate on having so compassionate and understanding a father. 'Thank God Sir Owen is Irish,' said Andrew, 'for the Irish, like the Poles, have always had the "feel" of underground fighting and of resistance work. It's in their blood.'

After luncheon Tommy, the Ambassador's PA, was sent to bring Christine and Andrew to the Chancery, where they were handed over to the care of a pink-faced young clerk. He said, 'I have instructions to issue you both with British passports.' Christine and Andrew were dumbfounded. Never in their wildest dreams had they expected to be given *British* passports, which were the most valuable and unobtainable passports in the world.

The young man, unaware of the sensation he had created with his announcement, continued in a matter-of-fact voice to ask for details and photographs. Fortunately Christine and Andrew always carried a supply of passport photographs in their papers. Then came the question of names. Christine said, 'I should have a name to match my present initials "C.G."' 'Granville!' said Kate O'Malley, 'that's the right name for you. It has English and French connotations. What do you think?'

Christine was delighted with her new name. When it came to Andrew's turn he had already decided on his surname. Like Christine, he felt his surname must tie in with his present initials. He had remembered that during the Black and Tan struggles in Ireland, a great many Irish people had emigrated to Poland, mainly because it was a Catholic country. A distant cousin of Andrew's had married one of these Irish émigrés whose name was Kennedy. In a flash, Andrew Kowerski became Andrew Kennedy.

Later Andrew was to have doubts about the choice of this name for neither he nor Christine knew much English. Andrew's sole contribution in this language was 'double whiskey', and Christine had a few ordinary phrases. They spoke French with Sir Owen and Lady O'Malley, with Kate and Tommy. This worried Sir Owen, who was a perfectionist.

It was not long, however, before they had dreamed up what they considered a foolproof cover story. When the Revolution began in Russia a number of British engineers were working there, some with Russian wives and children. Most of these Englishmen were subsequently either executed or deported, their wives and children staying on in Russia. Christine and Andrew decided that if they were interrogated they would say that during the Polish War they had escaped from Russia, and were travelling on the British passports to which they were entitled through the nationality of their fathers.

The only problem was that in each of their passports it was clearly set out that Christine and Andrew had been born in London. So the cover story was amended to allow the Russian wives to have had their babies in London. It was a real Munchausen fabrication, but because it was so unbelievable, they hoped it had the ring of authority.

Exactly seven minutes after the pink-cheeked young clerk had asked for details, Christine and Andrew were handed their British passports. Andrew could still not believe that the beautiful brand new passport in his hands was really his.

Just then, Sir Owen walked in and said briskly, 'I've been thinking this whole matter over, and this is what you are going to do now. You, Tommy, will, as I told you, take my big Chrysler. You will put Christine in the boot and drive her to the frontier. Andrew should go with you; but if he prefers to go under his own steam that's his affair. I think it's risky, but that's his decision.'

Knowing that Christine would be safe in the ambassadorial car, Andrew thanked the Minister, but said he preferred to drive his Opel. Apart from the fact that he loved the little car, he knew that once they had crossed the border, they would need a car of their own. The Chrysler was a vast roomy vehicle; it seated eight and had a large roomy boot, which was important, since without sufficient ventilation, it would be impossible for Christine to have travelled in it.

Sir Owen, having some suspicions as to the integrity of his butler and chauffeur, sent them off on an errand and in their absence led his little party to where the big car was standing. Tommy opened the door, and Christine got in beside the driver's seat. Andrew got in behind, and Tommy took the wheel. There was nothing Christine and Andrew could say to express their gratitude. Sir Owen's magnificent gesture was one they never forgot. As they left the Embassy, the policeman saluted, and Tommy drove round the corner to where the Opel was parked.

'I say,' he said, 'HE is quite right. You'd much better leave your car here. I'll buy it off you. How much is it worth?'

'I'm not selling my car, Tommy. I need it and I shall drive it myself, so shut up like a good fellow and let's get on with our plan.'

'The plan was simple,' said Andrew. 'We had decided to drive to Lenti, my little frontier post. The scenery was beautiful and, though I knew the road by heart, I was always pleased to drive this way. I drove in front of the Chrysler. I knew that Tommy was anything but happy at having this mission of mercy foisted on him. He knew that if he was caught helping us to escape, the consequences would be serious and he would be instantly deported as 'persona non grata', which was the last thing he wanted to happen to him.

'We had previously agreed that we should stop somewhere and discuss our future movements. The road was practically deserted for petrol was available only for essential journeys. We stopped, and Christine left her seat. Tommy opened the boot and she crawled in. I made her a sort of nest of overcoats and rugs, and she nestled in them, looking quite comfortable. We then closed the boot, and asked her whether she could breathe properly. She said, 'I'm fine', but she had begun to cough again. I said, 'Christine, for God's sake, watch that cough. If anyone hears that noise in the boot of the car, we're all for the high jump.' She gave a stifled sort of giggle, and then there was complete silence.

'It was arranged that I should have a fifteen minutes' start on Tommy so as to arrive at the border in time to test the reactions of the soldiers. I had made up my mind that, if the Hungarian soldiers tried to stop me, I should simply try to crash through the frontier. I had the bottle of brandy carefully wrapped beside me, and I drove on hoping that everything would work out. It struck me that it would be a good move to warn the Hungarian soldiers that I had passed a grand English car on its way to the frontier. I would say I thought it might be carrying a high official because it was flying the British flag. I knew that this would create a diversion and that the little soldiers would forget me, and start polishing their buttons and tidying themselves up for the arrival of the high official.

'I arrived at the border with my heart beating like a drum. I took a quick look at the smiling faces of my Hungarians, and said gaily, "Hello there, what about a drop of brandy?", with which I produced my bottle. "We've no time for jollifications now," said one of them, "there's serious business afoot; we've just had a message that the British Ambassador is crossing over to Yugoslavia." This was good news. I began to appreciate Sir Owen's efficient powers of organization. He had left nothing to chance. He had even asked the Foreign Ministry – which he was entitled to do – to let the frontier guards know that he was leaving Budapest. But there was absolutely no reason why he could not change his mind, and send his First Secretary in his stead.

'"Look," I said, uncorking my bottle of brandy, "this car is going to Yugoslavia, how about letting me push it over now?"

'One of the soldiers said, "May I see your passport?" I showed it to him. "There's no exit visa?"

'"That's no problem, is it?"

'"What have you got in your car?"

'"Nothing much. A little petrol, luggage and some bits and pieces that belong to friends."

'"That sounds all right," said one of the Hungarians, "but we can't attend to you right now. You will have to wait until the Ambassador has gone through."

'On the dot, Tommy appeared driving the enormous car. He was deadly pale, with eyes as big as saucers. I had said, if I pull my nose, it means everything is all right, and I was tugging away at my proboscis like mad. A bit of colour came into Tommy's face. The Hungarians saluted and respectfully circled the ambassadorial car. I closed my eyes, praying to God that Christine wouldn't cough. The Hungarians moved back, saluted, the barrier was raised and the car went smoothly through to the Yugoslav border.

'The normal procedure for a Polish car with a triptique was for it to be pushed over the border to Yugoslavia where it was picked up by a driver. The driver of the car who had brought it to the frontier returned to Hungary, as the Hungarians would allow this manoeuvre only if he were *not* possessed of a Yugoslav visa.

'I watched the Chrysler speeding away into the distance, and suddenly felt vulnerable and terribly lonely. Then I pulled myself together, and went over to the soldiers, and said, "Is it in order for me to push this buggy over to the other side? I'll come straight back and we'll have a drink together. I've plenty of time, as I have to wait until I'm picked up by a friend who is coming from Budapest to fetch me."

'They raised no objection, and I pushed the car over the frontier into Yugoslavia. I then produced my British passport complete with visa, and, with a mocking wave at the Hungarians on the other side, climbed into the Opel and was off to catch up with the Chrysler.'

Tommy stopped the big car a few miles down the road. Andrew had a quick and loving reunion with Christine who had by now been released from the stuffy confines of the boot. She got into the Opel and the little cavalcade set off for Belgrade. Though Christine and Andrew were delighted to have left the Gestapo behind them, they were sad at leaving Budapest which held so many nostalgic memories.

They got to Belgrade in the evening. Tommy went to the British Embassy, while Christine and Andrew put up at a comfortable little hotel. They planned to spend a fortnight in Belgrade, relaxing and preparing for their long journey. They had many friends here, among them Andrew Tarnowski, one of Andrew's rescuers when he was trapped in the snow by the avalanche. Andrew had spent many happy times with him and his wife on their estate near Cracow.

Everyone was pleased to see Christine and Andrew, who were taken to some of the Russian nightclubs which were a special feature of the city. There was only one momentary cloud on their happiness; Christine discovered that she would be unable to leave Yugoslavia, as she had no entry visa on her new passport. As she had arrived in the country in the boot of a car, this was not surprising. However, when Christine confided her difficulty to an SOE contact called John Bennett, he managed to get the required visa without too much trouble from the Yugoslav authorities.

There was a memorable evening spent by Christine with two of her 'boys'. These were the Cockney soldiers who had escaped from Dunkirk to Poland, and who had been convoyed out of Poland to Hungary by the organizations of the Musketeers. The lads had quite a story to tell. They were the first of the prisoners taken at Dunkirk to escape. They went from Germany into the part of Poland which had been taken over by the Germans. But even there they were helped.

They walked to Warsaw, mainly along the railway tracks. On one occasion a German guard tried to stop them. One of the Cockneys went for him with a Rugby tackle, and left him doubled up in a ditch. In Warsaw the Underground took care of them. Since they could speak only English, it was arranged that they should pretend to be deaf and dumb until they crossed over the border into Hungary with their guides, who posed as Red Cross officials. Once in Budapest they were collected by the valiant Kate O'Malley and taken to her father, who organized their passports and trip to Belgrade.

After a short rest, Christine wanted to get back to work. She had to re-establish contact with the organization in Poland, and make arrangements for their couriers to find new routes. The Musketeers had shown their mettle and were firmly in the driving-seat in Poland, but who was now to 'feed' them from outside? Andrew could not return, nor could Christine. So many lives depended on the choice of their successor that they could not afford to make any mistakes. The person who replaced them must be entirely trustworthy. Christine and Andrew discussed this problem in depth; but, from the very beginning, Christine said that the only person who really filled the bill in every respect was her husband, George. Andrew was somewhat baffled by her reasoning. He said, 'But my darling Kitten, if you send for George and he discovers that you have left him for me, there will be ghastly repercussions and complications.'

Christine laughed. She said, 'You don't understand the first thing about George. He was my Svengali for so many years that he would never believe that I could ever leave him for good. George wouldn't pay much attention to my having a physical affair, as long as I told him about it. Also George hates oppression and will do anything to combat it. Remember how he volunteered to go to Finland to fight, first the Russians and afterwards the Germans. He comes from the Ukraine and has never forgotten what the oppressors of the Russian Revolution did there. George is his own man, and he of all people is the one I want to replace me.' 'If you have such complete faith in George,' answered Andrew, 'I must accept that what you say is true.'

Christine said, 'George is undoubtedly the most difficult man I've ever known, but he is also the most efficient and the most uncompromising. He has his own codes of honour, which can be tricky, but where work is concerned, he is unique.'

Christine and Andrew discussed the matter of replacement at length with friends like Bill Morrell, John Bennett and A. G. G. de Chastelain.[3] The latter was at that time looking after the Rumanian Section and the possible sabotaging of Rumanian oil. Everyone was agreed that George was the ideal person, but it was thought that he might react adversely to the idea. Christine was firm. 'If I say George will come, then you can be perfectly sure that he will.'[4] She then wrote to him in England, explaining in detail what was required of him and asking whether he would join her in Istanbul. This important letter was sent by diplomatic courier.

Meanwhile preparations were going ahead for the journey to Turkey. The little Opel, which was finally to become famous all over the Middle East and even in Italy, was again loaded to the roof with petrol and extra luggage – winter gear and every imaginable thing they thought might be needed.

Just before they were about to leave, a courier brought Christine a consignment of important microfilms. She had no idea what the microfilms contained, but was determined to take them with her to Istanbul. Already her infallible instinct warned her that they might be a valuable asset at a time when she needed evidence of the Musketeers' good work.

Early in March, Christine and Andrew set off. It was pouring with rain, and Andrew, though he said nothing to Christine, was somewhat dismayed at the prospect of the journey ahead. He, like many ardent motorists, had heard of the famous Belgrade–Sofia Rally, which always took great toll of both cars and participants. The road, as such, did not exist. There was a river of mud along which the poor little Opel toiled gallantly. Andrew was used to driving in bad conditions, the Polish roads were generally poor, but this road was appalling and Andrew was justifiably terrified. Not so Christine. Having absolutely no knowledge of – or interest in – things mechanical, she had no idea of the dangers and was as happy as a lark.

'She was a marvellous companion,' said Andrew, 'except that she did not like the radio. It was one of the things that always astonished me about Christine. She really wasn't very musical, and when I turned on the radio, she said, "Please, darling Cat, turn it off. It makes such a noise." This was annoying, as on long, tiring and difficult journeys such as this, I liked listening to musical programmes. I compromised with Christine by listening only to the news which, from hour to hour, became increasingly gloomy. We arrived in Sofia in a state of complete exhaustion. The Opel had lost nearly all her vital underpinnings and I never knew at which point the exhaust-pipe was wrenched off, but the gutsy little car did her job well, and managed to get us to our destination.

'We booked into a comfortable hotel, and found a message inviting us to call at the British Legation. Before so doing, we cleaned up a bit and had a look at our precious microfilms. When we realized the implications of these films, we stared in amazement at one another. The Polish Underground had produced a startling document showing hundreds of trains, regiments, divisions and ammunition, all massed on the Russian border. It was evident that Germany was on the point of attacking Russia. Further evidence was an impressive list of petrol depots, adding up to millions of litres of petrol, more than enough to drive many thousands of Volkswagens to and from Moscow many times!

'We went to the British Legation, where we were received by a handsome Air Attaché called Aidan Crawley.[5] Besides being a first-rate sportsman, he was also extremely intelligent and had charming manners. He was a Socialist, which amused me. His father was a Canon of Windsor, and he had a brother in the Scots Guards.'

Aidan Crawley was immediately captivated by Christine's charm and listened with interest to the story of their activities in Poland and Hungary. He was already aware of – and impressed by – the work that had gone into the liberation of the British POWs, and in the rounding-up of the impressive number of fighter-pilots who had been brought out from Hungary to fight in the Battle of Britain. Once the Polish contingent had been exhausted, there had been others, among them brave Czechs and Austrians.

Christine had decided to hand the microfilms over to Aidan Crawley. He said he would see that they got to London as quickly as possible.[6] He also warned his new friends to get out of Bulgaria with all speed to avoid being trapped by the Germans, who were moving into the country, adding wryly that, as Britain was about to sever diplomatic relations with Bulgaria, neither he nor any member of the Legation would be able to help if Christine and Andrew were arrested.

Early next morning, Christine and Andrew tucked themselves into the Opel, which in the course of time was to become their refuge and mobile home. The road from Sofia to the Bulgarian border was even more treacherous than that from Belgrade to Sofia. Andrew, never the most patient of drivers, was in a perpetual frenzy of frustration owing to the lackadaisical habits of the Bulgarian peasants. He was certain that they owed their much vaunted longevity less to their intake of yoghourt than to the pace of their oxen. These patient, plodding beasts were generally up to the ears in treacly mud, and as they struggled to pull the carts along, the motorist had to contain his rage, halt his car and pray that it would start up again from its bed of slush.

It was getting late when Christine and Andrew reached the village nearest to the border. Andrew was worried that it might already be closed; but to his relief he was told that, though the frontier was supposed to close at eight o'clock, it was, in fact, open all night.

'We must get over that border as quickly as we can,' said Andrew. 'I can feel the Germans breathing down my neck.' They arrived at the frontier post just as it was getting dark. The frontier guards came out to meet the car.

'They were a good-looking lot,' said Andrew, 'but not what one would call very *simpatico*. These boys were brutes! I was still driving with my Polish number plates and with my Polish triptique. In those days a triptique was mandatory. As Poland was still recognized by countries like Turkey and Bulgaria, this triptique of mine was valid. The strange thing was that the Polish number plates were similar to the German ones. They were white number plates with dark lettering. At first glance, they looked the same, so when the Bulgarian Tarzan came over to the Opel with a torch and flashed it on our number plates, he thought it was a German car. I said, "Is the border open?" "Yes, Sir, it is open all night," and he spoke in German. "Thank God for that," I replied in the same language, 'I need not have hurried so."

'I handed him our British passports. He shone his torch on them and without changing his expression said, "The border is closed." "But you've just said it is open." "I made a mistake," he said coldly, "it is closed." I was just about to lose my temper and bawl him out when I felt Christine squeeze my hand. "Be calm," she said in French. She was absolutely right. A brawl with a Bulgarian soldier on their frontier with the Germans in possession of their country would not have advanced our journey.

'"What time does the frontier open tomorrow morning?"

Christine asked. "Seven o'clock in the morning. It'll give you plenty of time to empty your car because we're going to inspect every single bit of your luggage. You'd better get going. We'll want everything taken to the customs post."

'I said, "You mean you want us to take everything out of the car?" "Yes," he said arrogantly, "I said everything, and I meant it."'

Andrew and Christine unpacked the car and carried their luggage to the shed. The soldiers stood looking on. Nobody lifted a finger to help, even with the petrol container which was immensely heavy. One of the soldiers asked why they were carrying so much petrol. Andrew replied, 'Because in your country petrol is unavailable. This is also the case in Turkey, and we have to get ourselves to Istanbul somehow.' He said, disagreeably, 'Why must you get to Istanbul?' 'Because it's a neutral country, and as I have only one leg there is no reason for me to be caught up in all this upheaval.' From the look on his questioner's face, Andrew realized that he had touched the right chord, and invited him to take a look at the said wooden leg. As the Customs shed was on top of a hill, this leg was causing him considerable pain.

The soldiers began their search expertly and professionally, but solely in order to enrage the British travellers and thus provoke a row. Knowing this, Christine and Andrew sat watching in seemingly relaxed fashion while every single bit of luggage was picked over. They overlooked nothing. They squeezed the tubes of toothpaste, spilt Christine's facepowder all over a table, shook out every single garment, and having peered into every nook and cranny of the car and of the luggage, said, 'Now go and fetch the tyres off the car.'

Andrew thought at first that they were joking, but they were in earnest and watched him, as he toiled away by himself, removing the tyres and staggering up the hill with them. Having examined the tyres, they then told him to go and put them on again. This took a long time and caused the soldiery exquisite amusement.

Christine was waiting for the comedy to be over when a guard walked in with a large black Alsatian dog on a heavy leather lead. The first thing the dog did was to make a dive in Andrew's direction. The guards roared with laughter but the handler said, 'Don't try and touch him. He's the fiercest animal I've ever had.' At this moment, Christine walked up and calmly put her hand on the great beast's head. He looked up at her and wagged his tail. The guards could not believe their eyes, and to add to their mortification, the dog made friendly whining noises while Christine sat down, scratched its ears and talked to it. Christine had a special way of sitting down Oriental fashion on her crossed legs, and there she remained in complete control of the situation. The handler was puzzled, while the soldiers were furious. They began to jabber among themselves, obviously impressed with Christine's power over the dog. Andrew said, 'Can we go now?' 'No, you will leave tomorrow morning.' 'At what time?' 'The border will be open at seven a.m.' 'Where can we sleep?'

'In your car. You'd better go to it at once. We're shutting up this place for the night.'

'You can't be serious,' said Andrew. 'How can we sleep cramped up in that tiny car? Have a heart, look at the girl, she's ill. She must have a proper rest.'

Christine was deathly pale, her whole body was shaken by violent attacks of coughing. An elderly, more humane soldier took over. He talked to the other men, and must have convinced them that Christine was really unwell for he said that she could spend the night on the floor of a room which happened to be empty.

Andrew carried in their suitcases, and, pillowing their heads on their luggage, they tried to sleep. At seven o'clock in the morning the elderly Bulgarian guard came in with cups of hot coffee. After that nothing happened for a long time.

At last Andrew could bear the suspense no longer. He addressed himself to one of the guards. 'Can we go now?'

'Not yet, we must telephone Sofia.'

'Why, is there something wrong?'

'We don't need to make explanations to you.'

By eleven a.m. Andrew's patience snapped. 'I want to talk to the British Legation,' he said, flying a kite, for he suspected that the guards were not very well informed, and he himself was not certain whether Britain had broken off relations with Bulgaria. 'If you get no reply from the British Legation,' he said, 'I'll speak to the Swiss Ambassador, who is a personal friend.' This was a lie.

An hour later nothing had changed. Andrew was in great pain as he had been unable to remove his leg all night. Christine looked as if she were about to pass out. Suddenly, the soldiers announced that they were free to go. The no-man's-land between Bulgaria and Turkey was about three or four miles of unmade sandy road. In the driving rain it looked exactly like a ploughed-up beach. Christine and Andrew tried to get some order into the car in which the luggage had now been jumbled pell-mell.

Half-way across no-man's-land, Christine asked Andrew to stop. He did this unwillingly, and she got out. She stood there in the rain, whistling, and suddenly, unbelievably, the big black Alsatian bounded joyfully towards her. She knelt down and it nuzzled her face. The Bulgarian dog-handler stood helplessly waiting for her to decide what she was going to do with his animal. It was a moment of triumph for her. There was no doubt that the dog wanted to follow her. But she realized that it would be impossible to travel with a large, ferocious dog, who needed regular and large meals. Andrew drove back towards the Bulgarian frontier, and Christine waved ironically to the guards. The dog ran back to his handler.

This was the first experience Andrew had of Christine's power over animals. He said, 'She was talking to dogs all the time. There wasn't a dog she wouldn't approach. Animals loved her instantly, and there is no doubt that she communicated with them.'

Christine was so weary that she hoped they would be

allowed through the Turkish border with no fuss. She was bitterly disappointed. Ten soldiers were quartered in one dismal little hut. They spoke no known language; Andrew and Christine tried out their Turkish, and got nowhere. They began to think that they would have a repeat performance of their troubles on the Bulgarian frontier. The only difference was that, instead of scowling, the Turks were smiling, which was encouraging. Evidently the guards were refusing to recognize the Polish triptique, and wanted to confiscate the car. Christine tried to explain that the Opel had already passed without hindrance through Hungary, Yugoslavia and Bulgaria, and that it was simply *in transit* through Turkey. They continued to grin from ear to ear, and were adamant. Finally it was decided that a Turkish soldier should accompany them to Istanbul, some 120 kilometres away.

'Where,' asked Andrew, 'is the soldier going to sit?' The soldiers gesticulated, and grinned ever more widely. Finally, the soldier appeared complete with rifle and bayonet, and was somehow bundled into the car where, to Christine's consternation, he sat perched nearly on her knees. The poor little Opel was by now so overladen that she could scarcely crawl along. The Turk stank to high heaven, and by the time the party arrived at Istanbul, Christine longed only to be separated from her guard.

They were guided to the European side of Istanbul, to a superb Customs Hall. Built entirely of marble, it was luxurious in the extreme and was swarming with employees, most of them fluent in some European language or another. Andrew had reluctantly to agree to leave his precious car in the care of the Customs' authorities. They were given a receipt, and, feeling very relieved, took a taxi to the Park Hotel, recommended to them by Aidan Crawley. This was then the most beautiful modern hotel in Istanbul. The only fly in the ointment was, as they were to discover, that the hotel was in the shadow of the German Consulate, a vast building employing a staff of over six hundred. Nearby was the Soviet Consulate with a staff of eight hundred. But even this discovery did not spoil their pleasure in the comfortable rooms they were allocated, with a wide view over the Bosphorus. As soon as they had bathed, they ordered an enormous brunch, complete with toast, marmalade and great pots of coffee. Ten minutes after they had finished their meal, they were fast asleep.

They were woken by the telephone. It was a courtesy call from the British Consulate, who had had advance notice of their arrival from Aidan Crawley, welcoming them to Istanbul and making a date for the following day. That evening, when Christine and Andrew went down to dinner, they found that the dining-room of the Park Hotel was the chic rendezvous of 'le tout Istamboul'. Italian, German, Russian, American, Canadian and British patrons all relied on the harassed maître d'hôtel to seat them as diplomatically as possible out of earshot of those diners with whose countries they were at war.

By the next day, refreshed after a good night's sleep and enchanted by the beauty of Istanbul, Christine and Andrew visited the Consulate, where they talked to a number of interesting people in the same line of business as themselves, some of whom would re-enter their lives in Cairo, and after the war. There were long interviews with various important contacts. Christine was particularly anxious to make sure that the courier routes from Poland were still in perfect order. Also she wanted to make certain that her contacts there were supplied with money and information. Everyone seemed to be very helpful, and were flatteringly complimentary about the successful 'exfiltration' of the British POWs. Christine managed to send more funds to the Musketeers in Poland, and she and Andrew received a further consignment of microfilms from a Pole who was driving through Istanbul on his way to join the Polish Army.

At this particular moment, Christine and Andrew were happy. They were doing valuable work, and could hope it was being recognized as such by the organization they served. They were tireless in their efforts to further the cause, and when the working day was over, they found it easy to relax. No sooner had diplomatic relations been sundered between Britain and

Bulgaria, than their new friend, Aidan Crawley, arrived in Istanbul. He was going to England on a new assignment but, in the meantime, he did everything possible to smooth the way for Christine and Andrew.

Another welcome encounter was with an old friend of Christine's, a Polish diplomat called Szczerbinski. A fount of knowledge, M. Szczerbinski was an expert guide and took Christine and Andrew exploring the wonders of Istanbul – the Hazia Sophia cathedral which since 1453 has been the main mosque, the obelisk of Theodosius, the Suleimanije mosque (most exquisite of all Ottoman buildings) and the famous former palace of the Sultans, the Top-Kapi Serai.

This agreeable round of sight-seeing was interrupted by news which was to have considerable bearing on their future lives. George Gizycki had signified his intention of joining his wife. He had accepted her offer to act as her replacement, and was coming out to take over from her. Christine did not seem to be worried about his impending arrival. Indeed, she was impatient to discuss with him the many problems involved in exfiltrating the prisoners of war waiting to get out of Warsaw, among whom were a number of fighter-pilots. Andrew, knowing something of George's reputation, was astonished by Christine's attitude, and was distinctly uneasy about how her husband would react when he discovered that his wife had acquired an official lover.

CHAPTER SIX

On the morning that Christine was going to meet her husband, Andrew said, 'Kitten, what are you going to tell George?' Christine went on combing her hair. She looked at him standing there unhappily, and crinkled up her eyes. 'George is such an unpredictable man that if I told him that I was madly in love with you, he might well turn round and take the next boat back, and that wouldn't be any good to our organization. We need George.'

Andrew drove Christine down to the port to meet George Gizycki, whom he had met so briefly and so long ago at Zakopane. He watched him walk down the gangway, not very tall, but immensely broad and powerful looking, and then drove away, leaving Christine to greet her husband alone.

For security reasons George had been booked into the Pera Palace Hotel, and Christine stayed with him until the evening, when she rejoined Andrew. She looked calm, relaxed and happy. She said, 'Everything is fine. George is as anxious as we are to get on with the work. I've told him all about you, and you'll meet him tomorrow. I think that when you meet you'll understand what an extraordinary man he is.'

'I met George,' said Andrew, 'he was absolutely charming, though charming is the wrong word for a man who looked like an eagle. He had a pair of very chilly grey eyes, and I don't remember his ever smiling, certainly never with his eyes. He was an incredible character. He'd been everywhere, seen everything, done everything. He had begun by being a cowboy, then switched to working in zinc mines. He'd been a trapper in Canada. He used the knife and the lasso like a professional. One Sunday we went for a walk in the country. A stray turkey crossed our path. "Watch!" said George, uncoiling a length of rope. In a moment he had lassoed the protesting fowl. I was tremendously impressed.

'We talked at length about our work and of the various pitfalls he must avoid both in Poland and Hungary. George said that he felt that our efforts were not getting as full support as they deserved from the British organization. This had certainly been one of our grouses, but I told him that since Christine had done so well in helping to exfiltrate British POWs, they had begun to take us seriously and to show a greater interest in what we were doing. I added that Sir Owen O'Malley was a tower of strength and would do all he could to help him in any emergency.'

George was anxious to get to work. There were more and more rumours of impending war between Russia and Germany, and when Yugoslavia was invaded on 6 April 1941, people said Germany was too fully occupied to take on the Russians. George had become friendly with de Chastelain, with whom he had much in common. He was indubitably a near-genius, but he was inclined to glower and to gloom, and Christine sighed with relief when she said goodbye to him.

Soon after George's departure, Christine and Andrew went to Ankara. They stayed at the British Embassy and it was at this juncture that they met young Julian Amery.

We also worked closely with Czech and Polish organisations. Among the Poles was Christine Granville, who had been smuggling members of her organisation out of Poland. Many had travelled across the High Tatra and the Carpathians in the boots of cars driven by Andrew Kennedy. Kennedy had an artificial leg and many valuable rolls of microfilm were brought out in it. Christine was one of the gentlest looking girls I have ever met, and it was hard to credit her with some of the bravest clandestine achievements of the war.[1]

Superficially, everything seemed to be going well for Christine and Andrew. What they could not have foreseen was that at that very moment the Polish Deuxième Bureau were inaugurating a campaign of spite and jealousy against them. The Deuxième Bureau's attitude was baffling, for they must have known from the beginning that Christine and Andrew were dedicated patriots who had never hesitated to serve their country at the risk of their own lives; their only crime was that they seemed to have been doing very well without official backing.

Spring was close. The breaking off of diplomatic relations between Britain and Hungary, with members of the British Embassy being sent back via Russia and Tokyo to England, meant, of course, that Christine's lines of communication were temporarily interrupted; though, in spite of extreme difficulties, her people still managed to get through on forged passports, bringing out valuable information. Andrew was used to an active life, and he was becoming bored by a diet of mosques, museums and meals in the Park Hotel. Christine, as usual, was relaxed and interested in life in Istanbul. Finally Andrew announced that he was going to leave, and would drive through pro-Vichy Syria. This decision was greeted with concern by their friends. 'Anyway,' they said, comfortably, 'you won't get a visa.'

Christine said, 'Don't worry, Cat, I'll get the visas.' Andrew replied, 'But you've absolutely no contacts in the French Consulate, and, naturally, the Consul is pro-Vichy.' 'He's still a Frenchman,' said Christine, 'and a man, so I'll go off and see what I can do.'

At ten a.m. Andrew accompanied Christine to the French Consulate. At noon she reappeared, smiling happily. She had obtained transit visas through Syria for both their passports. Everyone thought this an extraordinary feat, and so did the

Deuxième Bureau, who made great capital of it in their anti-Andrew and Christine campaign. Only German spies, they said, could possibly have got these visas.

Feeling very pleased with themselves, Christine and Andrew went off to the Customs to reclaim the Opel. There was great activity going on in the sheds where an endless succession of crates were piling up for the German and Soviet Embassies. Judging from the number of men needed to move them, Andrew was certain that they contained arms and ammunition.

When Andrew took out his receipt for the Opel, and asked to have the car back, a jaunty Turkish Customs official shook his head. 'No, you cannot have your car. This car will be sold, according to the agreement.'

'I made no such agreement,' stormed Andrew, 'I was told I could collect my car any time I wanted.'

The man was adamant. In despair, Christine and Andrew dashed off to the British Consulate to ask what to do. The Consul said, 'Come off it, Andrew, you'll never get your car back unless you produce a substantial amount of *baksheesh*. You've got to grease their itchy little palms. You're a novice around here. You know what they say . . . "To beat a Turk, you need a Greek, to beat a Greek you need an Armenian". So, we'll produce a magician for you. Come back at ten tomorrow.'

When they returned to the Consulate they were introduced to a plump, friendly, dark-complexioned fellow, who could have been Greek, Armenian or a mixture of both. He spoke French and declared immediately that there was no use in returning to the Customs without a substantial quantity of cash. He said that Andrew must fill his pockets with two-and-a-half-pound notes.[2] Back they went to the vast, luxurious marble building, down whose middle were thirty grilles behind which sat a motley collection of employees. Christine and Andrew were told to wait. The Turks, they observed, have a sign language the opposite of what they themselves could understand. Everything appeared to work in reverse: when they beckoned, they meant stay put.

The Greek went from window to window doling out his two and a half pounds. Finally, he returned beaming with satisfaction.

'Now all is betters,' he explained. 'If they agree, the motor-cars will be transferred from this sheds to other side of Bosphorus, and as cars will be arriving from this side to Asia, you can then claim you are driving from there.' From this garbled explanation, Andrew gleaned that all was now well, but it had cost them a great deal of money.

The Opel was then safely loaded onto a train, while its owners sailed down the Bosphorus to meet it on the other side. Two days later they reached Iscandria (Alexandretta), the border town between Turkey and Syria. They found a small hotel and, as they were tired, they went to bed early. In the middle of the night Andrew was woken by angry shouts from Christine. She was waging war against an invasion of bedbugs.

She was so badly bitten that she ran a high temperature, and had reluctantly to endure the hotel for another two days.

It was the first time that Andrew had ever travelled in the Middle East, and he was enchanted with the beauty of the landscape. He had not bargained with the great heat and, to Christine's amusement, told her that if it increased he would have to turn round and go back. Just before they crossed the border into Syria they saw thousands and thousands of storks preparing to fly back to Poland. They sat silently looking at the great birds which, unlike themselves, were going home.

As they started on their drive to Beirut, Andrew grew more and more uncomfortable in the sweltering heat. The tinny little Opel was not well ventilated, and to add to his troubles a khamsin was blowing.[3]

One of the main traffic arteries in Lebanon is the north–south coastal highway, a route of almost unsurpassed beauty. The coast of Lebanon is dotted with sites of history. The Crusader castles follow the coastline from Tyre to Tripoli against a stunning background of mountains and sky. Andrew was to become familiar with this road, but he never forgot the first impression it made on him.

Christine was delighted by his enthusiasm. They stopped in the villages and bought fruit from the markets and delicacies such as goats' cheese, honey, and ground nuts made into a paste with grape juice.

By the time they reached Beirut, Andrew felt he was about to expire with the heat. They drove straight to St George's Hotel, which they had been told had a private beach and a fine view of the Beirut roadstead. They walked up to the reception desk, and immediately noticed a group of spruce-looking German officers sitting in a corner.

'They were obviously high-ranking chaps,' said Andrew, 'throwing their weight about in the usual arrogant way. We were stunned to see that the foyer was also full of French Spahi officers. I said to Christine, "How is it possible for members of a crack French cavalry regiment to be in the same hotel as the Germans who are occupying their country? Why don't they punch their bloody faces in?" Christine tried to shush me by saying, ironically, "It's a complicated psychological reaction." "To hell with that," I answered. "How can they sit there drinking double whiskys cheek by jowl with those arrogant German bastards?"

'Meanwhile Christine was asking the reception clerk whether a double room with bath was available. "For how long?" said the clerk. "For a night." "Could I have your passports, please?" he asked. We then produced our British passports. To my horror I heard the clerk saying in French in a loud voice, "Ah, vous êtes bien heureux, messieurs dames. Vous allez quitter cette saleté demain, tandis que moi je suis obligé de rester et de me vautrer dans la crotte."[4] Christine and I looked round to see whether this speech had reached the ears of the Germans. Seemingly not, for nobody moved, and the clerk calmly took down a key. As he walked towards the staircase with us he said, again in ringing tones, "Je vous donne la meilleure chambre aux prix normal, simplement pour le plaisir d'avoir des anglais ici dans l'hôtel."[5]

The clerk kept his word and gave them a splendid room. They were worn out with travelling. 'We'd better not sleep,' said Andrew, 'for I'm sure we're going to be arrested.' But except by mosquitoes which, according to Andrew, are as big as birds in Beirut, their rest was not disturbed, and they sat outside on their balcony, enjoying a bountiful breakfast and a sublime view. When they paid their bill, the reception clerk had obviously to restrain himself not to kiss them on both cheeks. In spite of his friendliness, Andrew still suspected him of being a German agent.

Their journey on to the Palestine border was uneventful. The approach from Syria was up a winding mountain road, its summit dominated by an immense Union Jack. 'It is really difficult to describe our feelings when we saw that flag,' said Andrew. 'We had for so many years lived in constant fear, and there was freedom, protection and friends. But we still had a few hundred metres to cross to safety. We came up behind a long queue of cars, whose occupants were mainly Arabs. They were queueing on the left, as in Britain. I said to Christine, "I'm not sitting here in this heat. It's too stupid. Hold on tight, we're off," and with this I turned the little car to the right, and rocketed straight across the border.'

Suddenly, two smartly dressed policemen, an officer and a sergeant, in immaculate shorts and dazzling shirts, barred the passage of the car. They looked cool and unhurried, but the expression on their faces was anything but welcoming. Obviously they did not approve of queue jumping. Then, taking a closer look at the occupants of the Opel, their faces cleared, and the officer, saluting smartly, said, 'Mrs Granville and Mr Kennedy, I presume?'

The British authorities in Turkey had informed the Palestine border police of the imminent arrival of this unusual couple, who, while holding British passports, could hardly speak a word of English. Andrew was deeply impressed with the cordiality and efficiency with which the border police looked after them. They were immediately issued with petrol coupons, ration-books and other vital documents, and instructed to drive down to Haifa and go to an hotel where reservations had been made for them. They drove away feeling happy and reassured. On their way to Haifa, Andrew saw a sight so strange, so unbelievable, that he stopped the car to watch it. It was just two o'clock, and the sun was flaming in the sky. Andrew saw a field ringed with onlookers, who seemed to be concentrating on the antics of a number of white-flannelled adult males, two of whom were facing one another with bats. The others were running about and throwing their arms in the air. Andrew turned to Christine.

'What the hell do you think they're doing rushing around like that?'

'They're Englishmen, and they're playing cricket!'

'In this heat! They must be mad. This is no place for me, Kitten, I'm going back.' Christine was helpless with laughter. Such was the manner of their arrival at Haifa.

Haifa, lying in the Bay of Acre under Mount Carmel, had much to offer travellers but Christine and Andrew were anxious to push on to Jerusalem. As they drove, Andrew could not believe he was passing through places the names of which he had first seen in his mother's Bible.

'The last part of the journey was very strenuous,' said Andrew, 'along a mountain road called the "Seven Sisters", whose seven great bends are a trial to the nerves of even the most experienced driver. The military traffic was already very heavy. At last we were able to look on the ancient city of Jerusalem. The setting sun struck the grey of the limestone houses, shading them with a glow of gold and rose. There is something special about this city; I was awed by the weight of history which seemed to seep from the very stones, and it was with difficulty that Christine and I dragged ourselves back to the mundane present, with its problems.'

They had been told to report on arrival to an office, where they were taken in tow by a pleasant young man from the organization called Porter. He was to become their guardian angel and a devoted and much esteemed friend. He had booked them into the cool and pleasant Eden Hotel.

Superficially, at least, all was milk and roses. They were in excellent spirits, rapturously in love with one another and in a pleasant country whose climate was in such contrast with the rigorous weather they had endured in Hungary. Christine was a true daughter of Sol, and asked for nothing better than to bask in his rays. Andrew had reservations. Excessive heat tired him and, though he said nothing, he was increasingly worried about the pains in his leg.

It was not long before Christine got in touch with her great friend Sophie Raczkowski.[6] A woman of exceptional beauty and intelligence, said to speak thirteen languages, she was the daughter of one of the founders of Israel, Nahoum Sokolov, with whom she had travelled the country promoting the cause to which he had dedicated his life.

'Beautiful Sophie,' said Andrew, 'lived with her husband and son in an old Arab house in the hills overlooking Jerusalem. It had been a gift to her father, and with its immensely thick walls and large cool rooms was as pleasant a haven as one can imagine. Sophie and her husband were very hospitable, and in their house we met many interesting people. Their young son, Joseph, was a brilliant boy and a dedicated patriot. Christine fell in love with the family dogs, two fine boxers, which we used to take for drives. Among the many people we met were some of our English friends but, though they were all very nice, polite and congratulated us on our good work, they were exceedingly guarded in talking to us. We both felt that something was very wrong.'

After two weeks in Palestine Christine and Andrew were summoned to Cairo. They left immediately. It was a long drive through the mountains along very twisty roads until they reached the border, where the police had, once more, been told to expect two non-English-speaking British nationals. They then embarked on the long drive – 400 kilometres on a straight road which ran through the desert to the Suez Canal. This was a most unusual road, convoluted in such a way as to resemble waves, and driving on it was like sailing a boat in a choppy sea. Andrew had had his fill of sand by the time they reached Suez, and had to be restrained from jumping into the water for a swim. When Christine informed him that the waters were shark-infested, his enthusiasm for a bathe cooled at once.

Though Christine's intuition warned her that something was seriously amiss in their world, she tried to sublimate her apprehensions so as not to spoil Andrew's enjoyment and reactions to the Middle East. 'Christine enjoyed every moment of my pleasure,' he said, 'and this was another wonderful facet of her personality. She could switch off her own emotions, and enter wholeheartedly into those of others.'

Finally, the gallant little Opel reached Cairo, and Christine and Andrew, acting on instructions, went straight to the rambling Continental Hotel with its wide shady verandah to which they later became greatly attached. Their friend Porter soon arrived and told them that he had been asked to give them a message: they were to rest and relax after all their difficult experiences and not to worry about anything. When they asked him what their future activities were to be, he became vague and non-committal, repeating that their orders were to take it easy. He also added that the organization (he did not specify which organization) would pay them a monthly salary while they were in Cairo and while their future was being decided.

When their guest left, Andrew and Christine sat talking late into the night. All their worst fears had been crystallized by Porter's obvious reluctance to give them any definite information. They were puzzled, hurt and apprehensive. They had been so sure that the organization which had backed them in Europe would continue to support them in the Middle East. Each tried to cheer the other by saying that British red tape was more difficult to disentangle than any other, and that in due course their real work would begin.

But when the Polish Ambassador, who knew Christine well, cut her dead they began to get really worried, and when several officers from the Deuxième Bureau, whom they saw in the Continental Hotel, looked straight through them, they knew, though they had no idea why, that they were definitely 'out in the cold'.

'Cairo,' according to Andrew, 'was very like Nice, rather Frenchified and fin-de-siècle, with white buildings and palm trees. The first impression was one of gaiety, though, on further examination, it was an unreal, flashy sort of gaiety.' The British military presence was predominant, which was not surprising since Cairo was not only one of the main theatres of war but also the 'crossroads of the Free World'. The officers seemed to congregate mainly at Shepheard's Hotel, an old fashioned, rambling place, 'with dark oriental halls, ebony women with richly curved rotundities, holding aloft frosted lights, pearl inlaid furniture, palms, drab hangings, marble corridors, brass bedsteads and Arab servants.'[7]

Christine and Andrew 'took in' Cairo, like the tourists they were pretending to be, but their hearts were heavy, and great was their relief when the Carpathian Lancers arrived in from the desert; in command was Colonel Wladyslaw Bobinski,[8] Christine's old friend whose horse she had ridden when she was fourteen. In this regiment were many of Andrew's friends, such as his cousin Ludwig Popiel and Andrew Tarnowski. Ignoring rumours, they all spent as much time as they could with Christine and Andrew, much to the discomfiture of the Deuxième Bureau, whose poison-pen reports were beginning to have a serious effect on Christine and Andrew, for, according to the Deuxième Bureau, Countess Christine Skarbek (Granville) and Lieutenant Andrew Kowerski (Kennedy) were German spies.

Their friends laughed immoderately at this *canard*, but it was no laughing matter to Christine and Andrew. Living in the shadows was no joke, and they were immensely grateful to people like Bill Bailey, Head of the Yugoslav Section, who ignored all damaging reports about his friends, and continued to be as helpful and kind as he had always been.

'Then,' said Andrew, 'one day we met Colonel Guy Tamplin.

He was a remarkable person. He had worked in British Intelligence for a long time, spoke fluent Polish and Russian, and was in charge of Polish affairs. Tamplin was very candid with us. He told us immediately that the Poles had objected to our working with, and for, the British. I said, "Please, Colonel, tell us what this is all about, we're completely in the dark." He replied, "The Polish Government in exile suspect your group was infiltrated by the Germans!"

'Christine and I were appalled, not only because of the implications of the accusation, but that our fellow Poles could have harboured such suspicions. I said, "Surely the honourable thing would have been for the Deuxième Bureau to send for us and to give us a chance to explain ourselves. They must be aware by now what my country means to me, and what a great patriot Christine is."'

The Deuxième Bureau had no intention of coming out in the open, but continued to play mean, subversive tricks on two people who could never hit back. Furthermore, their attitude seriously jeopardized Christine's and Andrew's work, since they could no longer pay couriers to go backwards and forwards as in the past. None the less, microfilms and information continued to be filtered through by people who came to join the Polish Army and had managed to conceal the microfilms from the Deuxième Bureau. At one stage, indeed, this organization got their lines so crossed that they pulled in one of the finest officers in the Polish Army, and, assuming he was a German spy, grilled him for hours.

The whole situation was ridiculous, and was summed up crisply by Colonel Tamplin when he found Christine and Andrew steeped in gloom. 'Don't be depressed. Working for the Poles, my friends, is like working in a theatre. One never knows whether the play is to be a tragedy or a farce. Today I received two reports. One states that Andrew Kowerski is a German spy; the other announces that this same man has won the Virtuti Militari. Is it a Polish custom to give their highest decoration to a spy?'

Christine still had some old microfilms hidden away, as well as some new ones showing further concentrations of arms and ammunition on the Russian border. She said, 'If we're persona-non-grata, there's not much point in our handing over these microfilms. As we're supposed to be German spies, they won't believe the evidence of their own eyes.'

Then, suddenly, the gloom lifted. Christine and Andrew were told that a top man was being sent out from London specially to deal with their problems. They were relieved. At last somebody would be able to straighten out the whole hideous muddle. Andrew said, 'In spite of our being "under a cloud", we were allowed to circulate pretty freely in Rustem Building, headquarters of MO4, one of the branches of SOE. Rustem Building had always been a secret and mysterious place to us until we discovered that all Cairo knew what went on there. All you had to do was to take an Arab taxi, and say to the cabby, "Drive us to the Secret Building", and immediately you were deposited at its door!

'One fine day we were told that a Major Peter Wilkinson[9] had arrived in Cairo specially to see us. We were summoned to Rustem Building. We walked in shaking with nerves and excitement, and found ourselves facing a young English officer. He asked us to sit down, and then said, "I have to inform you that we are dispensing with your services. I imagine that Mrs Granville could work in the Red Cross, while you, Mr Kennedy, should have no difficulty in joining the Polish Army." He did not add a word of explanation as to why we were in disgrace. We were stunned. Then I got into a furious rage. Christine was pale and silent. Suddenly, I remembered the microfilms and said, "I suppose you would not be interested in some micro-films we have. We think they are pretty important." Major Wilkinson stood up. "Your microfilms are of no interest to us. Good-day."[10]

'I realize, of course,' said Andrew, 'that Major Wilkinson was sent by London, and only carrying out his instructions. But it seems to me that there was no valid reason for the harsh way in which he handled the situation. The reasons for our being sacked were quite clear.

'The Polish Government in exile was made up of Poles who were, and wanted to remain, ferociously independent of any other groups, no matter how well-intentioned. At the beginning of the underground fighting in Poland, many groups were formed, including that of the Musketeers,[11] under the leadership of Witkowski. I've no doubt at all that he was an old Intelligence man, and he ran his group very efficiently. Then when the Home Army began to be organized from London, they made haste to get rid of independent groups. I believe that all the Musketeers accepted the orders from London and were integrated into the Home Army; but Witkowski continued to act on his own. He disappeared mysteriously, and nobody knows what happened to him.'

In spite of the reassuring attitudes of Guy Tamplin and Bill Bailey, who went out of their way to minimize the shock of Major Wilkinson's interview, Christine and Andrew were deeply depressed. The only redeeming feature of their life in Cairo at that moment was that they were together. This happy state of affairs was clouded when, summoned by de Chastelain, Christine's husband George arrived suddenly in Jerusalem.

As soon as he heard of the outcome of the meeting with Major Wilkinson, he flew into one of his famous rages, declaring categorically that he, for his part, would have nothing more to do with an organization which treated its people so shabbily. 'They're nothing but a mutual admiration society,' he said, 'and you're well rid of them.' Naturally, the question of Christine's future had to be discussed, and one day Christine returned to Andrew after seeing George. She was pale and distressed.

She had told him firmly that she did not intend returning to him, and that she was in love with Andrew. The explosion she had so long dreaded took place. The blazing volcano inside George erupted with terrifying violence. Yet, even though she was mortally frightened, Christine's reaction was one of overwhelming pity for her husband. He simply could not believe that the woman he loved would never return to him. Finally, after writing her a very cruel and bitter letter, he left for London.[12]

Christine was greatly upset by his abrupt departure. Fortunately, at this moment, she and Andrew were distracted from their anxiety about George's grief and their depression over the Wilkinson interview by being sent on a mission to Syria and the Turkish border. On 12 July 1941, the Syrian Armistice terms had been initialled at Acre after a conference between General Sir Henry Maitland Wilson with General Catroux, and General Verdillac, representing General Dentz. The terms were accepted by Vichy, and on 15 July, British troops entered Beirut; Syria and Lebanon came under Allied control.

In October of the same year, Christine and Andrew set off again in the Opel. The common frontier with Syria was Turkey, and nobody had any idea of what Turkey was going to do. The Germans were making frantic efforts to bring her over to their side. The Allies were doing all they could to keep her neutral, for they were aware that, should Turkey throw in her lot with the enemy, there would be no way to stop the Germans getting to the oilfields.

Christine and Andrew's mission was to make a reconnaissance of the bridges of the Tigris and Euphrates, and to evolve some sort of plan how to blow up the bridges, should this be necessary.

It was a long and tiring journey. They had refused military transport, since Andrew held the view that it was safer to depend on one's own car, and drove to Beirut. From there they took the beautiful coast road to Aleppo. 'This,' said Andrew, 'is one of the most extraordinary cities in the world. It is the most remote from Western influences, and is the most Oriental, the most Arab, and yet the largest Christian city in the Middle East. There are eighteen miles of covered-in souks, which present insuperable problems to the tourist, and are child's play to the *Bedou*, who have been stopping off at Aleppo, the terminal point of the great caravan routes from the East, for centuries.'

Christine was enchanted with Aleppo. They were booked into the Baron Hotel, whose proprietor, an Armenian called Koko Muzlumian, had been at Oxford and made no secret of his pro-British feelings. The hotel was a cross between the Randolph at Oxford and any typical English country pub. During the German occupation, Koko manifested his loyalty to Britain by playing polo by himself, on the only polo pony left in his stables. A gay and lively host, Koko was immediately captivated by Christine, and in her honour produced one of the two bottles of whisky he had been hiding from the Germans. The other he had handed over to the first British soldier who walked into his hotel.

Headquarters at Beirut had booked them into the hotel, so Koko treated Christine and Andrew as VIPs. Their immediate boss was Captain Mitford, a solid, efficient Scottish boffin, whose main job was testing new explosives. He, Christine and Andrew became very good friends.

On one very cold November day, Andrew, who was experimenting with a certain explosive, threw it into the water to see if it would work. There was no doubt that it did, for in a moment the river surface was filled with trout. Mitford wasted no time. Fully dressed, he dived in after the trout, and that night they had delicious fresh grilled fish for dinner.

All about Aleppo were stationed a number of Indian regiments, among them Prince Albert Victor's Own Regiment, Skinner's Horse, the Bengal Lancers, all the romantic names associated with past splendours of the British Raj.

Among the officers in Prince Albert Victor's Own Regiment was the son of the Emperor of Afghanistan, who had been toppled by Amanullah. Hissam was proud that his dynasty had governed what is now Pakistan for something like two thousand years. He was a fierce-looking soldier, and became very attached to Christine. He was always with Christine and Andrew and, as he was witty and entertaining, they grew fond of him. He had a fund of amusing anecdotes, mostly relating to the bad old days when his grandfather, the Emperor, was at daggers drawn with the British. One of the stories concerned his signet ring, a gift from Queen Victoria to his grandfather after their countries had signed a peace treaty. It was engraved with the words, 'Enemy to Enemy, Friend to Friend!'

Andrew said, 'We played a stupid little joke on Hissam. I was messing about with some magnets which I was using for explosive charges. Christine took off her Habdank ring with its sliver of steel, and picked up one of my magnets. Naturally, the magnet attracted the steel and picked up her ring. Hissam then tried the magnet on his ring, which being of solid gold set with some precious stone, did not budge. We told Hissam that this was proof positive that Queen Victoria had cheated his grandfather by giving him a ring that was not of gold. He was furious. We did not tell him about the sliver of steel for a long time.'

When they were not working, Christine and Andrew were enjoying themselves. They rode, they drove, they fished, and Andrew went shooting. The beautiful, stony, so-called desert was alive with wild life. Andrew saw birds there which he had supposed to be indigenous to the Ukraine and Poland, among them that truly *rara avis*, the bustard.

Andrew always felt that the few weeks they spent in Aleppo and Syria were among the richest and happiest in all their time in the Middle East. Christine could indulge in an outdoor life with people she liked; she explored the ancient souks, attended the birth of a camel, and was guest of honour at a local feast. She met and became friendly with grave Arabs who drove in from the desert in broken-down Cadillacs.

When, finally, they returned to Cairo, Christine, being an adaptable creature, worked out a design for living; a way of life that suited her until such time as she should be given a mission of consequence. She made the Gezira Sporting Club her headquarters. Owned and run by the British, the club had beautiful, spacious grounds. Its swimming baths and terraces appealed to Christine, who could generally be found 'lying like a salamander baking in the sun, with a book in her hand'. After swimming or tennis, it was pleasant to chat with friends who flocked to the club in a 'tide of gossip and pungent cigarettes'.

Few people knew that Christine loved small children and was good with them. It came to her knowledge that one of her colleagues, 'James Hill', who was often away on missions, had a problem. While he was away there was nobody to care for his five-year-old daughter, Irene. She was made a ward of the British Government, and for some time, Christine made it her business to look after the lonely little girl. 'I was living in a Catholic board-ing school at Heliopolis,' says Mrs Irene Atayan.[13] 'My childhood memories tell me that Christine looked after me, and that I adored her. I seem to remember her taking me to this convent, and presenting me with a huge teddy-bear for consolation.'

Life in Cairo was not expensive and there was no black market. Most goods were imported from the USA and Sicurel's, a large department store which resembled Harrods, had a daz-zling assortment of items almost forgotten by women shoppers who had lived so long in countries engulfed in the austerities of war. Fruit, too, was relatively cheap.

Shoppers in the Moski found quantities of lemons, oranges and Lebanese apples, but Christine and Andrew had little money for luxuries, and at times even accommodation was an acute problem. Once, when Andrew had to be away on an expe-dition and Christine was temporarily homeless, 'Pussi' Deakin invited her to move into the little flat she shared with a Czech girl.

Pussi found Christine both fascinating and mysterious. In those days of quickly ripening friendships, there was no time for the usual overtures and tactics. Agents had to accept one another without the usual background of information as to country of origin, family or past experiences. All the usual small exchanges which go to the gradual building up of a relationship were eschewed, so that friendship, desire and even love under these hothouse conditions blossomed rapidly, and as quickly faded and died.

Nobody was more adept than Christine in giving only that

which she wished to give. Those who did not know her well – her critics were invariably women – were irritated by the impact she made on most men; by her antinomian attitude to conventional rules and regulations, and by her disinclination to be pressed into an ordinary mould.

Thus they made it their business to distort even the most platonic of her friendships, so that finally a whole area of her life has been shadowed by a question mark.

The truth is simple. Christine was a healthy, vital young woman whose early background and education had, in a sense, inhibited and shackled her approach to sexual matters.

Clearing her mind, at last, of prejudice and rejecting all old-fashioned taboos was, to her, one way to approach the total freedom she always craved. As her life progressed and she was subjected to greater and greater pressures, she decided that sex was a part of living, an appetite to be slaked, but not to be dwelt upon, picked over or discussed.

Throughout her life Christine retained an aura of purity, and when she gave herself 'it was like holding a shaft of sunlight or bathing in a crystal cold mountain stream'.

On 22 June 1941, the Germans invaded Russia. A few days later Mr Litvinov made a broadcast in English from Moscow in which he said that Great Britain and the USSR must strike together, 'now, without respite, untiringly'. This news produced a violent reaction in Cairo, and particularly in the circles that had sent Christine and Andrew to Coventry. It was now patently obvious that German spies would hardly have been so stupid as to pass microfilm, detailing their preparations for war on Russia, to Britain. The icy atmosphere around Christine and Andrew began to thaw, and a further incident hastened the process.

During one of Andrew's periodical visits to the Hotel Continental, he heard that General Kopanski, who had been his commanding officer in Poland and now commanded the Carpathian Brigade, was coming to spend a few days in Cairo.

Andrew knew that recognition on the part of this brave and distinguished man would do much to remove the stigma attached to himself and to Christine.[14]

Andrew timed his arrival at the Continental to coincide with the General's. On one side of the foyer were representatives of the Deuxième Bureau, on the other some of Andrew's friends from the Carpathian Lancers. The General came into the hall, and Andrew, with his heart in his boots, walked across to meet him.

The General, opening wide his arms, cried out, 'Andrew, for Heaven's sake, what are *you* doing in Cairo?'

'Having troubles, General.'

'What kind of troubles?'

Andrew nodded towards the sneering group from the Deuxième Bureau, and, using an old Polish expression, said, 'Please, General, may I speak to you between four eyes?'

The General stepped back. 'You know this is impossible.'

There was audible jubilation among the Deuxième Bureau contingent.

Andrew stood there, unable to believe his ears, and the General added gaily, 'You know very well, my boy, that I've one glass eye, therefore, we can only speak privately between *three* eyes, so come along to my room.'

When he heard what had been happening, the General was furious. He sent for one member of the Deuxième Bureau after the other, asked whether they had anything against Andrew Kowerski, and why he was being victimized. In each case, the men replied negatively, and Andrew, having warmly thanked the General, left the hotel feeling considerably relieved.

However, even General Kopanski's favourable intervention did not bring offers of employment from SOE. Then, just as Christine was beginning to wonder whether she would have to spend the rest of the war in the Gezira Sporting Club, Guy Tamplin was appointed to a new post dealing with the Balkans generally. His replacement was named Patrick Howarth. Major Wilkinson had chosen him to replace Colonel Tamplin, and his posting to Cairo was the turning point in both Christine's and Andrew's careers, for his friendship and belief in their potential was finally to bring them in from the cold.

Educated at Rugby and Oxford, where he read Modern Languages, Patrick Howarth wanted to be a writer and his first job was editing a learned quarterly magazine called *Baltic and Scandinavian Countries*, run by an organization called the Baltic Institute, which received a subsidy from the Polish Government. Part of the Polish Government policy then was the establishment of a *cordon sanitaire* between Russia and Germany, and they wanted to persuade the Baltic and Scandinavian countries in the North – Howarth was in Gdynia – and they also had a Balkan Institute in the south with the same idea. It was a good idea, but it did not work.

Howarth stayed in Gdynia for a year and in the latter part of his time there became unofficial, unpaid PRO for the Polish Government. The Germans had a tremendously efficient propaganda machine churning out stuff, while the Poles relied on the good offices of a charming young man who could not speak good Polish.

Howarth got out in the last ship going to Copenhagen. He went into the Army, was commissioned in the Intelligence Corps, and went through various courses, as the result of which Peter Wilkinson, who had been at school with Howarth, spotted that he spoke Polish. So he was taken on the strength of that.

At first he was just the general dogsbody in the office in charge of files, but in December 1941, Howarth was sent off to Arisaig in the Western Highlands where James Young, Commandant of the Training Camp, instilled two simple rules into his young officers: sink half a bottle of whisky and appear next morning on parade. Rule II was to learn to dance an eight-some reel.

Howarth was then twenty-six, and as he said, 'My elevation to this new post was something of an ordeal. I had only spent six months in SOE, and found things in Cairo a bit of a strain.' However, he knew all about SOE's maverick couple, and had an open mind about their so-called German proclivities. He had also been asked by a mutual friend, a Pole called Major Richard Truszkowski,[15] the section bio-chemist, whose judgement he trusted, to look after Christine and Andrew. In a poem, 'Play back a Lifetime', written by Howarth, he described his first impression of Christine.[16]

'Here at last,' said Andrew, 'was a man who made his own decisions.' Patrick Howarth arrived in Cairo in August 1942, when Rommel was still near its gates. He had been halted; but it was by no means certain that he would not thrust on again. The general atmosphere was uneasy, and it was virtually decided that Secret Headquarters should be transferred to Jerusalem. It was there that he had first met Andrew. He was, in his own words, 'a civilian then, and had some sort of a job as transport officer for SOE. He was on their payroll, and made himself generally useful.'

After his first encounter with Christine through Major Truszkowski, he had seen her again in Colonel Tamplin's office, and had been taken aback when she flatly turned down a job in connection with codes and ciphers, but which had nothing to do with SOE. 'Naively, I thought that, as there was a war on, everyone should do anything they were offered,' he told the author. 'When I met her again at Gezira, and asked her whether she really did not want the job offered her, she replied, "J'ai tant d'endurance physique, mais pas intellectuelle." It made such a tremendous impression on me that I later incorporated it in my poem. When we first met we spoke French. Her English was not very good; but, as she worked at it, it rapidly got better and better. Truszkowski was a bio-chemist of some distinction. He had attached himself to the first Military Mission in Warsaw with General Gubbins, and had come out through the Balkans with them. He also spoke fluent Russian, and Peter Wilkinson sent him to Kuibishev, the idea being to see whether he could do anything to stimulate Polish resistance from the Eastern side.

'In fact, there was nothing much that could be done, for the

Russians were mainly concerned with spreading Russian power and not only in fighting the Germans. So Truszkowski wisely decided he was wasting his time, and was ordered back to London. He returned there via Cairo, where he was told to stand in for Tamplin until I arrived. When I did, he became my guide and mentor. He had a first-class mind, it was so brilliant that he could always see the reasons for not doing anything!

'Just before he left he asked me to look after Christine and Andrew and, while I had faith in his judgement, I was still very much on my guard because of my study of the files in the SOE office in London, in which I had discovered the involvement of Christine and Andrew with the suspect organization of the Musketeers. Then I learned that both Christine and Andrew were *still* on the SOE payroll. It was a small sum, but it was sufficient to live on without frills. This arrangement had been made by George Taylor, one of her first SOE contacts.'

It did not take long for Patrick Howarth to discover that some of the Poles he dealt with officially were hostile and suspicious towards Christine and Andrew; this, he thought, might have been partly because they did not take kindly to Christine's devotion to Britain. There were, of course, many Polish organizations Christine could have worked in; but she had always a special feeling of obligation towards Britain, which had enabled her to go on her first mission; also she had a much broader view than most Poles, who tended to be intensely nationalistic. Furthermore, she and Andrew were a partnership which tended to ignore all red tape, and to take matters into their own hands.

Howarth said, 'I liked them both more and more. I got on well with them at different levels. I talked more to Christine; but I enjoyed drinking with Andrew. They were living in a boarding house in Zamalek – a fashionable suburb of Cairo. It was a pleasant place kept by a couple called Katz, and while Andrew seemed to mix mainly with Polish cavalry officers, Christine had her own friends. There was Ted Howe, then in uniform and working for SOE. Another of her familiars was a Polish major by the name of Gauze. But, at all times, Christine and Andrew were very close, united by a deep mutual trust and confidence which enabled them to go their own ways.

'Life in Cairo was rather like life in the colonies. The meeting places were Gezira, the Turf Club and Groppi's, renowned for its superlative ices. There was a vacant room in the boarding house at Zamalek, and Christine and Andrew advised me to take it as I was looking for accommodation. Once installed, I found I was virtually living with my new found friends, and it was a wonderfully relaxed and rewarding relationship.

'I was fondly under the illusion that I was keeping secret from them what I was doing. A very important part of the organization of the Resistance army in Poland was the land-link, insofar as this could be achieved – you could drop things from the sky, arms and people; but it was a hellish long time before you could land a plane, and actually pick people up. Though this did eventually happen.

'At this particular moment there was a considerable area of Yugoslavia under the control of General Mihailovitch, the representative of the legal Yugoslav government, with whom we were in contact. A man called Bill Hudson had been with the General for months. This was before there was any serious fighting between Mihailovitch's Chetniks and Tito's partisans. The Polish Sixth Bureau found a Russian-speaking officer, a Captain Maciag, and between us we worked out his mission, and dropped him in the northern part of Yugoslavia into one of Mihailovitch's groups, the idea being that he should develop courier lines such as Christine had through Hungary into Poland. He was a very gallant officer, and, while he was developing his main mission, he became involved in a skirmish with Germans and was killed. The Poles grew more and more enthusiastic about the possibilities of penetration and we got a couple of officers trained; but, of course, the time came when we, the British, withdrew support from Mihailovitch and concentrated on Tito. But the Poles would have no truck with Tito.

'Suddenly one day – it must have been about a year after I came to Cairo – Christine told me in exact detail (and a good deal more besides) about these top secret missions! By this time I had come to the conclusion that, in spite of the rumours floating about them, Christine and Andrew were above reproach as far as their loyalties were concerned, and I felt that their particular talents were being wasted. It was quite obvious that they were anxious to get back to work, and the more difficult and dangerous the work, the happier they would be.

'Christine helped me in many ways. For example, we learnt that the Germans were drafting foreign workers in large numbers – including Poles – into the Balkans. I discussed this with Guy Tamplin and we agreed that there was a real chance of getting Poles to defect to our side. I sent some officers to Greece, where they did very well, and I was looking for someone to go to Albania for the same purpose. Christine produced Michael L.[17] He went to Albania where he got the MC. Christine it was who guided me in the intricacies of Polish politics and clandestine warfare, and if anyone converted me from the innocent to the sophisticated in this field, it was she.'

Christine felt it would be a great asset in getting back into action if she could operate a secret transmitter; so Howarth arranged with the SOE Signals Officer for her to have a course of training. A young sergeant, Dick Mallaby, later to be parachuted into Italy, became her instructor.

Andrew had an obsession about doing a parachute course, so that he could eventually be dropped into Poland. Christine refused to discuss this dangerous notion with him; but he convinced Howarth that he was in earnest, and finally pressurized him into sending Andrew to the SOE Training School at Ramat David in Haifa.

Andrew had, for a long time, been in pain with his leg, which was still running with pus; and one day, at a luncheon party at Sophie Raczkowski's, he met a quiet and charming Israeli doctor. As a result of this conversation Doctor Jaski examined Andrew's leg and, before he could decline, he was taken to the famous Hadassah Hospital and operated on by the great Viennese surgeon, Doctor Meyer. Andrew was in hospital for

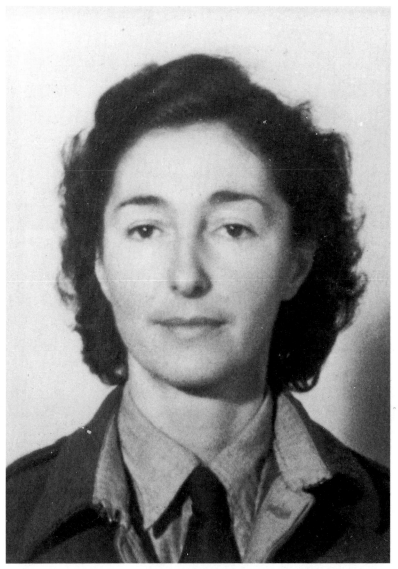

Official photograph of Christine from her file at the National Archives. The photograph is untouched and shows a strong and purposeful woman ready for action (NATIONAL ARCHIVES)

ID card, one of Christine's few and most treasured possessions (MIRRORPIX)

The Skarbek coat of arms (SKARBEK FAMILY COLLECTION)

Christine had a striking affinity with animals (MIRRORPIX)

The inside of Christine's passport, showing an elegant
19-year-old and signed Krystyna Skarbek

With Andrew in Syria. This was a time when the couple were deeply happy together (MIRRORPIX)

In Palestine, 1942

Christine loved
nature and was an
indefatigable walker
(MIRRORPIX)

Francis Cammaerts owed
his life to Christine, and
she found in his leadership
and friendship a brave and
dedicated '*preux chevalier*',
a brave and faithful knight
(FRANCIS CAMMAERTS)

With the Maquis and British officers in the Haut-Savoie, August 1944:
(left to right) Gilbert Galletti; Capt Patrick O'Regan; Capt John Roper;
Christine; and Capt Leonard Hamilton (IMPERIAL WAR MUSEUM)

Both sides of Christine's SOE code card, created by Leo Marks

Christine's decorations: (from top, clockwise) Order Virtuti Militari; Parachutist's Wings; Croix de Guerre avec Étoile d'Argent; George Medal; 'Chamois' of the Association Nationale des Pionniers et Combattants Volontaires du Vercors; Order of the British Empire

Christine's grave in the Roman Catholic Cemetery at Kensal Green, London. Andrew (left) and Ludwig Popiel pay their last respects

A rare moment of relaxation for Christine (GETTY)

two weeks, and it took him another two to learn to walk properly again with his artificial leg.

'I suppose it was a crazy idea,' said Andrew, 'a one-legged man insisting on learning to jump from a plane. I had a lot of trouble with the medicos, not because I had only one leg, but because nowhere in King's Regulations is it said who will pay compensation for an artificial limb broken in the course of a parachute jump. All my promises that I would pay the damages myself cut no ice, until I found an Irish doctor who understood what I was after. He said, "You bloody foreign fool, you'll probably jump from a lorry if I don't give you the necessary certificate, so here it is; now go ahead, and don't break your neck."'

For his first jump Andrew had an impressive audience. All safety precautions had been doubled. There were *two* Red Cross lorries, and *two* standing by to pick up the pieces. In the event, Andrew was the first to jump and was calmly rolling up his parachute when everyone converged on him. He waved them aside, and they rushed off to attend to Number Three, who had broken his collar-bone, while Number Five was found to have twisted his ankle.

When Andrew finished his course he was made a sort of glorified instructor. The general idea was that he should be featured as a star pupil, a one-legged man who had made the grade without trouble. He was there 'pour encourager les autres', and indeed this piece of elementary psychology worked well, calming the fears of many nervous beginners.

'In those days,' said Andrew, 'many important pupils attended the Parachute Training Course: among them were two generals, Davis and Armstrong. One was bound for Albania, while the other was going to Yugoslavia. Neither was as young or as supple as the average parachutist. But, seeing that I came to no harm, they soon learned to jump magnificently and without any problems.'

When Christine heard about Andrew's parachute course she was horrified, and annoyed with Pat Howarth for having arranged it. But she could do nothing to stop him, and soon after he had completed his course, Andrew was sent to Benghazi, where there was a starting point for planes, while Christine went to Ramat David to do a parachute training course in her turn.

CHAPTER SEVEN

The Polish embassy had again opened its doors to Christine and Andrew, though she never wanted to attend official functions. She much preferred small private parties and was selective in her choice of friends. Among her favourite hosts were Madeleine and Ashlan Catawe Pasha. He was an Egyptian Jew of great wealth and culture. His mother was lady-in-waiting to King Farouk's mother. In their home, Christine and Andrew met the 'haut gratin' of Egyptian society as well as a number of international celebrities. Here, too, they met and became friendly with Aly Khan and his English wife, Joan.

'Aly and Joan,' said Andrew, 'were always kind and helpful. Aly had a great sense of humour. He was very active as a liaison officer between the French and the British. His was a demanding job which he did well. Most of our old friends pitched up in Cairo sooner or later.

'We had a great reunion with Eddie Lobkowitz, old *Masque de Fer*, who had volunteered to join the Czech Forces. He was sent to Tobruk where he got a bullet in his backside. This was the subject of ribald jokes on the part of his friends, but it was, in fact, an extremely painful wound. Another old friend who suddenly appeared was Ledochowski. He had been badly wounded in the arm in the desert, and had been packed off to Cairo to convalesce. We did not see as much of him as we should have liked, for he was whisked off to his new job in Ankara, and we temporarily lost sight of him.'

Just before Christmas 1943, Andrew was sent to England for

briefing before going to Bari, and then on to Ostuni, where the Polish school for parachutists to be dropped into Poland had been established. Andrew was to be liaison officer in this school.

Andrew had not returned to England since 1937 and, in spite of the grim and austere war conditions then prevailing, he was delighted and exhilarated by the experience. He was received with open arms by the O'Malleys, who had returned home and treated him like a son of the house.

By the time he was ready to leave he was more than a little in love with a girl in London whom he had known previously. This romantic attachment on his part was to lead to much unhappiness later when Christine heard what had taken place in London. Andrew's lame explanation that the girl was young, innocent and in love, cut no ice with Christine, and Andrew was never allowed to forget this lapse. This was a fact which he found bewildering, since he and Christine were separated for over a year, and led independent lives. Furthermore there were repercussions with Sir Owen O'Malley, who did not take too good a view of Andrew's philandering ways. 'I am not proud of the way I behaved,' said Andrew. 'The girl was adorable, and I should have been more strong-minded than to embark on an affair with someone who seemed sincerely to care for me. I know that she had a happy marriage, and I hope that at this remove of time she has forgiven me.'

The exact date when Christine became an SOE agent seems impossible to establish, although it is evident from her official record that she worked first for British Intelligence, and then sporadically for SOE almost from its inception.

Any biography of Christine Granville would be invalid without a brief account of the secret organization whose workings and ramifications, although brilliantly collated by the historian M. R. D. Foot,[1] by their very nature created the aura of mystery which still surrounds those who worked for Special Operations Executive.

As early as 25 May 1940, the desperate state of the French

nation, which appeared to be in imminent danger of collapse, precipitated a revolution in British strategic thinking. The Chiefs of Staff submitted to the War Cabinet that should France collapse 'Germany might still be defeated by economic pressure, by a combination of an attack on economic objective and on German morale and the creation of widespread revolt in her conquered territory.' To stimulate this revolt, they added, 'was of the very highest importance.' A special organization would be required and plans should be prepared, and all the necessary preparations and training should be proceeded with as a matter of urgency, 'otherwise we would have no chance of contributing to Europe's reconstruction.'

On 3 and 5 June, Major-General F. G. Beaumont-Nesbitt put forward papers that proposed a War Office directorate of *irregular activities* exercising a 'measure of control' over the most secret services and with liaison with the Admiralty, Foreign Office and Air Ministry.

Sir Anthony Eden, then in charge of the War Office, forwarded the scheme to the Prime Minister. The idea of irregular warfare appealed tremendously to Churchill. He demanded instant action, urging that a single body should run this new venture. After many discussions with the Chiefs of Staff and informed bodies responsible for the various clandestine organizations, Lord Halifax called a decisive meeting in the Foreign Office on 1 July. Next day Dr Hugh Dalton, Minister of Economic Warfare, wrote to Lord Halifax: '. . . We have got to organize movements in enemy-occupied territory comparable to the Sinn Fein movement in Ireland, to the Chinese guerillas now operating against Japan, to the Spanish Irregulars who played a notable part in Wellington's campaign or – one might as well admit it – to the organization which the Nazis themselves have developed so remarkably in every country in the world. This "democratic international" must use many different methods, including industrial and military sabotage, labour agitation and strikes, continuous propaganda, terrorist acts against traitors and German leaders, boycotts and riots.

'It is quite clear to me that an organization on this scale and of this character is not something which can be handled by the ordinary departmental machines of either the British Civil Service or the British military machine. What is needed is a *new* organization to co-ordinate, inspire, control and assist the nationals of the oppressed countries who must themselves be the direct participants. We need absolute secrecy, a certain fanatical enthusiasm, willingness to work with people of different nationalities and complete political reliability. Some of these qualities are certainly to be found in some military officers, and if such men are available they should undoubtedly be used. But the organization should, in my view, be entirely independent of the War Office machine.'

Dr Dalton had set down the guidelines. After the inevitable intrigues and haverings which bog down all original concepts, Churchill invited Dalton to implement his project. This was on 16 July 1940. One of the last acts of the dying Neville Chamberlain was to arrange all the details. On 19 July he signed a most secret paper which had been circulated in draft to the persons most concerned nearly a week earlier. This document became the founding charter of SOE. In it was laid down that, on the Prime Minister's authority, 'a new organization shall be established forthwith to co-ordinate all action, by way of subversion and sabotage, against the enemy overseas . . . This organization will be known as the Special Operations Executive.' Churchill's directive to Dalton was brief: 'And now set Europe ablaze!'[2]

If SOE did not immediately do so, it played a vital role towards this objective all the way to the final reckoning. At its peak in 1944, it consisted of some 10,000 men and 3,200 women, and no single division in any army, taking that figure as comparable in strength, exercised a tenth of its influence on the course of the war. Of necessity it was a top secret organization. Very few people in the armed services, and only those with special dealings with the Inter-Services Research Bureau or the Joint Technical Board – SOE's cover titles – had any idea of its real identity or purpose. It soon became a worldwide network, and although much concerned with operations in France, it had many other German-occupied countries to infiltrate with subversion and sabotage.

The chain of command ran thus:

The Minister in charge of SOE was known as SO. It was he who carried the can when his subordinates made an error of judgement. Under him was the Executive Director, known as 'C.D.'. His task was to lead and control.

When Sir Charles Hambro resigned from SOE in 1943, he was replaced by his deputy, Col. Colin McVean Gubbins (later Major-General Sir Colin Gubbins). Colonel Gubbins was a man used to responsibility. In 1940 he was promoted Director of Operations and Training at SOE, with full powers to oversee secret missions to Western Europe and to France. Gubbins was a tough and realistic man. He combined a Scottish Highlander's insight with a regular officer's tenacity, an acute brain and a background of diplomatic and intelligence experience. It did not take long for Colonel Gubbins to take over the reins at SOE. 'He soon sorted us out,' said a member of his staff. 'He had it all worked out, he and his crony, John Holland, a Major in the Royal Engineers.'

The task of SOE, its *only* task, was to contribute to the eventual defeat of Hitler's Germany by carrying out para-military operations in enemy-occupied territories by direct intervention and/or support of Resistance fighters amongst the nationals of the countries concerned. SOE was wholly non-political, and took no sides in the rival political parties' competition for power against the time when liberation came; a difficult task, since that eventual power was likely to spring from having done the most to sabotage German occupation. SOE had to harness and direct these efforts, whoever might be making them.

It became clear that of all the occupied countries it would be in France that this task was likely to be most effective for reasons various, but self-evident. Not least its geographical convenience immediately across the Channel and its historical suffering at the hands of Germany; its inhabitants were hostile, their resistance to enemy occupation likely to be fierce and prolonged. Encouragement and assistance to that resistance would meet fertile soil.

At first, after the Dunkirk retreat, we were separated from France by a seemingly impenetrable wall of silence, and all communications were fragmentary and unreliable. Gradually, the wall thinned, contacts with the French people resumed and became their lifeline for eventual salvation.

The literature of the period from both sides of this 'wall' makes it abundantly clear that the courageous stand of the United Kingdom sustained the morale of the French people. That this stand took place, and that there was being built up a practical and successful form of supporting, organizing and supplying the needs of the French Resistance with men and *matériel*, became a constant all-important factor in maintaining hope under the yoke of German oppression and exploitation.

But when it came down to the brass tasks of implementing its directive, SOE was faced with a difficult, complex and uncertain situation in France, despite that country's hatred and resentment of the Occupation. It was rent within by factions antagonistic towards the political aims and ideologies of one another, and it was SOE's continual problem to know in whom to place its trust. In retrospect, at the end of the long day that has elapsed since then, it appears that many resistance groups working in France consisted of people with totally different political and religious affiliations, all of whom worked together in perfect harmony. Very properly, the SOE briefing did not include a political briefing, so that the individual agent had to find his own way round the intricacies of local political situations from the extreme left to the extreme right.

Thus with Security – with a capital 'S' – the essential first principle for a clandestine organization, F Section[3] had greater problems in conducting operations in France than the other SOE country sections, not least of these being the fact that its security also had to begin at home.

General de Gaulle was firmly established in London with his Free French supporters, and, at first, seemed likely, as indeed he proved, to be the postwar leader of his country. But it soon became impractical to work closely with him; Vichy refused to recognize him, and he would have nothing to do with anything, or anybody, remotely connected with the Pétain regime. This was a situation of exploitable value to the Germans, and they set about infiltrating the Free French of whatever persuasion with French collaborators, who in the guise of anti-Nazis, could act as spies for them. It was, in short, a security risk of great danger for F Section to bring the Gaullists into the organizational and operational picture; apart from the political implications of backing them, there was more than enough reason to avoid all contact with them.

De Gaulle was by no means pleased when inevitably he discovered this, and to placate him, and at the same time continue to protect F Section, a separate liaison section (codenamed RF) was set up which was allowed contact only between its senior officers and F Section's, and these were carefully restricted. Its HQ was at 1 Dorset Square, not far from Baker Street, but far enough to safeguard F Section staff in its comings and goings.[4]

F Section HQ unit under Maurice Buckmaster was small when one considers its scope and responsibilities. It consisted of six people in charge of five divisions: recruitment and supervision of training programmes, Captain (later Major) Selwyn Jepson; Major Bourne-Patterson, Intelligence and finance; Vera Atkins, assisting Buckmaster and responsible for welfare and preparations for the field; Captain Coleman, supplies – arms, explosives, etc.; G. Morel and André Simon *fils* (agents from the early days), planning and operations.

The training of agents on behalf of the country sections and the staffing and administration of the various 'schools' up and down the country was carried out by a separate section with its HQ in Montagu Street, parallel with Baker Street.

At these schools a student-agent was taught everything he needed to know from the use of arms and explosives to wireless telegraphy and the skills of infiltration and living secretly in Occupied territories. These establishments were strategically separated from one another and the trainees of the respective country sections kept apart by sending them to the schools in classes at separate times.

In the same system of 'separation', recruits and trainees never came to SOE headquarters in Baker Street, and were only contacted in different places for different needs and purposes.

In the case of F Section, it used a flat in Orchard Court, close to Oxford Street, but within walking distance of Baker Street. Here agents back from the field were debriefed, newly trained ones briefed, cover stories rehearsed and clothes and equipment assigned to those going out.

Recruiting took place still further away in an office room in the War Office-commandeered Hotel Victoria in Northumberland Avenue, or, when Captain Jepson was initially doubtful about a potential agent's security or suitability, in a room at the Ministry of Pensions where he could interview under an assumed name and not in uniform. In any case, as the only member of F Section who had to come into the open, as it were, he did so as anonymously and evasively as he could manage.

Selwyn Jepson, a well-known writer, came to SOE by way of the Buffs and the Directorate of Military Intelligence. His 'particular flair' (Foot: pp. 41–2) for understanding people put him at an advantage in the delicate area of interviewing potential agents, not least in deciding whether they were capable of undertaking this difficult and dangerous work. He had always to feel his way, not revealing at first more than he must of the nature of the work, and invariably planned further meetings both to give the man (or woman) time for reflection on the general picture he had drawn of what their possible involvement might be in 'dangerous intelligence work', and for himself to obtain the necessary security clearance on the individual from MI5.[5] In the course of subsequent interviews he made it clear, as he explained the work in closer particulars, that joining the organization was voluntary, and would always remain so.

It was a job to give his talent-spotting ability full expression. Jepson found recruits through a network of contacts both inside and outside the armed services: War Office, Admiralty, Air Ministry, Central Registry and from other less official quarters. None of these contacts had to know more than that he wanted to be told the names and whereabouts of individuals, 'men or women under the age of forty-five inside or outside the Services with perfect French for specialized work in connection with the war effort'.

'Inside the Services' conveyed the fact that he would invoke powers to extract such people from whatever post or unit they were in if he found they were suitable for the work and willing to volunteer.

His interpretations of decisions to join SOE's work are interesting in terms of Christine's story:

'One has to remember the tremendous shock at the fall of France to those who loved her and more particularly to the people who by virtue of birth (a French mother or father but themselves British-born), whose sense of double allegiance, a twin patriotism, gave them a very personal relationship with what we called the war effort and an urge to become more closely involved in it than they had been up to the moment I met them, in the destruction of Nazi Germany and the liberation of France. In the main these were by far the best people for the work; rarer but no less valuable were those of wholly British origin with such close knowledge of France and the French language that they could pass as natives there.

'Of course when talking to them and digging deeper into this primary attitude I often came on a personality's desire to prove itself – to discover if it could function effectively in situations of greater demand on its capacities than it normally met. In short, to "overcome". And where was a better opportunity than this work I was suggesting? There were also the adventurous ones; simpler, more extrovert people who didn't doubt their capabilities in this direction and would enjoy exercising them to a fuller degree than hitherto. Sometimes I suspected the death-wish syndrome in this type; from these I slipped away without committing myself. To gratify it would surely have endangered other agents.

'Then there were those seeking escape or relief from domestic pressure. An unhappy marriage, loss of a loved one that might be assuaged by devotion to a cause; perhaps when the loss had been through the war simply to carry on where the dead had to stop.

'Above and beyond these personal motives one has to remember the basic fact that of all stimuli war is the strongest, enough to deny self in a common need to defeat the enemy.

'Women are not immune from it. They can be frustrated by the concept of warfare as an exclusively male occupation. I found this attitude in "civilized thinking" when I raised the subject of recruiting women as agents for SOE, to make it part of that aspect of my job. History is full of martial women and mythology even more so; also when it comes to personal danger women are singularly endowed with what I call "lonely" courage; they do not need, as most men need, comradeship in arms as support for bravery.'

Jepson met another hurdle in the shape of the Geneva Convention that forbade women active roles in war and which the women's branches of the Services were adamant in obeying even if their commandants were privately sympathetic to his needs. One difficulty was on the purely domestic level of what the women in training should wear alongside the men in their battle-dress and who had formal uniforms, badges and all, to sport when not in school. And ideally the women should have similar status by belonging to a recognized service.[6]

The problem was solved when Jepson called on the Commandant of the FANYs (The First Aid and Nursing Yeomanry) to enrol the women agents of F Section in that corps. She complied eagerly, sharing his views about the suitability of the feminine principle in active warfare and agreeing that the Geneva Convention took no account of the realities of modern war, with its wholesale involvement of civilian populations. As he put it, 'Air raid bombs that demolish homes and kill children bring to every woman by every natural law the right to protect, to seek out and destroy the evil behind those bombs by all means possible to her. Including the physical and militant.'

The machinery for enrolling FANYs in SOE as student-agents was already there; FANYs had come early into the organization in roles varying from drivers to forgers of false papers, packers of parachutes and containers of arms and equipment that were air-dropped to agents in the field. Thus women directly from civilian life or transferred from other services were commissioned in the FANYs and there was no more trouble with the Convention.

Exceptional in the recruitment of agents were what Jepson calls ready-made agents, men – and on two occasions women – who had worked or were working in the field. Generally they had been brought into SOE circuits by their organizers, and it would happen that F Section HQ in London wanted to take a personal look at them, offer them training in the latest techniques of clandestine operations, then to brief them for a return to the field.

Christine was one such agent, but was different from others in that she had been operating not in France but in Poland. For this reason and that – we come to this aspect in a moment – she could no longer function there. However, her qualifications for working in France were excellent; not only was she a fully trained WT operator but spoke French like a native and could assume the necessary manner and appearance of a Frenchwoman.

Furthermore, she needed no further training apart from checking her proficiency in handling a W/T set and operating it. Jepson remembers her and, on looking at her photograph, recalls with certainty his impression of her as coming into the category he regarded as 'dedicated', along with a great anxiety to get back into the war against the Germans which had been badly frustrated; a strong, resilient, efficient personality more than ready to go.

'Sexuality? Plenty, but that wasn't unusual. As I said earlier, war is the great stimulator of primary instincts. The basic, territorial; then reproduction. Early in my job I learned to expect it as normal in the circumstances and saw no disadvantage in its presence.'

Sections were created as and when the need arose, and were formed to correspond to appropriate action in the countries concerned. In the late summer of 1940 the Polish Section headed, initially, by Bickham Sweet-Escott, came into being. Later Captain (Colonel) H. B. Perkins, 'Perks', took over, while working under Captain P. A. Wilkinson, who was also supervising a number of south-eastern European sections at SOE Headquarters in London.

The Polish Section differed from the others in that it was practically autonomous, and, while it co-operated very closely with the Sixth Bureau of the Polish General Staff in London, its authority in Polish affairs was strictly limited.

All agents, couriers and parachutists who travelled from Britain to Poland were, from the moment they touched down on Polish soil, the sole concern of the Polish authorities to whom they had immediately to report.

'Every applicant who was selected and trained for operations in Poland took the same oath as was administered to the men in the "Armia Krajowa" – the Home Army, underground forces who took their orders from the Polish Government in London. As soon as he reached Poland he became, so long as he remained there, a soldier of that Army. Political couriers took a different oath and were subject to the authority of the underground Delegatura Rzadu (a political body headed by a delegate appointed by London).'[7]

According to the historian H. T. Willetts, in a paper presented to an Oxford conference on Britain and European resistance, the duties of the Polish Section of SOE 'were to assist the Polish Sixth Bureau in maintaining and developing communications with Poland, in training operatives, in obtaining supplies and in arranging the delivery of supplies and personnel.'

According to Mr Willetts, the Poles were the only foreign nationals allowed to retain the right of their own cypher for radio liaison with Poland. The code names which the parachutists chose for themselves and used while in Poland were known only to the Polish authorities, and the British had no access to them.

British Intelligence certainly had its own agents in Poland, and communicated with them by means of couriers and other representatives; but 'it is certain that no agent was dropped there by SOE without the knowledge of the Polish authorities.'[8]

Andrew was in Italy when he got a signal from Christine saying that she was going to Algeria, because, at last, she had an important mission. Immediately, he asked for two weeks' leave and flew to Algiers to join her. 'Christine was staying in a house near Algiers under the command of a lady called Betty Sale.[9] She was the Queen mother of the FANYs there, and immediately understood Christine's complicated mental processes. Christine got a temporary commission in the RAF, and was not wearing FANY uniform, but that of the RAF, in which she looked even more attractive than usual.

'Betty gave Christine as much freedom as possible, and during the two weeks I was there, I tried to give her lessons in pistol shooting and riding a bicycle. I was unsuccessful in both cases. Every time Christine aimed her pistol, she closed her eyes and said, "I hate the noise, I hate the noise, and, anyway, I could never bring myself to shoot anyone!" She took a deep dislike to the bicycle and after a while refused to ride it. She was in a very nervous state, for a good many reasons; but the main one was that she had a briefing officer who rubbed her up the wrong way.'

Francis Brooks-Richards[10] wrote: 'Christine was certainly one of the most remarkable people I have ever encountered. My connection with her dates from 1944, when I was head of "Massingham's" French Country Section in Algiers. At a time, probably in the early summer, when preparations for the Southern landing in France were in full swing, I received a signal from Cairo SOE proposing Christine Granville for a mission in France. From what I had heard of her, I accepted immediately, and she flew into Algiers shortly afterwards in FANY uniform.

'It fell to me to decide with whom she should work in France, and my choice fell upon Francis Cammaerts (Jockey) of the London Buckmaster F Section who it had been agreed should be turned over to "Massingham's" operational control in preparation for the landings in Provence. Christine had not been in German-occupied France, and I deemed it important that she should be briefed very carefully for her mission by someone with recent experience of conditions over there. I thought I had found the ideal person in Major Ben Cowburn[11], one of the most gallant and courageous SOE agents, who was temporarily available between two missions to France; but the arrangement did not work smoothly, as I had to intervene frequently and soothe Christine before briefing could continue. I think, in retrospect, that these were displays of temperament that were to be expected of a "diva", even when attending master-classes by another great performer, which Cowburn undoubtedly was; though it would have been difficult to imagine two more contrasting styles. Cowburn's external *persona* was quiet and apparently diffident; his ability not to attract attention to himself was one of his greatest strengths as an agent, and Christine's bravura was in total contrast.'

Her original mission was to mobilize her Polish compatriots in France, who were working in their thousands in German forced labour camps. Some had been pressed into units of the German Army. She had awaited the call to arms for so long that, when it finally came, her patience was all but exhausted and she was in a state of acute nervous tension, the reasons for which Major Cowburn did not at first appreciate. After a visit by Patrick Howarth, Christine immediately calmed down and concentrated on the minutest details of her preparations.

The cover story was the first important step in briefing. It was coupled with exquisite attention to details, and was as

nearly truthful as possible. Leeway was allowed for slight incon-
sistencies which under interrogation, would give an appearance
of verisimilitude to an alibi.

The candidate was invested with a whole new set of relations, most of whom had died and were, therefore, unavailable
for questioning. Pedigrees were carefully thought out, and care
was taken to choose places of registration of birth whose records
had vanished through fire, raids or evacuation.

'Every officer rejoiced in at least three pseudonyms: a training
name which was dropped when briefing began, an operational
code-name in which his parachute operations (or his radio messages) were registered and, finally, a Christian name by which he
was called by SOE when in the field.'[12] Christine's code name
was 'Pauline Armand' and it is by this name that she is known in
that part of France in which she became famous for her exploits.

In order to understand why Algiers had become so important
in the war game it is necessary to go back to the decisive Battle
of El Alamein, which was fought and won in 1942. In November
of that year, in a rapid follow-up of this victory, Anglo-American
forces landed in Morocco and Algeria, forcing the Vichy authorities there to abandon their attitude of neutrality.

Preparations for the coming of a great armada to Casablanca,
Oran and Algiers involved a tangle of intrigues with anti-Vichy
groups and personalities. The main diplomatic problem had
been to find a French leader who might rally the French
authorities in North Africa, without revealing Allied plans and
without prolonged fighting.

For this latter purpose, General de Gaulle and the Free
French were useless, since a former move at Dakar had proved
that the French Colonial administration remained, in the main,
loyal to Vichy. The Allied choice, therefore, lay at first with
General Henri Giraud, a distinguished veteran soldier, who had
escaped from internment in Germany, but had not joined the
Free French. He landed secretly in Algeria on 5 November.
The Allied armada swept in two days later. Only at Casablanca
was there any serious resistance.

The French and German reactions were instantaneous. Hitler immediately occupied the whole of France, while the remaining units of the French fleet in Toulon harbour were scuttled on sealed orders from Admiral Darlan to save them from falling into German hands.

To make things even more complicated, Darlan, Commander-in-Chief of all the Vichy forces, suddenly appeared in Algiers, ostensibly to visit his sick son. His arrival was the signal for the Allies to make overtures to him, which ended in a hasty scissors-and-paste agreement between the Allies and Darlan that Darlan should supersede Giraud and order an immediate cease-fire. This was done.

Under the agreement which Darlan concluded with Mark W. Clark, Eisenhower's deputy, the Admiral became 'High Commissioner' of Algiers, Morocco and French West Africa. The most vital clause in the Clark–Darlan Agreement was that which left the Vichy administration in North Africa to function as before.

Naturally, de Gaulle and his followers, who were just preparing to work with Giraud, were furious with the Americans for concluding a treaty with Darlan, whom they considered to be a turncoat, and worse. Morale dropped to zero until, on Christmas Eve, Admiral Darlan was assassinated by Fernand Bonnier de la Chapelle, a young royalist. Giraud was promptly named the Admiral's successor as High Commissioner, as well as head of all French armed forces in North Africa.

But by the year 1942, almost the entire Resistance had accepted the leadership of General de Gaulle. Giraud's association with Darlan had smirched his image, and his continuation of Vichy policies and maintenance in office of leading Vichyites was a continual irritation.

At the Casablanca Conference, which took place in January, Roosevelt attempted to bring about a 'shotgun wedding' between de Gaulle and Giraud; but its political terms were unacceptable to the General, and, finally, in mid-May, it was announced that the Conseil National de la Résistance, grouping all leading Resistance organizations, political parties and trade unions, had been formed. The CNR immediately issued a manifesto supporting General de Gaulle, and when it was discovered that there was a definite swing (which included some of the staunchest Giraudists) to de Gaulle, the delayed nuptials took place. The Free French National Committee dissolved itself, and, on 30 May, General Charles de Gaulle arrived in Algeria.

His victory over Giraud paved the way for the coming struggle for power in France itself. The Grand Charles had eliminated a contender who had held power only because he was supported by the Americans and the British. But the epic struggle, the final and decisive battle would take place in France at the time of the Liberation.

When Operation 'Torch' secured Algeria for the Allies in November 1942, a base for SOE was set up at Guyotville, just west of Algiers. 'Massingham' was its international code name, and its cover, 'Inter-Service Signals (Issu) 6'. Its first commander, J. W. Munn, had previously been in charge of training. He was replaced by Douglas Dodds-Parker in 1943.[13]

'Massingham' was, of necessity, involved in the tangled local politics of Algiers; it was quite separate from the OSS Mission in Algiers, though it worked harmoniously with them. Within 'Massingham' there were small country sections, as in London. Only AMF dealt with France. This had originally been under the aegis of Jacques de Guélis. It was a copy of F Section and dealt mainly with the Giraudists.

Francis Brooks-Richards took over from de Guélis in October 1943, and this section became an RF-type,[14] or completely Gaullist-orientated section. 'Massingham's' other chief importance was that the air range into Southern France from the Algerian coast was shorter than the range from England, so that operations could be better mounted and supplied from 'Massingham' than from the main base.[15]

'Massingham' was seventeen miles west of Algiers at Sidi

Ferruch. Situated among the sandy dunes of the Mediterranean shore, it was well protected from the undesirable by a hundred miles of barbed wire. The primary object of the SOE mission was to form a base for an advance operational unit with the First Army, to build up the Resistance Movement that could not be supplied from London, and to begin the planning of similar operations in Corsica, Sardinia, Sicily and Italy.

The first group of FANYs, who were the invaluable 'admin' back-up team within this organization, arrived in Algiers on 3 January 1943. They removed from their first camp east of Algiers, to a pleasant new home in the Club des Pins, some fifteen miles from the city.[16]

The FANYs did not waste their time. They worked hard, and played hard. 'They visited strange flats in Algiers for secret conferences, they made hair-raising jeep rides at night to stop small boats sailing for Corsican beaches known to have been occupied by the enemy that day; they escorted agents on their parachute courses, and to their aircraft before leaving for France.'[17]

Algiers was entirely different from Cairo. It was smaller, more authentic, and since the French presence in Algeria had lasted 132 years, had something of the atmosphere of a French Mediterranean port. Yet it also had its own indigenous charm reflected in the casbah and in the old town.

Algiers has the same climate as Cairo, but Christine preferred it. It was right on the shore, and all about were attractive places for walks and picnics. She could sunbathe all morning (she did not know how to swim), and in the afternoons could go skiing up in the Atlas mountains. There was something Biblical and timeless about the Algerian countryside.

In a letter home a FANY wrote: 'There are ants, a very determined variety who manage to insinuate themselves everywhere. Most beds have to stand in bowls of water. The Arab population is clean and friendly. The villas on the hillsides are spacious and beautiful and bougainvillea, which grows like a weed, flows like a bright-coloured curtain over the white walls.

'The Kasbah is a frightening place and we're not allowed in there except under armed escort. It is narrow and terribly smelly, honeycombed with mysterious passage ways. I have been looking for presents but there is hardly anything to buy.'

This cry was echoed from the heart by the distinguished British hostess and famous beauty, Lady Diana Duff Cooper, who came to Algiers in 1943 with her husband. Duff Cooper had been invited to take over from Harold Macmillan, and was to become British Representative to the French Committee of Liberation with the rank of Ambassador, 'and the prospect of going on to Paris as such in due course'.[18]

Lady Diana found that Algiers was 'totally bereft of any buyable thing'. Even essentials such as electric light bulbs, soap, lavatory paper and candles were nowhere to be obtained. Such stores as there were were not issued to the shops which opened their shutters for a few hours only each morning. All she could offer her husband and important guests for breakfast was tinned milk and acorn coffee.[19]

Christine wrote often to Andrew. In one of her letters she mentions that she had gone shopping for leather wallets. She bought three, one for her Big Cat, one for her friend Patrick Howarth and one for herself. She was quite unmoved by the meagre rations available. She had long since schooled herself to accept hunger and a lack of material comforts as part of her training.

She was determined to make a success of her mission from the moment she was parachuted into France, and listened attentively to all that the briefing officer was able to tell her. It was of vital importance that no detail of her papers or clothing should be faulted if she were picked up by the Germans. From Margaret Street, in the city of London, came the blouse, skirt and jacket she would wear when she landed in France.[20] A French coiffeur, of which there were many, was called in to dress her hair in the latest French style. A dentist was called in to examine Christine's mouth, so that any dentistry she had previously undergone should tally with her cover story.

SOE employed the services of a department of scientists who, deep in the bowels of the Science Museum, produced the right papers for each agent's area of operation. A spectacular range of forgeries were turned out to cover every emergency from ration-cards, essential to survival, to facsimiles of identity-cards and other vital documents.

'SOE had developed a range of sophisticated new "toys", many of which were to prove of the greatest value to the agents who made efficient use of such aids as compasses hidden in cufflinks, a Gigli saw, as used in brain surgery, which was sharp enough to cut through the stoutest prison bars; telescopes with eightfold enlargement, minute enough to be stowed in cigarette tips; and a tiny infra-red torch whose beams showed up a special "invisible" infra-red ink. There were maps printed on pieces of rice paper which could be hidden in the shaft of a propelling pencil, wrapped around the lead.'[21]

It was now that Christine made a new friend who would occupy a special niche in her affections. John Roper was to become another of the 'knights in shining armour' to whom Christine was a very special person to be treated with understanding and respect. John Roper said, 'Whenever I knew or thought I was going to meet her, I always tried to have a clean pocket handkerchief for her and, if possible, a twist of tea, for, although she neither drank or smoked, she loved tea.'

Those who spent time with Christine before her departure found her in a fatalistic mood. Havard Gunn, who sometimes accompanied her on the long walks she enjoyed, said she seldom discussed the future, and when she did so, it was without great optimism. She said she could not envisage what life would be in peace time, so she preferred to concentrate on the matter-in-hand, and on getting herself into the peak of physical condition. She was still bothered by what she considered to be her excessive thinness and, though she sometimes got cramps in her legs, she could outclimb and outwalk most of her companions. She had no idea what awaited her in France; but she was anxious to get away and begin her 'real' work.

In the meantime, the planning for the great 1944 invasion was going ahead, and the first half of this year was devoted to preparing the Second Front – 'Operation Overlord', which had been the surprise packet opened for Stalin by Roosevelt and Churchill at Teheran. The main commanders had been chosen in 1943 and had been working together and training their troops. General Dwight D. Eisenhower had been designated Supreme Commander of the Allied Expeditionary Force.

The whole of Britain was turned over to preparing for the invasion. One and a half million Americans were brought across the Atlantic to prepare for D-Day. An armada of over 5,000 vessels was assembled for the first phase; 1,200 naval vessels, including seven battleships, to bombard the coastal defences, sweep mines, to escort the invaders and attack enemy sea and aircraft; and 4,000 transports, barges, tugs and other seagoing and amphibious craft to convoy the armies with their tanks, armoured cars, and other sophisticated items of equipment used in modern warfare.

In the air, the Allies mustered 7,500 aircraft in direct support of the invasion and 3,500 bombers. At two o'clock on the morning of 6 June, the first invaders crossed the Channel by air and were dropped at some distance from the invasion beaches. By dawn, five separate groups moved up from the sea to the beaches. These men – 20,000 airborne and 70,000 ground troops – were the spearhead of an enormous fighting machine drawn from many nations.

Some time before the invasion a great wave of sabotage had crashed down on German coastal defences, radar installations, interior roads, railroads and airfields. The long-awaited moment was at hand, and all those who had waited and prayed for this hour of release were ready at their posts.

For the first time it seemed that the long nightmare might, at last, be coming to an end. Yet the war was far from over, and in France, 'Roger' – Francis Cammaerts – urgently requested that an agent should be sent to him to replace his woman assistant who had fallen into German hands.

At last Christine was under orders to prepare herself for imminent departure. 'She was pretty impatient,' said John Anstey, who had taken over the French Section from Douglas Dodds-Parker, 'and we had the awful dilemma when at a certain time of the month, her physical condition and the moon coincided. The MO said that she was not to drop in this state, and it took the whole of the unit to keep her pacified and occupied until the next month.'[22]

On 6 July 1944, the long-awaited moment came for Christine. Her parachute was fitted, and the rubber-lined anti-crash helmet. She was issued with a loaded revolver, which terrified her, a razor-edged folding cutting knife, torch, and the inevitable 'L' Tablet, a coated cyanide of potassium pill, which when bitten caused instant death. Her vital documents were rechecked, local identity card in the name of 'Pauline Armand', ration-coupons and a money belt stuffed with sovereigns. The last farewells were said. Christine was helped aboard the aircraft. It taxied down the runway and took off. The little group standing there watched it in gloomy silence. It was the first time a woman agent had been sent from Algiers to be dropped into France.

Once they were airborne, Christine was filled with exhilaration. As the plane flew over the Club des Pins on its way to France, she sent her friends assembled there, a final *envoi* in the form of an 'excessively rude message she tapped out in Morse on an Aldis lamp, which some of them recognized from one of her favourite songs.'[23]

PART TWO

CHRISTINE AND THE ARMY OF SHADOWS

The Battle for the Vercors

CHAPTER EIGHT

In the night of 22/23 March 1943, Lieutenant Francis Cammaerts and Captain Charles Dolan, who was returning to France on a second mission, stood on the tarmac of the RAF station at Tangmere, near Chichester, waiting to take off. Cammaerts' first mission was to replace the former organizer of a network in the South of France, Captain Peter Churchill, who had been recalled to London after the circuit *CARTE* had got seriously out of hand.

Cammaerts arrived in France straight from the exhausting, action-packed course of the Special Training Schools of SOE. This young man, who was destined to become one of the great figures in the Resistance, and a key figure in Christine Granville's life, was an exceptional human being.[1]

His father, the Belgian poet Emile Cammaerts, had settled in England and married an Englishwoman named Tita Brand, the Shakespearian actress, who was the daughter of Marie Brema, the second woman to sing Brünnhilde at Bayreuth. Francis was born in 1916. He was educated in England and early decided that he wanted to teach. He got an MA at Cambridge in his subjects, which were English and History. His first teaching post was in Belfast. Later, when he was teaching at Beckenham and Penge County School for Boys in South East London, he again met Harry Rée, a close friend of his Cambridge days.[2] Rée was a pacifist though he never registered as a conscientious objector, and his influence confirmed Cammaerts in his desire to become a conscientious objector in

1939. Like many of his friends and contemporaries, he thought war futile and terrible, and had no stomach for the killing of his fellow man.

A Tribunal directed him into agricultural work which he much enjoyed. But, in spite of his deep pacifist convictions, he became troubled by the rapid growth of the Nazi evil. He married in March 1941, and his first daughter was born in 1942. These family responsibilities which brought him closer to the community, together with the death of his brother in the RAF, were the main reasons for his changing his conscientious objector status and determining him to combat the enemy.

Cammaerts wanted to get into Occupied France. His friend Harry Rée, who had enlisted in Field Security, told him of an organization which he felt might have some use for a man of Cammaerts' calibre and special talents. He saw Major Selwyn Jepson in June 1942. The omniscient 'Mr Potter' immediately recognized that the tall, serious young man before him was a born secret agent with intelligence, flair, resource and a potential for command and organization. Furthermore, he was bilingual and as fit as any trained athlete.

Selwyn Jepson, recalling one of his interviews with Cammaerts, said, 'It was one of the most interesting talks of its kind I have ever had. This was a man of the highest principle working on the land. Put there by the Conscientious Objectors' Board. We discussed at length the principle of warfare and the principles of Hitlerism. Cammaerts' motives were absolutely pure and, therefore, he was one of the most successful agents we ever sent into the field.'

Some time in July 1942, Cammaerts joined SOE. It was not long before he showed his mettle. Donald Hamilton-Hill, recruited by General Gubbins into this organization, was second-in-command of the SOE Training Schools. In his book, *SOE Assignment*, he mentions an incident which throws an interesting light on Cammaerts' rapidly developing talents as a secret agent. At this time Cammaerts was attending one of the Special Training Schools whose curriculum was equivalent to a final Staff College training for those specially selected to fulfil key roles in the Resistance.

'Francis Cammaerts, one of our trainees, had to contact the manager of Barclays Bank in Bradford, also in the secret, and endeavour to persuade him to start a Resistance cadre in Yorkshire. This was to be done during a game of golf on the local links where they could not be overheard. He was duly picked up by the local police, Special Branch, and asked what he was doing. His cover story, which he had to invent for himself, was that he was on a sheep and cattle buying trip for the farm which was run by a group of conscientious objectors near Wragby in Lincolnshire.[3] The police checked by phone, and found out that, indeed, this was correct. Cammaerts' wife who had not seen him for two months had answered the call and his story was confirmed.'[4]

On arriving in France, Cammaerts and his companion were landed on a large hop farm near Compiègne, which belonged to a wealthy and patriotic Frenchwoman who had put this landing-ground at the disposal of SOE. Greetings were brief. In a moment Peter Churchill and his companion climbed into the Lysander, while Cammaerts, now 'Roger', and Charles Dolan were whisked away by their reception committee.

It was not long before 'Roger's' acute flair told him that all was not well with the members of the network 'Donkeyman' with which he was supposed to work.

Almost immediately on reaching Paris with Commandant Marsac, known as 'End', he had the shock of hearing of Marsac's arrest by the Germans, and instantly decided to leave Paris for St Jorioz in the mountains of Savoy. He knew that here he would find 'Lise'[5], 'Michel's' (Peter Churchill's) courier, with 'Arnaud'[6], his radio operator.

'Roger' was far from happy with the set-up at St Jorioz, which was crowded with Resistance men and stringers, who did not seem to be as security-conscious as they might have been. This made 'Arnaud' uneasy, and he went off alone to set up his transmitter in a nearby village. 'Lise' told 'Roger' of the approaches made to her by a Colonel Henri, a German Abwehr officer. He had told 'Lise' that he was strongly anti-Nazi, and wanted to get in touch with British Intelligence, as did many of his influential friends who hated the present régime. He wanted 'Lise' to arrange for a plane to take him and Commandant Marsac, whom he said he had been obliged to arrest for his own protection, to Colonel Buckmaster in London.

'Lise' was dubious and puzzled by Colonel Henri's friendly overtures. 'Roger' was frankly suspicious and told her bluntly he thought she might be putting herself and her companions at risk by continuing to have any contact with the urbane Colonel. 'Lise' and her friends were, of course, totally unaware of the real identity of the friendly, pro-British Colonel. His name was Hugo Bleicher, he was an NCO in the Abwehr, in the department dealing with counter-espionage, and his warm and friendly manner masked a cold and cynical determination to capture and destroy as many British agents as possible.[7]

While awaiting the return of 'Michel', Colonel Henri amused himself by trying to convince 'Lise' of his pro-British intentions. Meanwhile, 'Roger', scenting the approach of danger, beat a strategic retreat, so that when 'Michel' returned from London and he and 'Lise' were pounced on by Colonel Henri, 'Roger' was far away.

He went to a safe house at Cannes. Here he built up his cover as a schoolmaster recovering from hepatitis, from which he had suffered in December while in England. During this period of waiting 'Roger' made several important decisions. He decided to detach himself from 'Donkeyman' and the old network, and to create a completely new circuit of his own, whose security should be as tight and as foolproof as he could make it. One of the major rules he laid down was that he would never spend more than three or four nights in the same house, 'so he never went to a strange address without checking it out, or being personally recommended by a reliable member of the organization'.[8]

During this time, 'Roger' was making new friends in every *milieu*. Most of them would be vital links in the chain he was trying to forge. Also, he made a particular point of making a thorough study of the geography of Grenoble and its surroundings. This included the great natural rock fortress known as the Vercors. 'Roger' relied on local people, who never failed to provide guidance when necessary.

Gradually his new network, named 'Jockey', began to build up. He did nothing precipitately, 'and to ensure that as many as possible of the members of his organization were reliable, he watched their leaders with great care himself some weeks before approaching them and persuaded them to agree with him that no one else should even be approached until they had been watched for a while in their turn'.[9]

'Roger' was so security-conscious that the squad he built up, and which included two policemen, spent their time shadowing prospective recruits. Even 'Roger', 'le Patron' himself, was not exempt from their checks. From the beginning, he was popular with his men, all of whom were aware that he was a British officer. This was essential to give them confidence so that they knew of their danger. They did not, of course, know his personal identity, and he made a special point of never letting any of his circuit contact him. He always knew how to get in touch with them; but they had no idea of where he was living, and could only leave messages for him at 'letter-boxes'.[10]

By the early autumn of 1943, 'Roger' had established an efficient network of small independent groups up and down the left bank of the Rhône valley between Vienne and Arles, and inland between the Isère Valley and the Riviera hinterland.

By the middle of the year, 'Roger' commanded an area larger than Derbyshire, Yorkshire, Nottinghamshire, Lincolnshire and Lancashire put together. He had hundreds of men under his orders, and had established communications with brother SOE officers working their own circuits in neighbouring counties. He evolved his own systems, and found they worked. Travelling on foot or on an old bicycle, by train or bus – the luxury of cars came much later – he was always on the move, establishing dropping zones, seeing that arms were distributed in the right areas, and forming new groups by gaining the confidence of the men and women he found in the towns, hamlets and villages he visited.

'Roger' had an astonishingly varied circle of friends. He was equally at home in the salon of a château or in a shepherd's hut. He was used to working twenty-four hours at a stretch, dealing carefully and thoughtfully with each problem as it came. A man of infinite patience and resources, he inspired all who worked with him.

Colonel Maurice Buckmaster, who visited 'Roger's' territory after the war, met many of the men and women who had worked with him. He wrote:

> The wide area in which 'Roger' had to carry out his duties involved him in much travelling. Many were the hairbreadth escapes, the lucky chances of that period, for travelling was the most unhealthy of pastimes. Only 'Roger's' wide circle of friends saved him from certain arrest. Striding across the uplands, his tall figure caused the shepherds to call to each other, 'voilà le grand diable d'anglais', for among the simple, honest people of the region 'Roger's' nationality could not be hidden. Not a man among them would not have fought to save 'Roger'; not a woman who would not have hidden him from pursuit at the risk of her life; not a child who would not have undergone any form of torture rather than betray *l'ami anglais*.[11]

'Roger' had sent urgent and repeated requests to London for a woman assistant. His request for a woman agent was based on his experiences of two remarkable women, Jacqueline Nairne of 'Stationer' and the gallant Pearl Witherington of 'Wrestler' with whom he had worked at Clermont-Ferrand and Riom.[12]

Two new assistants were finally sent to him. One of them was Cecily Marie Lefort, 'Alice', an Irishwoman and a proficient yachtswoman married to a Frenchman, and the other was Pierre Reynaud, 'Alain', who was in charge of the South Drôme, and whom 'Roger' used as a sabotage instructor.

But in September 1943, forty-year-old 'Alice' was caught in the house of a corn-merchant at Montélimar. 'Roger' was away on one of his tours, while 'Alain' and Monsieur Daujat, the owner of the house, were talking in the garden. They managed to escape; but 'Alice' was hustled away to the Gestapo prison at Lyons, where she was brutally interrogated.[13]

'Alain' managed to reach 'Roger' to warn him that the SS had taken 'Alice', and were watching Daujat's house in the hope that he would return to it. They had become increasingly aware of 'Roger's' activities, and were determined to find him. Indeed, so incensed did the SS become each time he carried out yet another daring exploit that they put a price on his head. Owing to the quality of his friends he was never denounced.

In spite of 'Alain's' bad news, 'Roger' returned immediately to Montélimar to see what could be done to save 'Alice'. He soon found out that there was little hope of extricating her from the prison at Lyons. He also knew that by staying in Montélimar he was endangering not only his own life, but that of his assistants; so 'Albert' (Auguste Floiras), his faithful radio-operator, was sent to the house of Doctor Paul Jouve, whose surgery at Digne was used as a clearing house for couriers, and as a letterbox for messages.

'Roger, now hard-pressed, had asked again for another assistant to be sent to him immediately; but the fate of 'Alice' nagged at him continually, and though she had been sufficiently warned against going to Monsieur Daujat's house, he felt responsible for her, and spent a great deal of time pondering ways and means of springing her from her jail.

After an interminable wait during which he went to England for consultations and returned to France in February 1944, 'Roger' was told that someone had been found for him. But it was not until four months later that he received a signal saying that 'Pauline Armand', his new courier, was on her way to him.

In the night of 7 July 1944, Christine and her companions were having a rough ride in the plane which bucketed and lurched its way to France. With her was the French Air Force Captain Tournissa, 'Paquebot', heading the mission from which he had taken his name. There were also four French lieutenants.[14] Christine, who for months had dreamed of nothing but the moment when she could land in France, had not now a thought in her head. She felt as if 'her brains were stuffed with the clouds' banked all about them. Then it was her turn to jump. Her instructor's final words rang in her ears. 'Take a deep breath and let yourself go, slow, sweet and easy. Relax your muscles, relax, go . . . go.'

Down she went, a rag doll swirling in the turbulent airs. The landing was scheduled to take place at a spot in the Vercors called 'Taille-Crayon' – Pencil-Sharpener – at Vassieux; but Christine did not land with the others. One of them, a Lieutenant Billon, fractured his thigh and was whisked off to the Maquis hospital at St Martin-en-Vercors.[15]

Christine was blown four miles off course in a howling gale, and she hit the ground with such force that the butt of her revolver was smashed and her coccyx badly bruised.[16]

She had no idea where she was, but was pretty certain that the reception committee would be searching for her. Rapidly, she buried her parachute and the remains of her revolver in the scrub, and when the search party arrived they found a young girl in neat unpretentious clothes enjoying an early morning stroll. They asked her whether she had seen a parachutist landing in the vicinity. In colloquial French, Christine assured them that she had seen no strangers. Then, having satisfied herself by listening to their conversation that they were genuine members of the reception party, she gave the operational code word, and announced that 'Pauline' had come to work with them.

Two days later she was taken to meet her commanding officer, who had been on tour. 'Roger' saw a beautiful, slender young woman with shining wind-blown hair, delicate features and a resolute little chin. He knew, instinctively, that 'Pauline' would give him the support and help he needed.

The Vercors is a towering acropolis of rock rearing up into the clouds. It straddles the departments of the Drôme and the Isère, and in the next few months Christine, like 'Roger', would come to know many of the secret mountain paths, gorges, ravines, caves and thickly wooded areas which screened the Maquis from prying eyes.

Here on the heights the thyme-scented air was thin, pure and stimulating. It quickened the pulse so that danger became the norm, the very stuff of life.

This was a green and purple land, inhabited mainly by farmers, foresters and shepherds, whose sharp eyes, like those of sailors, were used to scanning the horizon. Many of them, constantly on the watch for straying beasts, used their powers of observation to report any untoward movement to the men gathered in the rough camps throughout the forests of the Vercors.

Geographically, the Vercors is a chalky mass forming a high plateau. Massive in formation, it is rich in forests of beech and pine and is larded with fields bitten into by the tributaries of the Basse-Isère and the Bourne in particular, whose gorges are reached by roads and hairpin bends carved out of the solid rock of the mountainside.

The altitude of this natural fortress is 900 to 1,000 metres, and its walls are 200 to 300 metres high for more than 120 kilometres, nearly its entire perimeter, with the exception of St Nizier, a wide breach in the mountains which gives comparatively easy access to the interior.

There are eight access roads to the Vercors, three of them reaching the peak, while others wind up through the gullies and gorges eroded in the rock. Many roads have been carved through the rocks, creating dizzy escarpments and aerial balconies hanging vertiginously out in space.

Only those who know the Vercors well are familiar with the tiny mountain paths, each of which has a name and a history.

This rocky citadel is isolated from the other massifs by well-defined cuts.

It can be said to be divided into two regions; to the north, Montagne de Lans, which looks towards Grenoble, while to the south the Vercors proper debouches on the Royans by the Grands Goulets. It is the Bourne which divides and limits these two parts.

This immense bastion commands important lines of communication, and provided a good jumping-off point for attacks on the Rhône Valley communications, particularly at the narrow point of Tain l'Hermitage.

Almost from the outset, from 18 June 1940, when General de Gaulle had called upon all Frenchmen to continue the fight against the enemy, the people of the Vercors had listened and reflected on this clarion call to patriots. It was not until 1942 that Resistance in the Vercors became properly organized.

There were three strands of recruitment for the Vercors Maquis units. Le Mouvement Franc-Tireur Dauphinois, a group which under the guidance of two doctors, Martin and Samuel, and a patriot called Aimé Pupin, had taken refuge in the deep forests of the Vercors.[17] These were followed by Eugène Chavant, 'Clément', after Martin's arrest, though Martin was throughout the *patron* of the Vercors civilians.

The third group was the ex-Armée de l'Armistice – regular soldiers who had been disbanded in November 1943, and came up to the Vercors from the barracks at Lyons. They included Thivollet on his white horse, the Senegalese company and many others.

These were the Armée Secrète and included 'Hervieux'. subsequently Military Commander of the Vercors, Descours ('Bayard'), Commander R. Lyon, and Zeller ('Joseph'), Commander R.1 and R.2. The Military and civilians did not see eye-to-eye on politics or distribution of weapons. Zeller, Yves Farge (Procureur de la République) and 'Roger' often had to make peace between Chavant and Thivollet (Capitaine Geyer) in particular. The spit-and-polish boys according to 'Roger', wanted spectacular parades and glory.'[18]

The idea of using the natural fortress of the Vercors as a citadel and recruiting ground, reception centre and safe refuge was put to General Delestraint, 'Vidal', the military representative of General de Gaulle, and to Jean Moulin, delegate of the CFLN (Comité Français de Libération Nationale.) They both warmly approved the project which then received the blessing of Allied Headquarters in London.

The first objective was to assemble the committee of the network representing Le Mouvement Franc-Tireur Dauphinois as well as the Réfractaires and to merge them into one unit.

This unit was finally to produce a core of resolute men and women of the Plateau, who were determined that the Vercors should be a trump card in the forthcoming struggle for liberation.

In February 1943, the first Camp des Réfractaires was established on the Ambel Plateau, and by April of that year, nine camps with thirty men in each were scattered in clearings in the forest. These maquisards were provisioned and sustained by loyal men and women, many of whom would eventually pay for these services with their lives.

The initial maquis of the Vercors was formed of people who for one reason or the other had fallen under the suspicion of the authorities, particularly in the nearby industrial town of Grenoble, Valence and Romans.

Many had as their recreation mountaineering and skiing and knew the area well. Recruited by trade unions, political parties and dissident church groups (it is perhaps not without significance that this is the edge of the Protestant area of France), they were drawn to this natural place of refuge, with which they were very familiar.

Very often in the first stages they went to live there but returned home by night to pick up extra clothing and other necessaries. They were also members of various organizations which had been declared illegal – voluntary, political and church and youth movements – and in the mountains they found refuge, revenge and adventure.

The German Occupation and the Vichy Government together broke down the whole social structure of French life, a fact which is often forgotten. Thus the most active of the major social organizations were concerned about their future and that of the children under the occupation; many of them refused to send their children even to church, lest they were corrupted.

To this group were also added the Service de Travail Obligatoire and the military.

Soon after the Armistice the Germans began to press for volunteers to work in Germany. A big publicity campaign made use of posters and of propaganda.

The posters, 'Germany offers you work', were backed by a deluge of fictitious letters written ostensibly by a spate of deliriously happy French workers in Germany, who were living on the fat of the land, being paid a handsome wage and occupying cheap, comfortable houses. In spite of these blandishments, there were few volunteers. Those caught up in the war machine seemed to accept their lot and made no trouble about working for their captors. From the start, however, they were determined to do as much damage to the German war-effort as they possibly could.

The Germans needed labour, and they intended getting it. Pressures were applied and special labour exchanges were opened.

In spite of the fact that they could plan to exterminate millions of Jews, the Germans could always find time to put the screws on the authorities to liberate a single convict in a French prison needed for one of their factories in Germany.

The pressures became fiercer, and the Service de Travail Obligatoire came into being. Thus the Germans forged the first of the weapons which would eventually help to destroy them, for almost instantly the STO became the Maquis's chief source of manpower. Gradually, as the war continued, a pattern of life in the Maquis was evolved. Given certain geographical differences in the disposition of the terrain, the *modus vivendi* was pretty much the same.

'Anyone trying to get to the nerve centre of a Maquis would be intercepted by a sentinel who was generally unarmed; then by a second armed guard wearing a cap and tricolour brassard decorated with a large black Cross of Lorraine. If the visitor's credentials were satisfactory, he would then be allowed into the camp proper. This was skilfully camouflaged behind brushwood and foliage.

'Generally the huts were built like woodmen's; some were used as dormitories, some as kitchens, some served as prisons. The hut of the Maquis chief was divided into two. One part was used for sleeping and eating, while the other served as an office run by a secretary who took care of the Maquis "archives" and files.

'Elsewhere, on the Plateau of Glières for example, the maquisards adapted the huts used for sheltering livestock in summer. Other makeshift tents were constructed of parachute silk, while, in other places, the maquisards lived in caves and grottos deep in the mountain.

'Day-to-day living was methodically planned according to military routine. In normal circumstances, the maquisards were called at 6.30 a.m. and, after washing, attended Colours. Since some of the camps had no bugle, these were saluted by an accordion. After which breakfast was followed by weapon cleaning and general camp duties. The camp cooks were always instructed to take special precautions against making smoke; in a number of cases ignoring the rule about smoke signals brought disaster to the camps.'[19]

Supplying the maquisards with food presented many problems. Having no ration cards, they were cut off from most normal sources of supply. But sympathetic farmers and neighbouring shop-keepers provided the necessary. As the war progressed, it became easier to get forged ration tickets. In the beginning, however, the maquisards were on short commons. A document which caused considerable hilarity among the French was translated by an English-speaking schoolmaster who had been given it by an Englishman. Prepared by British Naval Intelligence division 'for the use of agents and escapees who may find themselves at large on the Continent without food', it offered invaluable suggestions.

> *Rats and Mice (rats et souris):* Both are palatable meat. Rats cooked in a stew might be mistaken for chicken. Skin them, 'gut' them and boil in a mess tin; rats for about ten minutes, mice for five. Either can be cooked with dandelion leaves for a stew. Be sure to include the livers.
> *Dogs and Cats (chiens et chats):* Providing much food, they are worth much trouble in capture by friendly advances.
> *Sow Thistle (laiteron):* Of all the edible wild plants, the sow thistle takes the first place as a sustaining food. In many countries of Europe it is boiled for the table, and its disuse in Britain can only be due to ignorance of its qualities.

Thanks to the grapevine which provided the information that vans of foodstuffs, clothes or tobacco would be travelling from A to B, a convoy of maquisards would hold up the van or vans, remove the goods and vanish, leaving the vanman to raise the alarm in his own good time, and in the knowledge that the full price of the 'stolen' goods would later be paid to his head office.

Operation 'Potato', Operation 'Soap' and Operation 'Fats' gave way to Operation 'Transport' as D-Day drew near. Cars and lorries began to vanish, as if by magic. Once in the hands of the maquisards, they were made 'battle-worthy'. Petrol was a tremendous problem. It was one of the most difficult, most dangerous and most costly items. It could not be hidden, and it often had to be obtained directly from the Germans, either by *coups de mains* or on the black market. It could also be obtained from army depots with coupons stolen from Town Halls, and by raids on petrol stations, during which the maquisards disguised themselves as German soldiers.[20] The man responsible for supplies in the Vercors was George Jouneau, 'Commandant Georges'.

Adequate clothing was difficult to come by, and the maquis-ards in their thin civilian clothes were often cold and wet. Moreover, with the approach of winter, their sufferings became acute, since the Vercors was at winter sports altitude, and the snow was often so thick as to be almost impassable. Gradually, clothes more suitable to their way of life were acquired by divers means such as a raid on a warehouse which brought a magnificent haul of boots, haversacks and berets. This was accomplished by chloroforming the compliant watchmen, who delayed giving the alarm until the raiders were safely away.

A further source of supply was French Army equipment obtained with the connivance of non-commissioned officers in charge of stores. The standard winter uniform of a maquisard was a *canadienne*, a wool-lined lumberjack's jacket, worn over corduroy trousers, with as many sweaters as could be 'organized'. Stout boots and woollen stockings were a necessity. Some maquisards wore a beret, others preferred woollen balaclava helmets dragged down over their ears. Among the rules laid down for the maquis-ards were the following: A Maquis should have no more than 15 men on the strength, and never less than 10. A Maquis must be sited in a clearing which gives its men the advantage of seeing without being seen. It can only survive if it is constantly on the alert, which means it must have sentries posted everywhere, and at all times. A Maquis must be mobile. The moment it is approached by unknown individuals, the entire group must leave at once for a new hideout, and if one of the members of a Maquis deserts, the Maquis must shift camp immediately.

In the early days, weapons and ammunition were extremely scarce. No quantities were parachuted in until the Spring of 1944. It was during the hours of darkness that the maquisards moved to carry out their manifold tasks of ambush, sabotage and foraging. By the end of 1943, under the passionate and patriotic leadership of Eugène Chavant, 'Clément', a partisan army assembled in the Vercors, brought together from all over France to form an active force which would later be fused with the FFI (Forces Françaises de l'Interieur) .

General Zeller, 'Joseph', commanded FFI regions Lyons (2) and Marseilles (1). Colonel Descours, 'Bayard', commanded Region (2) in which Vercors was situated. Colonel Huet, 'Hervieux', commanded the whole Vercors military operation. Commandant Costa de Beauregard, 'Durieux', commanded the North, and Capitaine Geyer, 'Thivollet', the South.

'Roger's' own territory now stretched from the Alpes-Maritimes to the Ardèche, a 'manor' of approximately 20,000 square miles. Somehow or other, he had to keep in constant contact with his far-flung groups; to this end, he 'organized' a fleet of cars in which he circulated happily, respectably and safely, equipped with all the documents needed to permit an official of the Highways and Bridges (Ponts et Chaussées), or a Red Cross worker to move around freely under the noses of the enemy.[21]

'Roger' said, 'When the messages went out on June 6th at the time of the Normandy landings, it was agreed that certain zones of France would be taken over militarily and politically. This happened in the Vercors, so that when Christine was parachuted into the Vercors, she was in liberated territory, though she did not know this. From June 6th to July 21st, the Southern Plateau of the Vercors was totally administered by us, and no Germans could get in.'

On 6 June 'Roger' was travelling around in the Hautes-Alpes. The plan he proposed carrying out on his return – a plan which had been approved and was supported by SOE, London – was to form large numbers of self-contained, autonomous groups, each numbering 15–20 men. These trained men, armed and with their own parachute grounds, were to be issued with instructions which would allow them to operate independently if necessary. 'Roger's' relationship with these groups was to help them get their *matériel*, which involved both explosives and weapons; to train them to use that *matériel*, to give them the messages which would release their action so that, whatever happened to him or to his HQ, they would still be an effective force. These were the groups he had set up, having recruited the men himself over the whole of the south-east of France – the whole rectangle of the Rhône Valley, the Mediterranean, the Italian and Swiss frontiers as far as Lyons. London approved of this concept, and 'Roger' worked on it continuously.

'Roger' said, 'Christine and I were always on the move, going from one section to the other. The object of the exercise was to make contact with people sympathetic to our cause. In seven or eight weeks, Christine met all the people I had met in two years, and we had made contact with fifty or sixty centres. These were known only to Christine and myself. Our main job, of course, was to persuade everybody who was willing to help our cause to join us.

'Christine's personality was an enormous help. She made friends everywhere. In spite of the conditions under which we lived, she managed to enjoy herself. In the most difficult situations she would sometimes be shaking with laughter. She was a completely independent human being, answerable to nobody. Many of our troops were living Maquis lives; we ourselves were with families or friends in safe-houses,[22] but never in hotels or paid lodgings. I had found a little bungalow for Christine at St Julien-en-Vercors. It was known as "la maison de Miss Pauline."

'Christine travelled light. All her possessions were stowed away in a knapsack and in a large, soft, squashy tote bag. Yet she always managed to look immaculate. We were Headquarters staff, and our job was to lend a hand with every kind of problem; so, one moment we were helping with instructions, the next planning a campaign and sending messages to London and Algiers. Also the Piats and Bazookas needed a lot of instruction, and it was important for us to stop, listen and talk.

'Then things began to accelerate so fast that there was really no time for explanations. But Christine did not need explanations. She got on with the job in hand. She was absolutely reliable and trustworthy. Of course, there were moments when we relaxed and talked; but we did not discuss each other's identity, nor did we exchange family histories. I believe that the things that most mattered to her were the fate of her mother and Poland. She had a deep belief in individual freedom, and the German attack on Poland had profoundly shocked her.

'By the time we met she had seen and endured so much. She did not believe in political solutions, and had little patience with the Polish Government in Exile. She had an ironic respect for the British Government and a deep dislike for any form of pomposity or hypocrisy. In her book, there were only "good" and "bad" people. It was a good time for getting to *know* people for the great thing was that all human barriers were down. Normally, we live with barriers erected by money, family, tradition and within the context of one's background, or in ancient parlance "to the state to which God had called you"; but in war-time, in the Resistance these barriers ceased to exist. You worked with people with whom you had a total equality of sex, age and religion.

'Christine, like all people who are suspicious of rationalization, was highly intuitive. She was a romantic and often her emotions dominated her reason. But it was because of this she had antennae, which men have not.

'Here, I believe, for the first time, Christine found perfection,' 'Roger' continued. 'There is something very special in the extent to which French cultural education has penetrated the provinces. Once I sat down with the stationmaster of some tiny place, and we talked for five hours about Proust, though I was dying of fatigue, and he had left school when he was thirteen.

'Christine had one very special friend. Paul Herault ("Commandant Dumont"), after whom my son Paul was named, had left school when he was eleven. He was a cabinet maker in Gap, and had one apprentice. He was in his mid-thirties when we met him. He looked like a Red Indian; he was a lean wiry man. He was a great mountaineer, and was unmarried.

'On the day Pétain's Armistice was proclaimed, Paul Herault said to his friends, "We're not going to accept this situation." He had never had any leadership role. Within a matter of months he became the unquestioned leader of the whole

Department, and included among those who obeyed him were the hierarchy of the Roman Catholic Church, the General Secretary of the Communist Party, the Society of Freemasons, and every single poacher in the district.

'Ever since I first met him – and Christine felt the same – if I have had a "crise de conscience" – I have invariably said to myself – and still do – "What would Paul's judgement have been?" The Germans were well aware of his activities. They knew, too, that if he were arrested in the street he would fight to the death. They also knew that his flat, where I stayed on a number of occasions, was booby-trapped after dark, and that anyone attempting to force an entrance would be blown to smithereens with everyone inside the flat.

'Paul Herault died on one of those stupid road hold-ups, like the one we had at Digne later on, and when we entered Gap we all had tears pouring down our cheeks because it was Paul's day. There was an extraordinary significance in his being a carpenter. I walked for many, many hours in the upper mountains of Gap and Mountauphin with him, and he knew more about comparative religions than any university professor. Christine recognized the purity and perfection of his personality. She could work and live with people like Paul, and she needed this level of purity.'

'Roger' had many other friends in the South Drôme.[23] Among them were a courageous young couple, Jean and Sylviane Rey, who owned a silk mill near Crest. Jean Rey was an officer in the Maquis, while his wife was an active worker, first in general clandestine operations and then, as the fighting spread, in nursing. Both Sylviane and Jean had much to do with the recruiting, training and parachuting receptions in this area.

When 'Roger' introduced his new assistant to the Reys, Sylviane was immediately captivated by the charm of 'Pauline'. 'We met,' she wrote, 'for the first time at Saillans, a little town in the valley of the Drôme. We had a camp not far from there and we had come down from the heights to make contact with "Roger", who had brought "Pauline" with him. She was still in pain from a bruised back, the result of her uncomfortable parachute landing. But this uncomfortable drop seemed to have made no difference to her love of parachuting, and I was greatly impressed by the poetic way she described her descents. She said, "I could see the parachute opening up above me like a great flower."

'"Pauline" had small fine features and unusual almond-shaped eyes, which narrowing towards the temple gave her, in my view, the look of a Siamese kitten. She did not have an aggressive, thrusting kind of beauty, but she exuded a subtle delicate charm.

'When the meeting was over and she and "Roger" were getting ready to leave, they discovered that their car refused to start. They then discovered that water had been mixed with their precious petrol. I can still see the scene as clearly as if it were happening now; there we were, the four of us, "Pauline", Jean, "Roger" and myself, sitting on the ancient cobbles of the pavement chatting away like old friends. Indeed, one of "Pauline's" accomplishments was that she created a climate of warm friendship so rapidly that one felt one had known her for ever.

'Jean and "Roger" were discussing the merits of a pistol which belonged to my husband. "Pauline" and I talked about Egypt, and about what she called her "inherent laziness" and the pleasure she took in spending so much time lying "on the sun".[24] The fact that she was able to relax so completely coupled with her almost limitless vitality and energy whenever she had a definite purpose, was, I think, as feline as her charming triangular little face, and was probably the reason that she was so well-balanced.

'Subsequently, we met quite often. Like all those who had the privilege of knowing "Pauline", I would not for the world have missed any opportunity of being with her. She was always calm, smiling and happy, and she was full of fun. She was modest about her own achievements, and generous in her praise of others.

'On 14 July 1944, "Roger", "Pauline", Jean and myself met

to attend a national day ceremony at Die. We gaily watched the arrival of a number of planes which were, we knew, about to parachute urgently awaited supplies of ammunition into the Vercors; and we were relieved and happy at the thought that the long nightmare was about to end. We had no idea that another, and more hideous nightmare, was about to take place up there.

'A little later a German reconnaissance plane flew over and sprayed us with a hail of bullets. Everyone made a dash for cover – everyone except "Pauline". She stayed where she was, and she seemed so serene and unconcerned that I wondered what all the commotion and rushing around was about.'

While Christine, 'Roger', Sylviane and Jean Rey were happily saluting the British aircraft on their way to Vassieux with their vital cargo, Joseph La-Picirella, with rage in his heart, was noting in his diary the events of 14/15 July in the Vercors.[25]

A parachute drop was expected for this day on the Vassieux landing strip, and I had asked the planes coming from London to 'buzz' the civilian population to cheer them up. In the early hours of the night of the 13th of July we had prepared for the planes to drop their containers. We then got the strip ready for the early morning drop. At 4 a.m. all was in readiness and the wireless operators were on stand-by. I went off to La Britière, returning to Vassieux at 7 a.m., and in spite of the heavy mist covering the whole plateau, made certain that everything was in readiness for the drop, checking and rechecking every detail for the reception. By 9 a.m. everything was absolutely ready.

At 9.30 a.m. we heard the drone of the engines which got louder and louder. Our planes had arrived! There were about a hundred of them flying in groups of twelve and the fighter planes circled around the Halifaxes and the Flying Fortresses. The noise filled the whole of the plateau and must have been heard in the plain of Valence. The Fortresses flew over the landing strip

while fixing their positions, and then they flew off in the
direction of Valence and returned to us flying low. Then
the parachuting began. From 72 Flying Fortresses
poured a stream of 15 to 20 containers each. It was a
splendid spectacle. A pilot dropped a packet of Camel
cigarettes encircled with a tricolour band on which was
written, 'Bravo lads. Vive la France!'

The planes which had jettisoned their cargo stooged
around waiting for the whole operation to be completed.
It was around 10 a.m. when the last Flying Fortress
vanished into the clouds. A few minutes later our trucks
arrived to pick up the harvest of containers and
parachutes. All the patriots of the Vercors were
celebrating their National Day by watching the fairylike
sight of the shower of coloured parachutes floating down
from the sky. But their pleasure was short-lived.

While they were helping to load the containers on to
the lorries, two fighter-planes suddenly appeared.
Everyone thought they were English planes, but, as
they dived towards the landing strip, the dreaded
Swastika was plainly visible. They dived to about eight
metres on the open plain where everyone was standing
and opened fire at point-blank range. This was only the
beginning of the horror. Bombs began to rain down on
the landing strip and on the village. An hour later our
communications were cut, and we were completely
isolated on our plateau. No vehicle could possibly have
run the gauntlet of that merciless fire, nor could anyone
come to our help. One maquisard did manage to get
through to us, but although we appreciated his courage
in taking such a risk, he did not think to bring any kind
of weapon.

Having sprayed us lavishly with bombs, the enemy
planes then inundated the plateau with dozens of
grenades calculated to rough up the terrain so badly that
it was unusable. To make matters worse, one of our

heavy machine guns had seized up, and in spite of the bombing, we had to take it to pieces to clean it.

Vassieux was on fire, so, of course, was my shelter. So I installed myself with a few men in a shell hole, using it as a battery post. Meanwhile, 'Paquebot' (Captain Tournissa) was organizing the western defences of Vassieux. Hardy was responsible for defending the eastern sector. In the meantime, we kept making dashes to try and grab the white parachutes which made such excellent targets.

There was no let-up in the bombing. Fighter planes and bombers flew over us in waves. As soon as one lot left, the next took its place. Their base was only 20 kilometres away as the crow flies.

Fearing that the Germans might invade the village with a battalion of parachutists, we decided, Hardy, Paquebot and I, to keep a company of Chasseurs Alpins as a reserve force hidden in the forest, leaving Vassieux to be defended by those who were already there and in possession of machine-guns and other weapons. Unfortunately, one of the heavy machine-guns was put out of action once we had fired the few rounds of ammunition in our possession. There was no way of getting any more.

During this vicious attack the enemy spared nobody. The population, livestock, houses, the roads, even the harvest, all were ruthlessly destroyed. Death and fire took over. The first objective of the enemy pilots was Vassieux. By 3.30 p.m. the church was a mass of smoking ruins, and the incendiary bombs were still falling fast.

Towards five o'clock the enemy concentrated on another target. While an ambulance was transporting the wounded to the hospital at St Martin-en-Vercors, the Germans started to bomb La Chapelle-en-Vercors. Yet, in spite of heavy casualties the people of Vercors went out by night to gather up the containers on the plateau.[26]

Even in wartime there are moments when the only important things in life are trivial ones: a hot bath, a good meal, a cup of real coffee, the sound of well-loved melody. Christine and 'Roger' both knew how to savour each good moment in its proper context. There was a great rapport between them, and together they explored intellectual uplands and made spiritual discoveries which would enrich their lives.

Christine, like 'Roger', grew to love this region of France. The Drôme, with its splendid mixture of Alpine and Mediterranean scenery, had none of the garish glitter of the smart resorts of the Midi. It was unsophisticated and resolutely old-fashioned, and its villages were real villages, each with its ancient church and market-place and cafés set about with plane trees.

In the lee of the mountains in the hot dry summers the only sounds to be heard were those made by the cicadas, and by the drone of the bees as they pillaged the fields of lavender spread like blue sheets in the sun. The breezes carried the scents of lavender and honey and of wild flowers.

There is something magical in the light of Provence. It is a distillation of gold, azure and amber, and the landscape has something of the veld, while the ruined castles and forts clinging to rocky eminences are medieval and as Italianate as the background to a Nativity by Uccello or Bellini.

Though the Germans ruthlessly took the cream of every crop, sweet melons, apricots freckled with gold, and large hard peaches were still to be found. Life went on in the farms, and in the cafés which were cool, shuttered against the harsh sunlight, and primitive with rudimentary sanitary arrangements, a hole and two pedals and a stench of urine to grab you by the throat.

Behind the bead curtains, which clicked in the breeze, the old men sat in the cafés drinking the local wine from little thick glasses. They sat, gnarled hands thumbing the greasy Belote cards or moving dominos around. They talked of crops, of the weather and of that 'other' war of 1914. That war in which the old Maréchal Pétain had so magnificently distinguished himself, that war in which he should have fallen with his *poilus* and not lived on to bring the shame of an Armistice with the Boche on his name and that of France.

The 'other' war, they said, was bad, but this was worse. It was terrible and inhuman for the enemy was all around, looking, listening, waiting to pounce. The old men often disappeared to rejoin their sons and grandsons 'up there' in the forests of the Vercors. Their knowledge of the terrain and of the mountains was invaluable.

The old men and women were a force to be reckoned with in the Resistance. Those who did not actually fight helped supply food and services, and even the presence of the enemy could not halt the progress of the seasons. The harvests, whatever their kind, were divided into two lots. One for the farm, and one for those 'up there'. It was from these little farms that the Maquis obtained some of their fresh provisions: bread, a newly butchered pig, chickens, eggs and fruit.

Even the fear of reprisals did not prevent the farmers from doing all they could to help the maquisards. The signals differed from week to week; but those who could read the code knew that a pot of white flowers on a windowsill, or a coloured rag hanging from a nail, meant that the 'fridolins' were out of range, and that it was safe to knock on a hospitable door.

CHAPTER NINE

On 8 July 1944, the morning of Christine's arrival in the Vercors, J. La-Picirella's diary of events reported a good deal of activity in the region.[1] A train loaded with merchandise attracted the attention of the 10th Company, who signalled their sharpshooters to get themselves to Crest as quickly as possible. Thanks to the help of the railwaymen, the operation took place in broad daylight, and without hindrance from the enemy.

'Thirty tons of sugar, tobacco, and sixty thousand litres of alcohol were rapidly "liberated". During the operation the place was swarming with housewives who, ignoring all danger, rushed to get at the sugar. On the afternoon of this same day, twenty-seven students and professors of the Polish Lycée at Villers-de-Lans arrived at St Martin-en-Vercors to enrol in the ranks of the FFI.'[2]

Twenty of them were sent to join various combat units, while seven others were directed to Vassieux, where, under the direction of Christine's travelling companion (Captain Tournissa) 'Paquebot', they joined the workers who were busily preparing a new Dakota landing-strip.

Christine was given certain well-defined jobs. Among them was that of acting as a kind of 'recruiting officer' among Italian units who had turned against their former Allies. Such a one was the 51st Alpini Division who engaged the Germans in a skirmish at the Mont Cenis tunnel. The Germans briskly disarmed some 45,000 Italian troops, and sent them off as a labour force to work on fortifications in France. A number of them deserted to the Maquis, and some of them found their way into 'Roger's' units.

It had not taken him long to discover just how valuable an assistant she was. Not only had she the gift of tongues, but she knew how to keep her own counsel, and to carry out her work with the minimum of fuss. 'Roger' said he never saw her anything but unhurried and unruffled. Her reflexes were trigger sharp. 'On one occasion she was trapped on a road with a German patrol in front of her. She was in full view so that any attempt at evasion or turning aside would have aroused their suspicions. She realized she had in her pocket one of the silk maps with which people who went into the field were often equipped by SOE – a map printed on very fine silk which could be easily carried or even crushed without coming to any harm. On an impulse, Christine whipped the map from her pocket, and tied it round her throat like a scarf where it looked perfectly normal, and attracted no attention from the Germans.'[3]

Every hour of every day was dedicated to preparing for the Allied landings in the south. Those concerned with this massive piece of strategy had every move worked out; but a number of key Resistance men, among them 'Roger', were provided with only the sketchiest information. This did not make the implementation of his programme any easier.

The plan, approved by Colonel Buckmaster, was to take possession of practically the whole of the south-east of France, with the exception of the coastal belt and large towns, which could easily be isolated by a complete break-down in communications.

By this time, 'Roger', in his capacity as the envoy of the Inter-Allied General Staff, had within his organization 10,000 men, among whom were mountaineers and skilled ski-instructors. He had plenty of work for them all. He had been told to cut communications with Italy, so, to the impotent rage of the Germans, his teams enthusiastically and repeatedly cut the Simplon railway route and the Rhône Valley lines. 'Roger' deployed his men brilliantly over a wide terrain. Teams of railway-workers caused troop-train derailments, while flying squads in the Drôme ambushed enemy columns.

But it was the Route Napoléon which taxed 'Roger's' ingenuity to its fullest extent. He had made up his mind that the Germans should not make use of this vital Route Nationale. Nor did they, for whenever a column of Germans appeared on this road, their progress was halted by 'avalanches' of rock crashing down from the mountain, or by gigantic obstructions in the form of earthworks created by a massive charge of explosive. When, or if, the survivors tried to find another way out, they were subjected to constant and expert fire from Sten guns used by determined maquisards hidden on the heights.

By now rumours of liberation were rife, and it was becoming difficult to prevent the maquisards from taking matters into their own hands. Every day rumours reporting Allied landings at Marseilles, Fréjus and Cavalaire sent everyone into a frenzy of anticipation.

On 5 June, 'Roger' received a message for action. He was to join his troops with those of the FFI, and specifically be Chief Liaison Officer with General Zeller in Regions 1 and 2. This meant more to 'Roger' than just setting up his own groups for action, because he already had knowledge of the activities of the other groups.

The first signal he received instructed him to put all his troops at the disposal of FFI (Zeller's forces). Then locally, within two days, he got an appeal for help in the Valley of the Ubaye. It was at this point that Zeller and 'Roger' met for the first time. 'Roger' realized immediately that his plan for autonomous guerilla groups would not fit in with the French plans of occupying strong points like the Ubaye and the Vercors. On the one hand there were the French, and on the other, SOE London. Between SOE London and SOE Algiers, and possibly between the Allied High Command and SOE, there were wide divergences of views and strategy. Clearly the French organization supported F and RF Section.[4] 'Roger's' allegiance was to F Section. FFI, London and Algiers had agreed to the Policy of Points Forts, which were envisaged in the various plans of action to be taken; but these were never revealed to 'Roger'.

The moment 'Roger' arrived outside the Town Hall at Barcelonette and saw the Tricolour boldly flying with the Cross of Lorraine, he realized that someone had jumped the gun. Excited maquisards told him that he had arrived just in time to hear that the Valley of the Ubaye was to be proclaimed a Republic.[5]

Inside the Town Hall 'Roger' met General Henri Zeller, regional commander of the FFI. To 'Roger's' consternation, he announced that the Normandy landings were definitely expected within the week. Algiers, he said, had promised that liberating columns would come to their aid within ten days. In view of this magnificent and encouraging news, he had mobilized their people in the region.

'Roger' could not quite conceal his dismay. Diplomatically, he questioned the General, asking him whether he had had further assurances from Algiers. The General turned to the group of officers about him, and asked one of them to step forward to confirm the news. This was Captain Edgar, a British officer, seconded by Algiers HQ to General Zeller's command, in anticipation of the Allied landings. He had been dropped a week previously by parachute on one of the reception grounds controlled by the Gaullist network.

'Roger' said firmly that he had received absolutely no information from London relating to immediate Allied landings. General Zeller was beginning to get a little apprehensive, and with reason, since the orders from Algiers were different from those issued by London. He suggested that 'Roger' should immediately contact London or Algiers, and tell them to send a massive drop of arms. 'Roger' realized that all his carefully laid plans were about to go to the wall, for it was crystal clear that Zeller's inadequately armed units could not possibly hope to hold out against any serious German offensive, and it was equally obvious that the Germans would instantly move in to crush any kind of open defiance.

On 15 June the German tanks and armoured cars thundered into the little town and mowed down the men who tried to stand in their way. Captain Edgar managed to destroy two tanks and an armoured car before being gunned down. Thus did the newly-born 'Republic of Ubaye' perish with 150 of its defenders. 'Roger' and General Zeller, with some of their men, made their way as rapidly as possible to the Vercors, where they established their headquarters.

Some time after D-Day, Colonel Descours, 'Bayard', had arrived with his general staff and chief radio operator, Captain Robert Bennes, 'Bob', who had come from Algiers some time before. His job was to maintain radio contact with SPOC (Special Projects Operational Centre), which was staffed by American and French officers. The British SOE contingent was headed by Colonel John Anstey, who had been responsible for sending Christine to 'Roger'. The SPOC centre at Algiers was attached to Field-Marshal Sir Henry Wilson's Allied Headquarters Mediterranean, and its aim was to make use of all the strategical and operational plans of ANVIL to co-ordinate all action in the FFI regions of southern France.[6]

Colonel Descours' radio operator in the Vercors was in constant touch with both the SPOC Headquarters in Algiers, and with de Gaulle's Headquarters in London. The object of this double radio link was to ask and to arrange for the dropping of urgently needed arms and ammunition. The maquisards were also short of soap, tobacco, pistols with silencers, benzidrine tablets, torches, batteries, woollens, food and money.[7]

London at this time was inundating 'Roger' with messages, some by radio, and some in code on the French programme of the BBC. Many of them were less welcome than the one that had come the year before when it was noticed that 'Roger', who very seldom showed any emotion or anxiety of any kind made a particular point of being present whenever the BBC programme was turned on. It was obvious that the personal messages were of the greatest significance to him. On 10th August 1943, when 'Roger' was at Montélimar, the announcer read, 'Joséphine ressemble à son grandpère, je repète, Joséphine ressemble à son grandpère.' 'That is the message I've been waiting for,' said 'Roger'. 'London promised to announce the birth of our child. If it had been a boy they would have said "Joseph ressemble à sa grandmère".'

The packing arrangements in North Africa were far from satisfactory, and 'Roger', who did not mince words, described 'Massingham's' packing as 'shocking', and reckoned that more than a fifth of the supplies dropped to him were lost, either because the parachute did not open or because the containers burst on impact. Once he reported furiously to London that, 'at last delivery parachutes failed to open as usual containers fell on house and crushed back of mother of one of the reception committee this bloody carelessness absolutely inexcusable you might as well drop bombs stop relatives did not even complain but my God I do'.[8]

It was evident that the Vercors were under close surveillance by the Germans, and that serious trouble would soon follow. The command of the Vercors, which had been reorganized on 6 June, was well aware of the lack of arms to oppose the enemy tanks which were coming closer each day.

On the evening of 20 July, 'Roger', with Christine standing by, sent this signal in the name of General Zeller:

FIERCE BATTLE FOR CAPTURE OF VERCORS IMMINENT
STOP WITHOUT YOUR HELP RESULT UNCERTAIN STOP
URGENTLY REQUEST REINFORCEMENTS OF ONE
PARACHUTE BATTALION AND MORTARS STOP REQUEST
ALSO IMMEDIATE BOMBING OF ST NIZIER AND CHABEUIL
STOP COME TO OUR AID BY EVERY MEANS.

On the 21st another SOS was sent:

MASSIVE ATTACK BY AIRBORNE TROOPS LANDED AREA
VASSIEUX IN VERCORS FROM ABOUT TWENTY AIRCRAFT
EACH TOWING ONE GLIDER STOP STRONG INFANTRY AND

TANK STOP OTHER ENEMY UNITS ARRIVING ON ROUTE
NATIONALE 75 STOP WE HOPE TO BE ABLE TO MAINTAIN
RADIO LINK.

No help was forthcoming, and Zeller, Yves Farges, 'Roger' and
Christine were involved in sending an historic signal to Algiers:

LA CHAPELLE VASSIEUX ST-MARTIN BOMBED BY GERMAN
AIRFORCE STOP ENEMY TROOPS PARACHUTED AT VASSIEUX
STOP WE PROMISED TO HOLD OUT FOR THREE WEEKS
STOP TIME PASSED SINCE TAKING UP ACTION STATIONS SIX
WEEKS DEMAND REVICTUALLING MEN STORES
AMMUNITION STOP MORALE OF OUR PEOPLE EXCELLENT
BUT THEY WILL TURN AGAINST YOU IF YOU DO NOT TAKE
ACTION IMMEDIATELY STOP THOSE IN LONDON AND
ALGIERS UNDERSTAND NOTHING ABOUT THE SITUATION
IN WHICH WE FIND OURSELVES AND ARE CONSIDERED AS
CRIMINALS AND COWARDS STOP YES REPEAT CRIMINALS
AND COWARDS.

The tragedy of Vercors was about to go into its final phase.
On the morning of 21 July, the Germans launched a full-scale
attack. Their advance was supported by artillery fire and mortars, and they were covered by planes. Waiting to repulse them
were inadequately armed men. 'Roger' and Christine remained
at Headquarters between St Aignan and St Julien-de-Vercors
until the morning of the 22nd.

In the Vercors the battle raged for three days, but the situation became so desperate for the Resistance that, on the 23rd,
the Military Commander of the Plateau, having held a council
of war with the military and civilian authorities, decided, with
black rage in his heart, to put a stop to the massacre, and
ordered the soldiers of the Resistance to disperse immediately.

Many returned to the Maquis, where for almost a month
they led a nomadic existence without supplies, and often
without water. Even so they still managed to harass the enemy

who, enraged at not having wiped them out, took a bestial and terrible revenge.[9]

All farms in the vicinity which might have provided refuge for the wounded or the hungry were set alight, the cattle were slaughtered and the women raped. While the maquisards were trying to get back to their bases, the wounded had to be moved to a place of safety. During the night of 21/22 July, Captain Ganimède, himself a doctor, and two other doctors, Ulmann and Fischer, 'Ferrier', took it upon themselves to evacuate the wounded. They found that the road to the south was blocked by the Germans.

It was then decided to make for a large natural grotto, the 'Grotte de la Luire', which was known to the locals and to Dr Fischer, who had made a mental note of its possibilities as a hiding-place. Forty able-bodied men acted as stretcher-bearers, or carried and supported the wounded through the smoking ruins of their villages, up the narrow, overgrown mountain tracks. There were sixty wounded, some of them very seriously hurt.

The ground in the grotto was strewn with sharp stones which would have cut into the stretchers, and so had to be collected and taken outside before the wounded could be brought in. Those in charge were under no illusions that the Germans would not hunt them down sooner or later. It was, therefore, agreed that those who could walk should try to escape, and rest in other caves and grottos which abounded in the mountains and whose whereabouts were known to the locals. Others chose to make for the forests.

Ganimède, Fischer, Ulmann, Father de Montcheuil of the Society of Jesus and six nurses stayed with the thirty stretcher-cases in the grotto. Among the nurses was Sylviane Rey, the friend of Christine and 'Roger'.

The days dragged by. It was impossible not to hear the noise of the machine guns being used to flush out the maquisards who had failed to get away. There was no food or water. Drops of moisture were gathered from crevices in the damp walls of the grotto. By this time the Germans were 200 metres from the improvised field-hospital, so that it was impossible to get out for a breath of air.

On the afternoon of 27 July, shots sounded a few metres from the opening of the grotto, then bullets ricocheted on the rock where the Red Cross flag had been erected. For three days the doctors had been looking after three wounded soldiers of the Wehrmacht. At the sound of the shots, the German patients dashed out shouting, 'Don't shoot, don't shoot!' They then explained that the only other occupants of the grotto were the wounded, as well as some women and children, and the doctors. The German soldiers insisted that they had been well treated. The SS Adjutant did not bother to hear them out. 'Out, all of you,' he ordered, 'out with your hands above your heads.' The stretchers were dragged out. The wounded were terrified, but relieved to be taken from the stench of the grotto into the warm summery air. Under the stained bandages, feverish eyes peered out at the enemy. Within seconds a hail of machine-gun fire had killed eighteen of the wounded patriots.

The following day twelve more wounded were shot down. Dr Fischer and Dr Ulmann were executed in Grenoble, as was Father de Montcheuil. Captain Ganimède, having been interrogated at length by his captors, managed to give them the slip and to get clean away. The six nurses in the grotto were deported. Sylviane Rey, having escorted her wounded men to a place of safety, finally managed to make her way back to Crest.

When it became obvious that, through sheer weight of numbers and equipment, the Battle of the Vercors was going to be lost by the Resistance, General Zeller and 'Roger' decided that there was nothing to be gained by letting themselves be slaughtered or captured. 'Roger' was responsible for his entire network and so, while the battle was raging, on the morning of 22 July, a small party composed of General Zeller, Christine, 'Roger' and Captain Antoine Sereni, 'Casimir', the faithful 'Albert' and a few maquisards scrambled down the rocky slopes of the mountain. The main members of the party then went by car to the Col du Rousset, and walked down the mountainside – because the firing was incessant and intense – to the valley of the Drôme. After crossing the valley they went up to St Nazaire-le-Désert and then eastwards towards Serre and to Savournon, one of their large reception centres. There they got a lift which took them for ten miles, after which they crossed the Route Napoléon to a little village, Monnetier-l'Allemand, where the local baker convoyed them, in an exhausted heap, to their base at Seyne-les-Alpes. They had covered seventy miles in twenty-four hours of almost non-stop walking.[10]

Secret agents were not encouraged to look upon any dwelling place as a permanent home when they were in the field, and certainly 'Roger' was too disciplined to infringe any rule laid down in the unspoken, unwritten code that governs the actions of a careful spy; but when at last he and his companions stumbled into the familiar and hospitable little house of Monsieur Turrel, who ran the local *bureau de tabac*, his relief was indescribable. Once he had made sure that his flock was in good hands, he flung himself down on his bed, and instantly fell asleep.

There was no time for anyone to brood over the horrors of the Vercors massacres. Almost immediately, 'Roger' and Christine were deep in their multifarious activities. 'Roger' knew that, as soon as the routine work and interviews were over, he must take to the road again.

Meanwhile, two new arrivals from Algiers had just been parachuted in to join his team. These were Major Xan Fielding and Captain Julian Lezzard, a colourful South African character, known to his intimates as 'Lizzy'. This irreverent and witty man, who was as averse to discipline as was Christine, was also cast in the heroic mould, though he concealed his courage under a cloak of flippancy and mockery. Unfortunately, 'Lizzy' was badly injured on landing, and Fielding stayed with him until help, in the shape of a young medical officer, arrived and took over the patient. As soon as Xan Fielding knew that 'Lizzy' was comfortable and would receive proper medical treatment, he went off to Seyne to Turrel's, where SOE had told him to contact his chief.

Naturally he had no idea of what 'Roger' looked like, and was astonished to discover 'a smiling young giant whose coltish appearance was exaggerated by sloping shoulders and an easy resilient poise. These features, to begin with, obscured the contradictory qualities of leadership and modesty with which he subsequently impressed me. It was only later that I realized that for him Resistance was tantamount to a new religion, which he had been practising and preaching with remarkable success for over three years.'[11]

Fielding's first impression of Christine provides the most lifelike pen portrait of a woman he admired so much that he dedicated his admirable book, *Hide and Seek*, to her.

> Ever since the military collapse of her own country, Poland, she had been employed on the most hazardous missions in other parts of Occupied Europe; and this reputation of hers had led me to expect in her the heroic attributes which I fancied I immediately divined beneath her nervous gestures and breathless manner of speech. Not that she in any way resembled the classical conception of a female spy, even though she had the glamour that is conventionally associated with one; but this she preferred to camouflage in an austere blouse and skirt, which with her short, carelessly-combed dark hair and the complete absence of make-up on her delicately featured face gave her the appearance of an athletic art student . . . She and 'Roger' were an imposing pair.[12]

Fielding, at that moment, did not have time to get to know Christine better, since she left almost immediately for Italy, where her mission was to make contact with the partisans.

'Roger' was loath to let her go so soon after her exhausting walk from the Vercors; but he need not, he says, have worried, for she went off gaily with her light dancing step, her eyes fixed on the grandiose rosy peaks of Les Evêchés and the Grande Scolane, which formed the backcloth of the pretty little village of Seyne-les-Alpes.

As always, Christine was to have many dangerous adventures before she joined 'Roger' again. It was his impression that Christine did part of her journey on the back of Gilbert Tavernier's motor-cycle. At all events, she crossed over into Italy, where she contacted and assisted the only 200-strong partisan group in the Italian Alps capable of upsetting the Germans, since they held the heights between the two main roads leading from France into Italy.

This mission was accomplished at great personal risk at the time of a large-scale offensive during which Christine had to pass the German lines in difficult and dangerous mountainous country. She then went on to influence the Russians serving in the 'Ost' or 'Oriental' Legion of General von Weise's Nineteenth Army.[13] Thanks to her powerful arguments and the impressive way she presented them, hundreds of these men deserted, and joined local Resistance units.

Not the least strange of Christine's adventures, and one which again showed her power over animals, took place one night when, trying to avoid a German patrol, she took refuge by the roadside under some bushes. The Germans, who were using police dogs, passed close to her hiding place. An Alsatian dog pounced on her. Quietly, without uttering a sound, she put her arm round his neck. He sniffed at her, licked her hand and then lay down beside her. She heard his handler whistling him in for a long time; but the dog did not budge. He remained with her that night and subsequently refused to be parted from her. 'Roger' said, 'The dog remained with us in the Hautes-Alpes until the Liberation. He was totally devoted to Christine and, though he was a trained "frontier" dog, when he was with her he behaved like a puppy.'[14]

Part of Christine's success as an agent was due to the way in which, when necessary, she could get into the skin of the part she was playing. During the time she was in the Italian Alps, she had decided that her role would be that of a naive and trusting young peasant girl. Twice she was caught by the Germans, but so convincing was her act that they let her go.

The third time she did not get away so easily. A frontier patrol caught up with her when she was guiding an Italian partisan to the nearest Maquis. Christine was told to put her hands above her head. Unhesitatingly, she obeyed. She had a live grenade in either hand. In idiomatic German she informed her captors that, unless they let her and her companion go free, she would blow them all up. It was obvious that this was no idle threat, so the Germans shambled off, leaving her and her Italian to make good their escape.

Christine's next important mission concerned the subversion of the garrison in the fort held by the Germans at the Col de Larche. This mountain pass, also known as Le Col de la Madeleine, dominated the surrounding terrain, and was used by the enemy to send reinforcements to Digne. When Christine discovered that the fort was manned mainly by Poles from Western Poland who had been mobilized into the German Army, she decided to climb up to the fort to talk to them.

The Col is 1,994 feet high, and the approach to it is through dense larch forests which cover the flanks of the precipitous mountain side. To reach the Col was a tremendous feat of endurance. According to 'Tatar'[15], Christine left Gilbert Galetti's[16] house by gazogene, and drove through the mountains to the spot chosen to take her through the forest. She left the road for a narrow track which curled upwards. She walked steadily on, though she was often halted by the difficulty of walking through a deep litter of larch needles. Sometimes, she slipped and fell, and the sharp needles scratched her legs.

It took her a day and a half to get to the top of the mountain. Once in the lee of the fort, Christine managed to attract the attention of her Polish contact there, and then with a loudhailer, she spoke to the Poles in their own language. The upshot was that she persuaded them to desert the Germans and come over to the Resistance. Had she failed to do so, German plans for an attack in force over the Col de Larche might have succeeded and held up the advancing American columns. Thanks to Christine's action, the Maquis were able to blow the road up, so preventing enemy motorized troops from passing through.

While Christine was doing her marathon climb to the Col de Larche, her chief was in serious trouble. On 11 August 1944 – three days before the Allied landings in the south – 'Roger', with some of his team, set off for Apt where they met some recently arrived senior French officials who handed over a large sum of money to 'Roger'.

Two days later 'Roger', accompanied by Xan Fielding, now rather grandly renamed 'Armand de Pont Levé', a French officer called Commandant Sorenson, code name 'Chasuble', and their driver Claude Renoir, son of the painter, returned from Apt to Seyne.

Xan Fielding was filled with admiration at the unconcerned manner in which 'Roger' and his group travelled through enemy territory in their Red Cross car, though he had been told, of course, that they were all equipped with 'genuine' false papers. So security-conscious was 'Monsieur de Pont Levé' that, having checked through his own personal documents and papers, he decided that he was carrying far too large a sum of money, and that, were he to be questioned, so much currency would certainly arouse suspicion. So, dividing the sum into three, he gave some to 'Roger' and some to 'Chasuble':

Our drive [wrote Fielding] was so uneventful and
enjoyable that I had to keep on reminding myself that I
was not on holiday but on active service – a fact which
escaped me at each of the delightful villages, where,
while 'Roger' conferred with each of the local leaders, I
drank a glass of wine outside the café under the plane
trees.[17]

This feeling of euphoria was to be of short duration. On the
return journey to Seyne, the party in the Red Cross car was
about to drive into Digne when an Allied air-raid began, and a
posse of 'Mongols'[18] surged around the 'official vehicle'.
Instantly, 'Roger' told Renoir to drop his passengers as soon as he
could, and then to drive round and meet them on the nearest exit
road to Seyne. The party split up and were careful to avoid the
'Mongols', who were still scurrying officiously around. As soon as
the all-clear sounded, 'Roger's' men rejoined their car which, as
arranged, was waiting at the rendezvous. Congratulating themselves on a narrow shave, they set off again in the direction of
Seyne.

Hardly had the car moved off, when they saw a road-block
ahead. It was manned by another posse of 'Mongols', who
brought their car to a stop. 'Roger' and Fielding produced their
impressive official-looking documents and the slit-eyed Cau-
casians, being unable to read them, decided to let the Red
Cross car proceed on its way.

But just as they were moving off again, Renoir saw a German
car drive up close behind them. It was a Gestapo car, and from
it jumped a number of armed SD men.[19] With them was a
young man in German uniform who directed a stream of questions at Renoir. These were simply routine questions, and it
looked as if he was satisfied with the answers and would allow
the party to continue on its way. Before letting them go, however, he insisted on checking 'Chasuble's' and 'Roger's' papers.
Finding them in order, he turned to 'Armand de Pont Levé'.

Though French was Fielding's mother-tongue, it was a long
while since he had spoken it, and he was conscious that it was
halting and rusty. The German officer, after interrogating
Fielding, asked for further papers. Algiers had supplied him
with a number of other documents which, with his money, were
in the wallet he handed over to the German. The date on one
of the cards had expired. The German ordered Fielding to get
into his car and, just as he was about to obey, asked him to
identify his travelling companions. Fielding said he had no idea

who they were – just two men to whom the driver had given a lift. Fielding then got into the Gestapo car, numb with horror at the way in which the situation was developing.

In the meantime, the German had told 'Roger' and 'Chasuble' to empty their pockets and produce their wallets and other identity papers. When Fielding was summoned from the Gestapo car to join his friends it was clear that something had gone terribly amiss.

The German said, 'You say these two men are total strangers to you?' 'Never seen them before in my life,' replied Fielding. The next question was addressed to all three men. 'Can you gentlemen explain how it is that the money each of you was carrying individually belongs to the same series? . . . No, don't answer. I don't want to hear any more lies. Into my car, the whole lot of you.'

Claude Renoir had been allowed to go, and hurried back to Seyne with the bad news. The others were driven to the Central Prison at Digne, according to 'Roger', 'a dreary barracks of a place'. After being made to stand for several minutes facing a wall in the courtyard with their hands above their heads, they were pushed into a basement cell, furnished with 'a half-filled bucket of excrement and urine, and four dirty bunks in two tiers, one of which was occupied by a recumbent figure.'[20]

For twenty-four hours 'Roger' and his friends remained without food or water. Finally, they were taken from prison, pushed into a car and driven to the local Gestapo Headquarters called the Villa Rose. Here they were again locked up until they were taken out, one by one, for interrogation. This process lasted for some time and, though Fielding was punched in the face and in the kidneys by one of the interrogator's strong-arm boys, the three SOE men, much to their relief, were again reunited. At once they decided to try and escape as soon as night fell. They had no chance, however, to put this plan into action, as they were driven back to Digne prison, and locked up in another, larger cell.

Early on the morning of the arrest of 'Roger' and his men, Christine returned to Monsieur Turrel's house at Seyne, to find a grim-faced Renoir with Dr Jouve and other members of the team discussing the possibilities of raiding the prison at Digne. Christine knew that it would be hopeless to try and get them out by force; so she decided to go to Digne as quickly as possible to see what she could do to save 'Roger'.

'Roger's' 'pianist', 'Auguste', had transmitted the news of the capture of 'Roger' and his friends to Algiers, and was awaiting their reply, when Christine came to one of her lightning decisions. 'Hold everything,' she said, 'and wait until I get back before trying to do anything.' With that, she wheeled out an old bicycle and, thinking back with gratitude to Andrew's cycling lessons, she wobbled off on the twenty-five miles' journey to Digne.[21]

From the moment she had heard of her chief's plight, her one thought was to get him out before the Gestapo discovered his identity and that of his companions. She was well aware that, if they discovered that the random spot check described by Renoir had brought about the capture of the famous and much wanted British secret agent 'Roger', he would be shot out of hand, and the others with him.

One of Christine's friends, John Roper, was in Briançon, where he heard the news of 'Roger's' plight. Rapidly he collected 'such gold coins and other monies as were available, and got down to Seyne by motor-bike to see if there was anything I could do. I arrived at the Turrels early. They and the locals (Jouve, Claude Renoir and some others) were sitting with their heads in their hands. They said Christine was about; but they did not know where. I sent a boy off with the gold to the place where she was most likely to be in Digne, and sat down with my head, too, in my hands.'[22]

Christine, arriving in Digne, wanted to make certain that 'Roger' had not been moved elsewhere. She made her way to the jail. A good many people were milling about, and Christine had no trouble in slipping through the gates. As she walked round the grim building she hummed, very loudly, the tune of 'Frankie and Johnnie', a song which she and 'Roger' liked, and which they had often sung together to keep their spirits up when walking or driving. For some time she circled the prison without the slightest response to her signal; then, all of a sudden, she heard someone singing, quite loudly. 'Roger', much to his companions' surprise, was bellowing out their tune in his stentorian voice.

Christine's next move was dictated by circumstances. Posing as 'Roger's' wife, she questioned the local gendarmes as to the possibility of being allowed to visit her 'husband', who, she said, had recently been picked up in a wave of arrests and taken to Digne prison.

Nobody seemed much interested in her troubles until she came across an elderly gendarme, who took pity on the fragile young woman with a dark scarf tied, peasant fashion, around her face. She asked him how she could get permission to take her 'husband' a few necessities such as soap and shaving things.

'Food would be more useful to him,' said the gendarme, 'but I can't help you to see your man. The only person who can is Albert Schenck, an Alsatian, who acts as liaison officer between the Prefecture and the Gestapo.' Christine demanded an interview with Schenck and came straight to the point.

'Capitaine, the Gestapo have arrested three very important Allied agents. One of them, 'Roger', is my husband. I, myself, am a British agent and a niece of Field-Marshal Montgomery. You may have heard that the Allies have landed not far from here, and that very soon they will be here. It will then go hard with those who have killed my husband and his friends. You can be perfectly certain that if our soldiers don't shoot you, the men of the Maquis, who are on the spot, will do it, if only to avenge the execution of so many of their comrades.'

Albert Schenck was aware that the war was going very badly for the Germans, and there were informed rumours that the Allies were close. Christine seemed to him to be a very resolute young woman. He decided to call her bluff.

'I can do nothing for you myself, but there is a man, a Belgian called Max Waem, who is "officially" the interpreter for the Gestapo. He *could* help. He might make a gesture, though gestures of this kind are dangerous, and they cost a great deal of money. However, if, as you say, you are so well-connected, there is no doubt that you will be able to get the necessary cash to make Waem's intervention worthwhile. I know for a fact that he wouldn't be interested in any sum under two million francs.'

'I see,' said Christine coolly. 'Well, Capitaine, you fix a meeting with Monsieur Waem, and I'll see what I can do.'

At four p.m. on 14 or 15 August, Christine sat waiting in Frau Schenck's flat for Waem. Time, she knew, was running out for 'Roger'. The door opened, and in came Waem, a small, mean little man with aquiline features; he was in Gestapo uniform, and carried a revolver. For three hours Christine argued and bargained with him and, having turned the full force of her magnetic personality on him, she told him that the Allies would be arriving at any moment, and that she, a British parachutist, was in constant wireless contact with the British Forces. To make her point she produced some broken and useless WT crystals.

Waem put his revolver down, and poured out a cup of coffee from the pot Frau Schenck had brought in. It was real, and not *ersatz*, coffee. Christine and Waem drank their coffee in silence. Both were thinking hard. Waem was obviously impressed by Christine's air of authority.

'If I were you,' said Christine, 'I should give careful thought to the proposition I have made you. As I told Capitaine Schenck, if anything should happen to my husband, or to his friends, the reprisals would be swift and terrible, for I don't have to tell you that both you and the Capitaine have an infamous reputation among the locals.'

Increasingly alarmed by the thought of what might befall him when both the Allies and the Resistance decided to avenge the many murders he had committed, Waem struck the butt end of his revolver on the table, and said, 'If I do get them out of prison, what will you do to protect me?'

'I promise,' answered Christine, 'in the name of the British authorities that if you do get my husband and his friends out of prison, everything will be done to protect you and Capitaine Schenck from the vengeance of the maquisards. Also, I will see to it that, as soon as the Allies arrive here, they are informed of the important service you have rendered them. As you can imagine, under such conditions, they will not imprison or punish you and, for my part, I will see to it that you are protected in every way.'

Christine could sense that she had won a reprieve for 'Roger', but knew that she must get hold of the money at once, before Waem could change his mind. She broke off the interview, got back to Seyne as rapidly as she could, and asked 'Auguste' to contact Algiers without delay. Her message to Brooks-Richards was that two million francs was the price of 'Roger's' life, and that of his companions. She added that there was not a second to lose. So certain was she that Algiers would respond to her SOS that she went off at once to arrange for a dropping ground for the container with the money.

Christine saw Schenck on 14 or 15 August. The money was parachuted in on the night of the 16th. Christine put the rubber pouch containing the money under her bed and slept fitfully until dawn, when once again she took the all too familiar road to Digne.

In the meantime, John Roper at Seyne had troubles of his own. With his Commanding Officer incommunicado, he urgently needed another source of authority. He, therefore, set off to walk down the hill from Seyne intending to make a detour round Digne, as he had done before, and pick up transport on the other side. He had walked a little way when Christine overtook him in a car and told him, briefly, that an escape was planned, and that, in consequence, Digne would be on the highest alert; that he would have no chance of getting through. She took him back to the Turrels and left him, while she went off again to Digne.

In their cell, the prisoners were becoming increasingly

gloomy. Though 'Roger' was never convinced that they were going to be shot, he knew that their lives were certainly at risk. During their four days' incarceration they were, says 'Roger', 'interrogated briefly and rather incompetently. Most of the four days I slept, and I think the others did too. A stool-pigeon had been put in with us, and that stopped us talking.'

At noon on the fourth day, the prisoners were given their first decent meal since they entered the prison. As they ate the hot vegetable soup and crusty country bread, they exchanged thoughtful glances, wondering what this change of diet could presage. Fielding and 'Chasuble' were convinced that it was to be their last meal on earth.

Late that afternoon, Max Waem, wearing the tunic of the Wehrmacht and a cap with the skull-and-crossbones of the SS, marched into their cell, and roughly ordered them out. They followed him apprehensively, for they thought he had come to escort them to the football ground which was used as a place of execution. Revolver at the ready, he marched his prisoners across the courtyard and to the prison gates. 'Just outside the prison gates,' said 'Roger', 'my memory is that Christine was actually waiting in the car. It was one of our cars, a *traction avant* Citroën. Christine was in the front seat. Waem, Xan and Sorenson scrambled into the back, and I got in and drove away. As we left, Christine said, "It's worked."'[23]

The car roared off at top speed, and 'Roger' made for the outskirts of Digne. The escapers found themselves once again faced by a road-block; but this time the sentries, impressed by Waem's presence, signalled them to proceed. They drove into the open country. At a certain spot, 'Roger' stopped the car and Max got out, motioning Fielding to follow. They were on the edge of a steep embankment. They slithered down the bank to the river, where Waem ripped off his cap and uniform jacket. He and Fielding then dug a hole. When it was deep enough they pushed the jacket and cap into it, replaced the soil and heaped stones and pebbles over it. Then they got back into the car, and 'Roger' drove off again.

At approximately 11 p.m., they stopped outside an isolated barn. Inside were the wireless operators and John Roper.[24]

There was tremendous excitement at this reunion. An hour after the arrival of the 'prisoners' and their escort, everyone listened to a BBC broadcast in which, among the 'messages personelles' after the news, were included the two sentences, '*Roger est libre. Félicitations à Pauline.*'

The return to Seyne was triumphantly celebrated by all those who had sweated out the hours until the return of Christine and her party. There was also the good news that the General commanding the American Armoured Task Force had taken Digne a few hours after the departure of Christine and 'Roger' and their companions. Havard Gunn, who had also been aware of the developments in Digne prison, had driven frenziedly to St Tropez in his tiny Peugeot car to try to get the Americans to hurry to 'Roger's' rescue; but they were too late; and it was, as he said later, 'unquestionably Christine's operation'.

True to the promise made in the name of the British authorities, Capitaine Schenck and Max Waem were given safe refuge until further plans could be worked out for them. In spite of warnings and advice given him, and on his own responsibility, Schenck, who had been given the two million francs by Christine, returned to Digne, where he was killed, doubtless for the money. Frau Schenck, who was in great danger, was not abandoned by Christine and 'Roger', but was given financial assistance to enable her and her two children to return in safety to Alsace.

Max Waem was later taken to the British Parachute Brigade at Nice, and 'Roger' then arranged for him to be sent in the protective custody of the British Field Police to Bari in Italy. Waem, later, volunteered for military duties in the Far East, and was finally sent as an internee to Australia. He returned, safe and sound, to Belgium, and nothing more was ever heard of the two million francs Christine had handed over.

The last word about the Digne operation must go to Xan Fielding. He wrote:

For Christine who had of her own volition risked the death penalty, the responsibility must have been almost beyond endurance. For apart from the consideration of personal courage, she had also to decide whether from the SOE point of view her action was wholly permissible. As an individual she would not have hesitated to barter her life for the lives of three others. As an agent, however, she was obliged to assess the value of those lives against hers; and if hers proved to be worth more, it was her duty to keep it.

In the assessment she made it was 'Roger's' life that weighed the scales in favour of the decision she took; for in comparison 'Chasuble's' and mine were of small account. Had not 'Roger' been arrested with us, Christine would have been perfectly justified in taking no action if action meant jeopardizing herself. Indirectly, then, I owe my life to him as much as I do, directly, to her.[25]

CHAPTER TEN

Almost immediately after the Digne rescue operation, the three men who had come so close to death, parted and went their separate ways. Major Fielding was posted out of the French theatre of war, and sent to Greece to join Donald Hamilton-Hill's outfit, where his knowledge of Greek and previous experience in Crete made him an invaluable asset.[1] Commandant Sorenson slipped quietly away to take up a senior position in French Military Intelligence in Paris. John Roper had already left on his motor-bike to go back to the north to get on with the business in his part of the world.

Christine and 'Roger' immediately set off together to look for Allied Headquarters, where they hoped they might be useful. They found an SOE liaison officer, a Captain Banbury, who took them to Sisteron, where they made contact with the American GSO1, who introduced them to the General commanding the Armoured Task Force.

Curt to the point of rudeness, the General dismissed 'Roger's' suggestion of help in a familiar locality with access to men whom he knew well, saying that he was not interested in the activities of private armies. Then, turning his back on his guests, he pretended to be absorbed in his maps.

'Roger' hurried Christine from the tent. He did not trust his temper and remained silent until they reached Gap, where the Germans were surrendering wholesale. The American Army, approaching the town along the Sisteron road, reached a high point above Gap and spent the night there. When Christine and

'Roger' joined them, they were preparing to fight a battle to capture the town. Meanwhile, the Secretary-General of the Prefecture in Gap, Serge Barret, a member of 'Roger's' Resistance group, had persuaded the Germans that all was over, and had incarcerated the enemy troops in the local cinema where they were guarded by Boy Scouts.

So the tanks rolled down into Gap at dawn to find no resistance at all, and the Boy Scouts proudly handed over their prisoners. 'Roger' and Christine, who had come down with the troops, took part in a great celebration, with no loss of life. It was strongly rumoured, however, that the Germans were preparing a counter-attack, and would come over the Col Bayard.

At this point 'Roger' and Christine were introduced to an American Captain, who said, 'Hell, I've got 2,000 Poles in German uniform right here in the valley.' Christine and 'Roger', remembering the Col de Larche, and the readiness of the Eastern members of the Wehrmacht to join the Allies, said, 'Let's have a look at your prisoners.'

After luncheon they accompanied the American Captain to where the Polish prisoners were encamped in a large field. Christine was given a megaphone. She went closer and addressed the prisoners in these terms:[2]

> 'We are threatened here by a German counter-attack.
> We hope that you will be the ones to lead us against the
> Germans. But you cannot do this wearing their uniform,
> and we have no others to offer you, so you will have to
> go forward *torse-nu* (naked to the waist).'

There was a moment of silence. Then the Polish soldiers tore off their uniform jackets and waved them in the air, clearly indicating that they were prepared to follow Christine.

Beaming, the American Captain said, 'Well, what about that? But we shall need the approval of the General.' So the three of them went to find him. His reception was again frigid. He intimated that 'Roger' and Christine had been interfering with his prisoners, and threatened to put them under close arrest unless they left immediately.

This left a nasty taste in everyone's mouth; but that same evening 'Roger' and Christine met a prominent American war-correspondent to whom they told their story. 'Whether as a result or not, I do not know,' comments 'Roger', 'but at all events, very shortly afterwards, the General left that theatre of war!'

'Roger' and Christine then drove down to the Headquarters of General Patch and reported to him for further duties. He received them very cordially, and told them that his main anxiety was the protection of his left flank on the west of the Rhône Valley. He asked 'Roger' and Christine to act as his liaison team with the Resistance forces in the Departments of Gard, Ardèche and Rhône, right up to Lyons.

They left the General's headquarters with official orders, picked up some of their friends in the Vaucluse, and travelled up through the three Departments to St Etienne and Lyons.

Just before 'Bambus' (Havard Gunn) left for Nice to organize a group called Liaison France-America, he and Christine went up into the mountains to talk with a group of maquisards. 'I was astonished by her physical fitness and reserves of strength,' he said. 'The going was pretty tough, even for a man, but Christine showed no sign of strain, though I'm sure there must have been moments when her muscles ached like fury. We did not talk much, but I got the impression that she was sad, and that she did not envisage the future with any pleasure.'

That final journey of 'Roger' and Christine through the loved familiar landscape was nostalgic, for it was clear that their partnership was soon to be dissolved, and both knew that never again in their lives would there be a relationship equal to that which had united them. Although they had not known one another long in terms of time, the very nature of their work together, of the dangers and stresses they had experienced together, had made it possible for them to skip the usual barriers and to reach, in one bound, the high peaks of mutual trust, friendship and understanding. They were well aware that this was the end of the work they had had to do together. They realized that others were taking over who might well not have the love and sympathy of their French friends. They realized that the barriers were already being re-erected.

Always 'Roger' would remember Christine. Not only because she had saved his life and given him back to his family and to his work; but because her conduct had proved that some of his theories about the gallantry of human beings in peace and in war were valid and true.[3] As for Christine, her affection for 'Roger' transcended everything except what she felt for Andrew. The sweetness and nobility of this man had opened new horizons in her mind, and she was grateful to him for his silent understanding of aspects of her own character which she revealed to no one else.

The stolid city of Lyons was in a state of complete euphoria when 'Roger' and Christine arrived. The Germans' power had been broken, and column upon column of dejected-looking soldiers and batches of prisoners shuffled past the windows of the houses whose inhabitants had, for so long, known only fear and sorrow.

Christine had the great pleasure of meeting Sylviane Rey again. 'I teased her affectionately about the number plate of the jeep in which she was being driven around,' said Sylviane Rey, 'it was MI5. We had luncheon together, talking like parakeets the whole time, and then walked to the Place Morand where "Pauline" suddenly discovered a run in her stocking. She was upset, as nylons in those days were as rare as snowballs in summer. Luckily I was in a position to provide her with a new pair. She was delighted. She was very feminine and fastidious about her appearance.'

Christine and 'Roger' met many old friends and acquaintances in Lyons. One of these was Peter Storrs,[4] whose first encounter with Christine had been a casual one at Sidi Ferruch in Algiers. Now he was to get to know her better.

'When we first met,' he said, 'I was a very minor creature

attached to Allied Headquarters in Algiers. Douglas Dodds-Parker was the head of our outfit, and Francis Brooks-Richards was my superior. At that time Christine, though very attractive in a slim, greyhound sort of way, was just another agent. It was only after we discovered what had happened to 'Roger' and his assistant in the Vercors that we in Algiers took a personal interest in this remarkable pair, and their welfare and survival became a matter of concern to all of us. After I heard what had happened at Digne, I was filled with admiration for Christine's audacity and courage.

'I landed with the Allied Forces via Corsica on a beach near St Tropez. Contact was made with "Archduke", our man on the spot. He found us a car and driver. The car had a parachute painted on the door. My job was to go round the country seeing the agents for whom we were responsible. We drove across the country to the Ardèche, and then to Lyons, where I had been instructed to set up a headquarters pending the arrival of Francis Brooks-Richards. This was to be an Anglo-American report and depot centre for the reception of massive quantities of arms and ammunition hidden in caches all over the country-side. I set up this depot in a large private house which, to the best of my remembrance, was in the Avenue de la Grande Brétagne. In due course, agents like "Roger" and Christine, reporting back on arms, equipment and people with whom they had been involved, began to trickle in to HQ.

'It was an interesting moment, for it was then that the *cloison étanche* (iron partition) came down between the RF and F Sections, and I had dealings with many colourful SOE charac-ters, including the legendary Tony Brooks.[5] We all spent much of our free time together, and I soon discovered that Christine was a true European, in that I am sure that she had fought for European values. Although she was loyal and uncomplaining under the most trying circumstances with a leader she trusted, she did not suffer fools gladly, as I well remember from the terse signals sent to us in Algiers from the field. She was cer-tainly the bravest woman I have ever known.'

This was the last time Christine would enjoy the life of action and danger that stimulated her. She was soon to be stripped of the protective male comradeship that meant so much to her. Also she was to lose the security of being part of an organization which, while it might demand her life, saw to it that, while she belonged to it, she would be kept, clothed and fed and provided with adequate transport and methods of communication, so that in the field she never had to worry about the mundane problems concerned with day-to-day living.

Having reported the completion of her mission to the regional HQ in Avignon, Christine met John Roper at the Crillon Hotel in Avignon. A few staff officers told him to hang about until he had been 'de-briefed'. He was not attracted by this prospect, so, after a night or so, she, John Roper and a brother officer borrowed a Resistance car and drove to Lyons where they hitched flights to London via Paris. Christine's few possessions had been sent in error to Northern France, and never caught up with her. Her sole luggage was a cumbersome moneybelt stuffed with gold coins which she had been unable to distribute to the maquisards for whom they were intended. She had no money of her own.

Christine knew this was the end of an important phase in her life, and she left France feeling vulnerable and lonely. Always in the past there had been the comfort of coming back to Andrew. This time there was nobody to greet her. All through the long Saturday of her first night back in London, a penniless Christine walked the streets of a grim grey city licking its war wounds.[6] This nocturnal vigil was a shattering experience, for it was then that she began to fear the future that might lie ahead. She did not turn to her religion for help, for the simple reason that, though she had been brought up as a practising Catholic, her faith was not strong enough to support her in time of stress, and this lack of spiritual confidence when she so desperately desired to *believe*, added to her sense of desolation.

It was at this period that Christine and John Roper met again and consolidated what was to be an important friendship for them both. 'It was then,' said John Roper, 'that she came to stay for the first time in my flat in London, which was temporarily tenanted by my aunt, the late Mrs Ffrench. Christine and I seemed to be more or less based on that flat during the next couple of months or so, before we went to Italy in preparation for the abortive Polish mission. I well remember the two of us going round to Baker Street to discuss that business. Above all it was in those days that Christine and I came to know one another well.

'She was, as is well known, very attractive to men. In my case, however, this was not the principal point. Although it would be absurd to say that her beauty added nothing, the fact of the matter was that she was an exceptional person with an exceptional capacity for friendship. She was friends with my current girl-friend, and she was friends with my aunt. But in neither case should this be confused with, for example, the kindness she showed to my cook, who adored her. Ours was a straight friendship. One may wonder why, after all these years, I still think of Christine as so close a friend, when I probably never spent the equivalent of a full month in her company. All I can say is that, if it had been I who had been killed, instead of her, I can honestly say that I think she would today still think about me in the way I think about her. The quality of her friendship was unique.'

Andrew Kennedy was in Italy, hoping that, somehow, Christine would be able to join him. He, too, had had his fair share of vicissitudes. He had first gone to Bari in Italy, from thence to Monopoli and so to Ostuni, to the Polish School of Parachutists, who were hoping to be parachuted into Poland.

He had had many adventures, not the least of them being an unexpected audience with Pope Pius XII in Rome. Andrew became a part of this audience only because a Dakota, flown by an Australian pilot, had landed in Poland and picked up a group of people, including General Tatar, then playing an important part in the Home Army, and a Colonel Hancza.

As this was the first time anyone had come from Poland and

from the Home Army, the Polish Ambassador in Italy had arranged for the General and the Colonel to have an audience of His Holiness. But the General had to fly to London for consultation, and the Colonel, who could speak nothing but Polish, asked Andrew to accompany him.

'We entered by the side door,' said Andrew, 'and were greeted by a guard of honour formed by the Swiss Guards. Then we went along enormous corridors to an antechamber filled with wonderful paintings. Here a Church dignitary, a Cardinal I believe, was waiting for us. He showed us round, and guided us into the room in which the Pope was sitting. It was a tiny room with white Louis XVI chairs. His Holiness sat on a plain chair. We walked in, kissed his ring and the conversation began. This was between His Holiness, the Polish Ambassador and myself, as the poor Colonel was unable to participate. I was very disappointed that the Pope would not follow our suggestion that he should say something about the cruelties of the Nazis against the Jews and the Poles.

'I was very bitter and forgetting all protocol said, "But, Your Holiness, surely the Catholic Church cannot just sit and watch these horrible atrocities being carried out – people being killed, taken away and gassed, without saying something?" His Holiness said, "Well, my son, you must understand that the Catholic Church must look after the whole world, and not one country only."'

In Italy Andrew was attached to Force 139. This section of SOE was under the command of Colonel H. M. Threlfall,[7] who in the autumn of 1943 had been transferred as Deputy Head under Lieutenant Colonel Perkins, to the Central Europe Section. This section covered Poland, Czechoslovakia and Hungary, and Force 139 had been formed early in 1944 to carry out operations to the Continent, all of which were now mounted from the Mediterranean theatre.

'The establishment of the main SOE base at Bari in Italy led to the possibility of expanding operations initiated two years earlier into Occupied Poland. Like the Free French, the Poles were represented symbolically in London by a government in exile, and together they formed the largest elements from Occupied Europe fighting on the side of Great Britain. Poland thus remained at war with the Axis. SOE operations into Poland, which had begun with one isolated mission in 1941, were conducted directly by the Poles themselves. It was their special pride to organize their parties independently of British control. These missions were even transported to Poland in aircraft flown by Polish crews. Until the very last days of the war no British mission, as such, landed on Polish soil, and the operations technically organized by SOE from Britain to Poland were essentially conducted by the London Poles acting as an independent power.'[8]

Andrew's peregrinations had taken him to London in 1943 where he met 'an important Pole named Nowak, one of the top couriers between the Polish Government in London and the Underground in Warsaw.

'I asked him to lunch with me,' Andrew recalls, 'and explained to him that in my view it was vital to have a British Mission in Poland who could report directly to the British Government. I explained to him that the British, being insular, distrust foreigners and trust only their own people. Nowak agreed with me. He said, "I know, as you do, that it is essential for us to have such a mission; but General Sosnkowski and the 7th Bureau have set their faces against the idea of having such a mission."'

From early 1941 until 1943, special operations to Poland in support of the Polish Secret Army were carried out by SOE from the United Kingdom. By the autumn of 1943 this Northern route had become difficult and dangerous to fly, and in September 1943 six aircraft were lost in two night operations. This was because the route to Poland traversed the night fighter and AA belt stretching from the north of Denmark well down into the centre of Germany, designed to protect Berlin from the heavy raids which Bomber Command were, at that time, carrying out. The loss of the six aircraft decided Bomber

Command, then in charge of Special Operations, that the Northern route to Poland was too dangerous, and it was suggested that Poland might be approached from the South.

The first proposal was to fly from North Africa, and, indeed, at the end of 1943 the Polish Flight of a number of Liberators and Halifaxes left the UK and as '1586 Flight' took up its position in North Africa. The first operation with three aircraft took place in early December; but bad weather forced them back. A further attempt later in December brought three successes.

It was then decided to transfer the Polish Flight to Southern Italy and as soon as the airfield at Brindisi became available for special operations the move began. By the beginning of January 1944, 1586 Polish Flight was established at Brindisi with 148 Squadron, RAF, together forming 334 Left Wing. All subsequent special operations to Poland, with the exception of one large American sortie from the UK to Warsaw at the time of the rising, were flown from Italy.

The transfer of flights from the UK meant that a signals station with direct communication to Poland had to be set up in Italy, together with the necessary Polish operations staff, and towards the end of 1943 this was established at Latiano. It was also decided that the many recruits for the Polish Sixth Bureau, who were coming forward from the newly formed Polish Forces in the Middle East, should attend this school. This training school, known as *Impudent* under Major Kritzer, was established at Ostuni. The operational base known as *Torment*, first under Captain Granowski, then under Major Jazwinski, was established at Latiano. Both stations had British liaison officers with them to conduct all necessary negotiations with the British Military Authorities to fit the Polish Special Operations into the general framework of SOE activity in the Mediterranean.

The Anglo-Polish base in Italy was concerned only with the training and operational side of Special Operations to Poland, and its direct communications with that country were limited to matters of vital importance. All questions of policy or intelligence were dealt with by the Sixth Bureau in London, which had its own W/T links direct with the field, a privilege enjoyed by the Poles alone among the Allies. There was also a direct Polish link between London and the Latiano base.

This set-up was finalized by the arrival of Colonel H. M. Threlfall and Major I. C. Klauber at the end of March to take up their duties. A headquarters was established at the little fishing port of Monopoli, halfway between Bari and Brindisi. 'I suppose you could call it picturesque,' said Colonel Threlfall, 'if you could ignore the poverty and disease which were rife. Andrew was one of my officers, and for a time was my Liaison Officer at the Polish Training School at Ostuni. I had heard about Christine, and when it was suggested to me that I might be able to use her, I was sure that someone of her calibre would be of great help.'

Monopoli did not offer much in the way of excitement or entertainment. The most imposing building in the town was a Cathedral dedicated to St Nicholas, which housed the pride and joy of the local inhabitants. This was a Madonna known as 'The Madonna of the Rafts', because a portrait of the Virgin Mary had drifted miraculously into the harbour on a raft. The Madonna was surrounded by an extensive collection of ex-votos, not the least impressive being an inscribed plaque thanking the Madonna for her miraculous intervention in preventing any single one of the sixty bombs which the British dropped on Monopoli from exploding.

Christine, having been given an honorary commission in the WAAF, was kitted out in RAF uniform and flown on 21 November 1944 to Italy. John Roper, who was also going to be involved in the Polish mission, flew out with her, and their excitement when they saw Andrew's little Opel in the street, and managed to track him down, was intense.

'It was a tremendously moving and emotional moment when I saw Christine again,' said Andrew. 'She looked terribly thin, she was a bag of bones; but she was glowing with success. She did not stay long. She had some plans to implement, and left again almost immediately for England. But even those few days with her were marvellous.'

On 1 August 1944, the Polish Secret Army in Warsaw, joined by the civilian population, rose against the Germans when the Russians were entering the suburbs across the Vistula, and appealed to the Allies for supplies of arms. At the request of the Polish Government in London, the Chiefs of Staff telegraphed to MAAF, asking for their opinion on the practical aspect. After major consultations, the plan was rejected and the fifteen aircraft, which were to have been flown to Warsaw on 4 August, were diverted to other Polish targets. Four failed to return, and two crashed on landing.

Balkan Airforce, which controlled all Special Operations from the heel of Italy, declared that operations to Poland during the moon period were too dangerous, and stopped them. Their reason was the German night fighter and radar belt protecting the Silesian industrial area. Thus, at the time of Poland's greatest need, not only was help to Warsaw refused, but all support of the Secret Army cancelled.

This situation did not last, for after the Commander of Force 139 had pressed the urgency of the situation, Balkan Airforce allowed the Polish Flight to operate to Warsaw. In the meantime, the Polish Prime Minister, Mr Mikolajczyk, who was in Moscow, appealed to Marshal Stalin for help from the Russians. This help was seemingly promised; but, in fact, no Russian help was forthcoming until the night of 13 September.

The second stage of help for Warsaw, a really large scale effort, resulted from renewed approaches from SOE, and desperate appeals by the Polish High Command direct to the Chiefs of Staff, and by the Polish Government to HM's Government. A telegram from Lord Selborne, Minister of Economic Warfare, responsible for SOE, to Mr Churchill, resulted in the re-examination of the position of MAAF, and in the allocation on 13 August of two squadrons of Liberators from 203 Group to supplement the efforts of 334 Wing.

Colonel Threlfall said, 'I had a great deal on my plate at the time. I was trying to help the Poles in every possible way. It wasn't always easy, and I was often the ham in the political sandwich. I had to pass on to the Poles the decisions, good or bad, made in London. At the same time, I was fighting like a tiger to get them what they wanted.'

Andrew said, 'Colonel Threlfall, who was a good friend to the Poles, in his usual efficient way helped to persuade the British authorities that the British Mission to Poland was necessary. I must say I have tremendous criticism of the Sixth Bureau, who only agreed to these missions when disaster had struck, and Warsaw was in flames.

'From Brindisi the planes started dropping on Warsaw. The cry over the radio from Warsaw to us was . . . "Supplies, supplies!" In the beginning, the pilots did return. Usually, they left at 5 a.m., returning at 5 p.m. The flights covered Italy, Yugoslavia, where the planes were battered by anti-aircraft, then across Hungary with more anti-aircraft potting at them; and then Poland, and dropping down over Warsaw, Warsaw in agony, Warsaw in flames. Most of their drops were useless as the supplies fell into enemy hands, because Warsaw was already divided into dozens of little enclaves. The loss of aircraft was colossal, and tragic. Many Allied pilots, having dropped supplies on Warsaw and finding that their planes had been severely damaged, were not allowed by their allies, the Russians, to land in their territory, although it was only on the other side of the Vistula.'

It was just after the Warsaw Rising that Christine came back to Monopoli. This had been a terrible moment for them all. Christine and Andrew and the Polish contingent had to stand by powerless while their country was being crucified. They were glued to the radio by day and by night and Christine was in tears because of her inability to help. This was probably one of the most traumatic moments in her whole life in the field, for the sufferings of her country had ravaged her emotions as nothing else had ever done. Her burning desire was to leave immediately for Poland.

There were to have been three teams in the Polish Mission. Only one team went; the second team to which Andrew, John Roper and a great mutual friend, Paul Harker, belonged never went; nor did the third, nor did Christine, whose role would have been as courier and liaison between the teams.

Colonel Threlfall said of her, 'I thought Christine a most interesting woman. She had brains, energy and drive. Unfortunately, we had no cut-and-dried job for her, but she was helpful in filling in the Polish background for the British officers we intended dropping into Poland.'

Christine was living in the Imperial Hotel at Bari, while the men were housed, for security reasons, in extreme discomfort in cold houses in the hills behind Bari. Andrew and John Roper shared a bedroom, but the latter saw little of his friends because he was working hard at Polish, and also had certain communications responsibilities twice a day which the others did not.

Almost from the moment Christine arrived the weather began to deteriorate. It was the worst winter Italy had experienced for over thirty years. As the weather got worse and worse, Christine and Andrew grew increasingly frantic at the news from Warsaw. Then Christine's mission to Warsaw was definitely cancelled, and she was desperately disappointed.

It was at this point that the close and passionate relationship between Christine and Andrew began to change. In spite of their mutual pact to lead independent lives, both protagonists in this long-drawn-out affair of the heart were deeply jealous and possessive of each other. Christine had never really forgiven Andrew for having become too deeply involved in London with a mutual friend, who wanted to marry him.

Andrew, too, had his grievances. Christine had often flicked his male pride on the raw, and her circle of admirers had many times driven him from her side. Yet, so great was their love and need of each other, that each time they were reunited, all peccadillos were forgotten in their mutual happiness.

Andrew, realizing how disappointed Christine was at the cancellation of her mission to Warsaw, decided to arrange a little break for them both. So much had happened in the past few months that he wanted time to re-establish their old intimacy, and to test Christine's reactions to a new plan he had formulated.

Christine said she was ready for a rest. Andrew had made all the arrangements. He found pleasant rooms in a picturesque little hotel which he thought she would enjoy. He had so much to tell her, and he had hardly had an opportunity of congratulating her on her exploits in the Vercors and in Digne. It was the first time Andrew had ever seriously contemplated relinquishing his liberty, and he was anxious to share this decision with Christine, whom it most closely concerned. He hoped that when she heard the good news she would revise her own somewhat jaundiced views on matrimony. So it was with an even keener sense of anticipation than usual, that he awaited the coming of his beloved.

At last she arrived. Even now, Andrew finds it difficult to talk about this brief and shattering meeting. Christine announced that she was leaving immediately for Cairo where she had been offered employment in the Movement Section of GHQ, MLF. This was the reason she gave for cancelling their holiday, and, if it was not the true one, Andrew was never given any other.

There is no doubt that the scene that took place on this occasion terminated their perfect physical rapport. The psychological bond between them was too deep ever to be endangered; but, from that moment onwards, Andrew considered he was no longer bound to Christine as a lover; and, although they were very often together later on, the savour had gone, and nothing was ever quite the same between them physically after the disastrous episode in Bari.

Christine's reasons for hurting Andrew as she did are inexplicable, for her own defection on this occasion did not make Andrew any less important to her. He was all that was left to her from the shipwreck of her life. He and she were exiles, and when she returned to him it was, and would always be, a coming home.

*

On 1 January 1945, Christine Granville was awarded the George Medal for having saved the lives of two British officers. For having saved that of Major Sorenson, the French awarded her the Croix de Guerre avec Etoile d'Argent. The citation by General Zeller which accompanied this award is reproduced on the page opposite.

Christine's most urgent desire was to return to Poland, and when she heard that her friend Patrick Howarth, whom she had last seen when they had been all together at Monopoli, had been posted to the British Embassy in Warsaw in 1945, she sent him a telegram urging him to get her a job there. 'I immediately went to our Ambassador,' said the faithful Patrick, 'and told him about the legendary Christine. Bill Cavendish-Bentinck was quite agreeable to employing her. I was delighted, and wrote off at once to the Foreign Office. But they would not play, so I had to tell Christine, who was very disappointed.'

In October 1944 in the Continental Hotel, Cairo, Christine met a young man who was later to become a close and trusted friend. Major Michael Dunford was an Englishman, a radar specialist and an expert in communication. He had travelled widely in the Middle East, had worked for the British Council, and in a civilian capacity had been involved in the press and public arrangements work for the Teheran Summit Conference in 1942.[9]

Major Dunford was instantly attracted by Christine, but at the time of their meeting she was still too spiritually bruised and uncertain of the course her future would take to enter into any kind of serious relationship. Also she hoped that, somehow or other, she and Andrew might eventually be able to paper over the cracks that had jeopardized their relationship after the Italian fiasco.

Christine remained in the Movements Section of GHQ, MEF until she was demobilized. She relinquished her commission in the WAAF on 11 May 1945 and was given a gratuity of £100. A grateful Government then forgot all about her.

- E X T R A I T -

de l'ordre général n° 211

Le Général Z E L L E R Henri, Commandant la

16° Région Militaire

C I T E

A L'ORDRE DE LA DIVISION

Madame G R A N V I L L E   Christine .

".De nationalité britannique, descendue en parachute sur le
" Vercors au mois de juin 1944, a montré jusqu'à la libération un courage
" remarquable, une volonté magnifique, une endurance surprenante.

" Parcourant toute la zone alpine, a réussi un grand nombre de
" missions de liaison périlleuses.

" Chargée plus spécialement de prendre contact avec les soldats
" polonais servant dans l'armée allemande, a conduit à la reddition la gar-
nison du col et du village de LARCHE.

" Est parvenue à sortir de la prison de DIGNE, un officier bri-
" tannique et deux officiers français tombés entre les mains de la gestapo."

LA PRESENTE CITATION COMPORTE L'ATTRIBUTION DE LA CROIX DE
GUERRE 1939-1945 AVEC ETOILE D'ARGENT.

Fait à Montpellier le 30 novembre 1945

signé: ZELLER.

EXTRAIT CERTIFIE CONFORME :

Paris, le   0 8 OCT. 1974

L'Administrateur civil B A L A T
Chef du Bureau des Décorations,
Commandant BATTINI,

SOE, the 'firm' which had always promised her some form of security, was no less cavalier in the treatment of its brilliant agent. Her own country, Poland, made no gesture to honour one of its most heroic women. Christine had immense difficulties in getting even the most humble employment. She had many loyal and dedicated friends; but so great was her pride and her anxiety to be independent and a burden to nobody, that she kept to herself the bitter anxieties that were beginning to haunt her. She had always found it difficult to discuss her private affairs, and even her closest friends had no inkling of the true state of her finances.

John Roper was in Germany until 1946, when he entered the Foreign Office and was put, by good luck, to work for the resettlement of the Polish Armed Forces. It was at this point that he became conscious that Christine's chief concern after the war seemed to be the troubles and problems of other people, rather than her own.

In the summer of 1947 he was posted to Athens; but before that Christine had come back from the Middle East, and he saw as much as he could of her. It was then that John Roper, together with a group of friends, began to look into the possibilities of finding Christine what they thought would be an appropriate job. The group contained two junior Ministers in the then Labour Government, and at least two future Conservative Ministers. They had several ideas between them; but they all came to nothing when Christine made it perfectly clear to John Roper that she was not prepared to accept any job which was offered to her on the basis of what she had done in the war.[10]

Christine now began to lead a peripatetic existence. For a while she joined Andrew, who, having finished his war in Hamburg, had gone to Bonn where Paul Harker was Agricultural Chief in the Military Government, and had co-opted Andrew onto his staff. Finally, Andrew decided to make his home in Germany. This decision was totally unacceptable to Christine, and she went off alone to the South of France, where she had an aged and indigent aunt, whom she felt it was her duty to support. She took a job with an estate agent; but after a while she came to the conclusion that it was not the kind of work she wanted. Her life was insecure, and she wanted security.

Andrew said, 'If Christine had had a private income she would have bought a place in the South of France. Maybe near Vence, or somewhere up in the hills. It would have been an old Provençal *mas* with no damp course or electric light. She would never have furnished it fully; but she would have acquired a family of stray dogs, cats and birds, and for the rest of her life she would have lain in the sun. She was, as I have said, a salamander for the sun.'

Ironically, Christine could have had such a property had she accepted the legacy of a house in London. This house was left her in the will of an English friend. At his death, his executors contacted her and told her that she was now the owner of this property. For mysterious reasons of her own, she refused this bequest, and when questioned by Andrew as to why she had thrown away a chance of security, she merely smiled, and refused to discuss the matter.

She returned to London hoping to expedite her naturalization. As nothing seemed to be happening on any front, she began job-hunting in earnest. It is difficult to understand why a woman of Christine's calibre should have sought for, and accepted, such uncongenial and menial occupations. But it would appear that at this juncture she was in a state of deep depression; there seemed to be a complete fragmentation of her personality; the reality of ordinary life was so unsupportable and the battle-fatigue she felt so intense, that for a time she seemed to have lost the will to struggle back to the light.

Though her appearances were sporadic, she continued to see her friends. Her sense of humour was unimpaired, and she entertained them with thumbnail sketches of the people she met in the course of her various jobs. For a period she was employed as a telephonist at India House; but the switchboard made her nervous. She then tried her hand at selling clothes in one of Harrods' dress departments. But her blunt and honest comments when plump clients tried to force themselves into garments that were too small for them, did not endear her to them, or to her direct superiors.[11]

Her next venture was to take over the care of the linen room in an hotel in Paddington. This was a surprising departure, since Christine was anything but an adept seamstress, and the piles of towels, sheets and pillow-cases which were in constant need of repair depressed her. So she took her congé.

A friend introduced her to the manager of a chain of hotels. At her first interview, he told her that only *married* women could be considered for this post. Christine asked whether this rule applied equally to men. The answer was in the negative. 'Right,' said Christine, 'give me a list of your unmarried managers, and I'll marry one of them.'

At last her most ardent wish was fulfilled. She was granted British naturalization. She had not been eligible because she did not have the necessary residence qualifications in the UK. Aidan Crawley was one of her sponsors, and as an MP and Junior Minister, carried great weight; but, at a time when everybody in responsible positions knew people who were clamouring for citizenship, it was decided to put up several Poles with outstanding war records together. Christine's was the first name on a list of ten Poles, whose cases were considered personally by the late Chuter Ede, then Home Secretary. He had no hesitation in ruling that their services to Britain fully justified overlooking their lack of residence qualifications.

In 1947 Christine was given her passport. She was delighted and felt sure that it marked the beginning of a new and more promising era for her. Clutching the new document, she went happily off to Geneva to be interviewed for a job with exciting prospects. Her future employer examined her new passport with care.

'Sorry, Mrs Granville,' he said, returning it to her. 'You're not British, you're just a foreigner who has managed to get a British passport.' Certainly the statement on the front page of the document was invidious. Christine was known as a 'British Subject by Naturalization. Certificate of Naturalization No. AZ

20605 Home Office. G 26822 of 23/11/46.' 'All those numbers made her feel like a convict,' said Andrew.

This was the last straw. Christine wanted to get out of Europe. Always she longed for the sun and for wider horizons; and when her friend Michael Dunford wrote and said that he had decided to settle in Nairobi, and liked the country very much, Christine, to his astonishment, wrote back and said that she would join him there. The thought of escaping from the grey, dismal postwar world of ration-books and queues to the great sun-washed spaces of Africa was an appealing one.

He did not really believe that she would come. To his great surprise, she arrived in Kenya a few weeks later; and in July 1947, they went to the Belgian Congo together on holiday. Immediately she began to regain something of her verve and joie-de-vivre. Michael Dunford was the right companion for Christine at this crossroads in her life. His kindness and understanding helped her to recover her health and equilibrium. She and he had many tastes in common for they shared a love of nature and of travel.

Christine had applied for permission to reside in Kenya, but for reasons which are obscure 'the Colonial authorities at that time were being obstructive in granting permission. On 20 July, she was told that her OBE and George Medal were to be presented to her by the then Governor of Kenya, Sir Philip Mitchell. In typical Christine fashion she made it known that she would not accept the honours from the representative of the King if, at the same time, His Majesty's Government regarded her as unsuitable to reside in Kenya.' Michael Dunford remembers that when she took this attitude, the administration was thrown into dismay, and it was only due to the intercession of the Commander of the RAF in Kenya, who appealed to her as an ex-WAAF officer to accept the awards for the honour of the service, that she went to Government House and was presented with the medals, and was granted permission to stay in Kenya.[12]

Sometime after Christine came to Nairobi, Mervyn Cowie,[13]

himself a legendary character in a land of 'characters', appointed Michael Dunford to look after a new organization he had launched. This was the Kenya Tourist Travel Association (KTTA), and was a forerunner of the East African Tourist Association.[14]

Soon afterwards Christine's passport was, once again, a bitter bone of recrimination against the authorities when she tried to get a job in Kenya.[15] The Kenyan Civil Aviation advertised for a ground stewardess, and Christine went to apply for the job. The official who examined her passport asked her why she was travelling on a British passport, and why she did not return to her own country. This so infuriated Christine that she returned to the official's office the next day with a lawyer, and asked him to repeat his statements.

Christine then cabled to Andrew to meet her in London. When she arrived she was still in an icy rage. She had determined to return her decorations and the passport, which she had been told was similar to that issued to 'second class citizens'. Andrew calmed her down, and they went to see Aidan Crawley again. He was very sympathetic, and took the matter up immediately with the Home Office. As the result of his intervention Christine and all those who had been in the same plight as herself became known as 'Citizens of Great Britain and the Colonies'.

Aidan Crawley and his wife, the writer Virginia Cowles, were devoted to Christine and were always happy to welcome her to their home. 'She was quite lovely,' said Aidan Crawley, 'fragile, small-boned and delicately made. She was very attractive to men but was not much interested in women. She often vanished but she always told us where she had been. She was kind and intelligent and she hated hurting people. This was finally to be her undoing. She was stifled by an ordinary climate of living. When I discussed bravery with her, she laughed and said that when she was in the field and a crisis occurred, she was generally too busy to be frightened. She was an eminently practical soldier.'

Christine returned to Kenya to resume her life there. Photographs taken of her at this time show her looking relaxed, pretty and serene. She was obviously content and enjoying her life. There were times when she seriously considered settling in East Africa. Although she and Michael Dunford travelled extensively in the Middle East and stayed for a while in Cyprus, where he bought land to build a holiday home, she was always relieved to return to Nairobi.

Andrew was never far from her thoughts, and she wrote to him constantly of her plans and projects. She wanted to build a house in the sun and she wanted him to join her. She was enthusiastic about the good new life they could build up together in this bright new world. Andrew, however, had no intention of living in Africa. He said, 'I was just beginning to enjoy all I had missed during the long years of war. The idea of boiling my brains in the sun did not attract me in the least. What should I have done out there away from the cultural life of Europe? Besides, knowing my Christine, I was sure that she would begin to miss her friends and want to come home.'

Christine was irritated by Andrew's uncooperative attitude about her plans for their future. Michael Dunford, waiting patiently on the sidelines, sensed, for the first time, that Andrew's hold over the woman he loved was weakening.

At this moment Andrew had a car crash which put him on the critical list. He was unconscious in hospital for a long time. When he finally opened his eyes, the first person he saw standing at the foot of his bed was Christine.

CHAPTER ELEVEN

It took some time for Andrew to recover, but his magnificent constitution stood him in good stead, and he was able to leave hospital earlier than expected. During his convalescence he and Christine had made many plans for the future. She had decided not to return to Kenya, but was uncertain as to what direction she wanted her life to take.

Francis Cammaerts said, 'There was a short-lived placement agency run by a naval officer. It had been started to help SOE people to find employment but was only allowed to operate for a few months. In that time Christine had been offered a variety of jobs, but none of them suited her. I often asked her what kind of a job she wanted, but she could only tell me what she did not want to do. She definitely did not want to become involved in administration, she did not wish to undertake a long course of training; but she did want to work with people.'

Though Christine was not much interested in money for herself, she wanted to repay Andrew for the financial help that had been always so readily available to her when she needed it, so, when she received a letter from a friend she had met in Cairo and who had emigrated to Australia, she was delighted at the thought of being able to put an interesting and profitable business proposition in Andrew's way.

Michalof, a Russian serving in the Yugoslav Army, had joined the Allied Forces before emigrating to Australia. In his letter to Christine he told her that he had joined forces with a partner called Norman Hamilton, an Australian pilot with wide connections. They had set up in business together, and thought that there was a great deal of money to be made by obtaining automobile agencies.

Andrew thought this an admirable idea, and wrote immediately to Michalof asking for his specific requirements. It was then arranged that Michalof and his partner should come to Europe to discuss the deal in detail, and, while Christine returned to London, Andrew busied himself getting the necessary contacts and connections in Germany.

Both Christine and Andrew had high hopes that this new business would be the basis of a profitable undertaking which would take care of all their financial needs. Andrew concentrated all his efforts on preparing the ground for the visit of the partners from Australia.

During the next few months there were constant meetings between Christine and Andrew, both in London and on the Continent; and in 1950 they made a wonderful pilgrimage through France, stopping everywhere and meeting Christine's old friends. The climax of their journey was a commemorative ceremony in the Vercors at which, much to Andrew's pride, Christine, whom they always called 'Miss Pauline', was the heroine of the hour.

By the time Michalof and Hamilton arrived in Europe, Andrew had arranged for them to have the agencies of several well-known automobile manufacturers, among them the famous Porsche motor car. The meeting was a great success. Andrew and Christine entertained their guests handsomely and, though the expense of doing so was very high, Andrew felt sure that he was making a sound investment both for Christine and himself.

Although the partners returned to Australia glowing with optimism, two unforeseen events ruined all their plans. Severe recession had just set in so that the sale of fast, expensive European cars was strictly limited; furthermore serious differences of opinion between the partners had arisen.

This news, when it reached Christine and Andrew, was a

great blow. To make matters worse, Andrew had invested all his available capital in expenses connected with launching the new project; and Christine was stricken with guilt at the thought that she had brought this mishap on Andrew by introducing him to Michalof. As by now both she and Andrew were extremely hard up, she could think of nothing but going to Australia to try to sort things out between the partners.

It was at this time she resumed contact with her first cousin, Stanley Christopher. 'She rang me up one day out of the blue. I had not seen her for a very long time. She suggested a meeting. I was delighted. She was still the same Christine, though she seemed to have lost a little of her "brilliance". Even so, she was more *alive* than most people. We had a kind of family reunion, and talked about Poland and our relations. Christine had loved her mother deeply and any mention of her upset her terribly. So we did not mention poor Stephanie.

'I knew, of course, that Christine had done very well during the war; but she refused to talk about the war years, or what had happened to her since we had last met. It was difficult to find out what she was actually doing, or what she hoped to do in the future. My wife and I had the impression that she was not very happy or settled. She appeared to cling exclusively to her Polish friends.'

This was not so. Christine saw many of her English friends, among them Francis Cammaerts and Patrick Howarth. Whenever John Roper was in London on leave, he made a point of seeing Christine; and when Andrew was in London, he and Christine 'popped in' on their mutual friends. They were an entertaining couple, and were always sure of a welcome whenever they appeared. There is no doubt that there was an aura of mystery about their movements, due in part to the lack of continuity of their visits, and also to the fact that Christine seldom discussed her private affairs, and never her financial worries.

Christine certainly did spend much of her time with her Polish friends. She was trying to find her way back to her roots, and she sought them among her countrymen. They, like herself, were beginning to realize that the world they had known before the war was buried forever beneath the rubble of the Polish cities destroyed by the enemy. Christine felt very strongly that the Poles in exile *were* her people, and their welfare her concern. It was natural that she should turn to them for reassurance, since the golden haven she had hoped to find in England had failed to materialize.

It was at this time that Christine had an accident which left her severely shaken. She was knocked over by a car at Hyde Park Corner. While she suffered no broken bones, she was badly bruised in body and spirit. Accustomed to being in peak physical condition, she was upset to find how this stupid accident had not only slowed her up but left her feeling depressed and confused.

'Pussi' Deakin, then living in Oxford, often saw Christine in the flat of mutual friends in Park Street, London. 'Pussi' was curious about many aspects of Christine's past, but she charmingly refused to answer any questions and inevitably changed the conversation. Once 'Pussi' asked her for details about the Digne Operation. 'Best leave it alone,' said Christine. Julian Dobski, who was in touch with all the Poles in London as he had been with them in Cairo, was worried about Christine, and tried, time and again, to find her congenial occupation. He was unsuccessful.

One day 'Pussi' arrived at Park Street to find Christine there in a very sombre mood. Julian Dobski said to 'Pussi', 'You talk to her. Find out what she really wants to do with her life. She's just drifting at the moment.' 'Pussi' tackled Christine. 'We're none of us as young as we were. The moment one's shape becomes slightly blurred, one has to begin thinking seriously of one's future. What are you going to do with yourself? You can't go on drifting from one job to another. Why don't you marry Andrew? He's been sitting around waiting for you. He won't wait forever.'

Christine burst out laughing. 'I'm not worried about my contours, blurred or otherwise. You should know that. As to my future, I'm going to do a lot of travelling from now on. You see. I'll send you sackfuls of pretty postcards.'

Christine had suddenly hit on a way of getting to Australia without incurring any expense. She would be a stewardess. Thus she would kill a number of birds with one stone. She would see the partners in Australia and straighten out the mis-understanding that had arisen between them. At the same time she would travel and see the world.

It was, therefore, with feelings of considerable relief that she was at last getting to grips with the problem that she approached the Shaw Savill Line to see whether they had any vacancies for stewardesses. She was taken on with no difficulty, issued with a Seaman's Record Book and Certificate of Discharge No. R 549975; and, with a large new suitcase, she made her way to the Victoria Docks on 12 May 1951, to join the 17,851 ton Shaw Savill liner *Rauhine* on her maiden voyage to Australia and New Zealand.

Leaning over the rail as she approached the gangway, was 41-year-old bathroom steward Dennis George Muldowney. He saw a slim young woman weighed down by a heavy case. He ran down and took it from her; and this meeting was the beginning of an association that was to end in tragedy for Christine Granville and Dennis George Muldowney.

The journey did not begin auspiciously. Christine, a second-class stewardess, was told that she was expected to wear the ribbons of her decorations, if any, when on duty. The dazzling array of ribbons she put up, albeit unwillingly, immediately aroused feelings of suspicion and jealousy among certain members of the crew. Some of the male Navy personnel resented the fact that they had never had the opportunity of acquiring similar gongs, and were resentful of the fact that they had been awarded to a *foreigner*, and to a woman to boot.

Some of the stewardesses were soured by Christine's air of breeding, by her reserve and by the fact that the passengers clamoured for her services. The undersized Muldowney was instantly fascinated by Christine, and, having become her self-appointed protector, tried to smooth her path as much as he could. She was deeply grateful to him, for she had never before encountered petty spite, unkindness and malice, backed with a strong determination to humiliate 'the foreign woman'.

While Muldowney was congratulating himself on having secured the attention of a war heroine, who was at the same time an attractive and charming woman with a sense of humour and a kind heart, she saw him plainly for what he was: another pathetic, scruffy, lame dog to add to her menagerie of seedy pets. But, though she did not know it, this was a new species. This was a dangerous animal.

Born in Wigan of Irish parentage, Muldowney had been raised in an orphanage, and had spent most of his adult life at sea. There had been breaks during which he had tried his hand at being a chauffeur-valet. He married young and begat a son, but was divorced by his wife in the child's infancy. Muldowney was a Catholic. He was sentimental and vain. He was also a schizophrenic, subject to sudden bursts of violent rage and to periods of sullen brooding. He had little to say for himself. He had never before met anyone so dazzling as Christine Granville and he fell violently and obsessively in love with the quiet woman with her shiny little nose, white teeth and reverence for life.

Christine was lonely. She had no friends on board, and her fierce pride would not allow her to show her distress at the way she was being victimized and humiliated. Muldowney was like an eager mongrel, helping her, protecting her, worshipping her. She became attached to the odd little man, and was genuinely grateful to him for his efforts to make her first voyage less difficult. When she discovered that he had no family, and dreaded being ashore because he was so lonely, she was overcome with pity, and determined that she would ask her friends to help this man who had done so much to help her.

Although Christine succeeded in seeing Michalof in Australia, it was too late for her to bring about a reconciliation between him and Hamilton; whatever the reason for the break-up of the partnership, it put an end to Christine's and Andrew's hopes for a secure future.

On 16 September 1951, the *Rauhine* slipped into Victoria Docks. Christine had wired Andrew to meet her. Their reunion was a joyful one for Christine had been away for four months. She looked well and tanned. She introduced Muldowney to Andrew, explaining that, but for his kindness, she would have long since been eaten by the fishes. Andrew understood immediately that Christine would want him to help her pay her debt of gratitude, and offered to take Muldowney back into London with them. From this moment he was introduced to their circle, and made much of. Nobody ever had any clear idea as to why Muldowney always tagged along in the wake of Christine and Andrew. Few of them paid much attention to the weaselly little man who never opened his mouth. Patrick Howarth remembers having tea with Christine at the White Eagle Club where she introduced her new friend to him. 'After a few abortive attempts at making conversation with him, I forgot all about him. He never made the slightest impression on me.'

But Muldowney *was* impressed. By Christine's intelligent, cosmopolitan, and grand friends. By a way of life he had glimpsed only from the servants' hall and from the Stewards' Square. True, many of Christine's closest friends were impecunious exiles, but they had breeding and a glittering past that seemed to furnish them with inexhaustible memories of great houses, shooting parties, horses and servants.

After each voyage Christine reappeared with Muldowney, and finally her friends became puzzled with this incongruous friendship. Countess Puslowska knew Christine well, having stayed in the same pension with her in Zakopane in 1939. She said, 'Christine was not with her husband at that time. I don't know where he was; but I do know that, in any case, she liked her independence. She was the sort of person who had friends from all walks of life. Society, *le beau monde*, as such did not amuse her. She liked a mixture of politicians and intellectuals.

She liked to be stimulated. She was bright, vital and full of odd ideas on life. She was fun. Muldowney was a curious little creature. I used to see him around with her at the White Eagle Club. It was obvious that he had a frightful inferiority complex. We used to wonder why he was with her. He did not come from her *milieu*, and he was definitely *not* her type. Christine always had a wide choice of stunning men, so why did she waste her time with a goblin like Muldowney?'

As time passed, and Muldowney became a constant in Christine's life, Andrew, though he was grateful to him for the care he had taken of her on the voyage, began to find the bathroom steward was becoming an unmitigated nuisance. 'Dennis was always around,' said Andrew. 'He was unbelievably thick-skinned. He was small, dark, insecure, and he was a mass of obsessions and neuroses. We thought him a dangerous simpleton; but none of us had any idea of just how dangerous he was going to become. He was like a dingo dog trotting at Christine's heels.

'One evening, we were all going to the movies. Muldowney and I were walking ahead of Christine and a friend. I have an odd habit of clicking my fingers quite loudly as I walk, and I was doing this unconsciously when Muldowney peered up at me, his ferret face crumpled with fear. "Andrew, stop, stop, there's something wrong with me. I can hear the most terrible noises in my head!"

'I said nothing, but walked on clicking merrily. A little later he clutched my arm. "Andrew, the clicking is getting louder all the time." Impatiently, I said, "Come on, Dennis, pull yourself together, man. Nothing, but nothing, is going on in your head. I'm making the clicking noises like this," and I snapped my fingers under his nose.'

Francis Cammaerts said, 'Muldowney was completely out of his depth in Christine's circle. I thought him a pathetic bore, but Christine explained his background and his futile, miserable life. She told me he would not leave her alone. She said the only thing she could do to escape from him would be to pretend to sign on for another trip, and then to get as far away as she could until he came to his senses. I rather agreed with her, as I could see that he was becoming intolerably clinging.'

Christine, herself, became increasingly worried by Muldowney's possessiveness and fits of jealous rage. At the same time, his total dependence on her pandered both to her power complex, and to her feelings of deep compassion for the little steward. He was so entirely her creature that she felt that she must not abandon him when his need of her was so great. Life had treated him so shabbily that she could not bear to destroy his faith in her. Furthermore, she felt responsible for having introduced him to a way of life that was so different from his own, but which had now become necessary to him. She said that his lack of intelligence made him vulnerable, and she hesitated to hurt him.

Had it not been for Muldowney, Christine might have enjoyed her life at sea. As it was the knowledge that he would always be waiting for her at the end of a voyage began to worry her. When John Roper was on leave from Greece, she said she would like to see his daughter, who was then between two and three years old. The night before the Ropers were going back to Athens, she came to their hotel in time to have a romp with his stepsons and small daughter, before dining with John Roper and his wife.

After dinner, he walked her home to her hotel, and they had a long talk. She told him about Muldowney, and said that she was frightened of him. Outside the hotel she kissed him goodbye, and said something in Polish, adding rather wistfully, 'That was a short prayer for you and your children because I do not think we shall meet again.'

In March 1952, Christine became both anxious and irritated at Muldowney's total lack of discipline where she was concerned. He had taken to following her everywhere, and would hang about her hotel and all the restaurants, flats, shops or private houses in which she was shopping or seeing her friends. On one occasion she phoned Ludwig Popiel, and asked him to meet her and escort her home as she dreaded having yet another scene with Muldowney, to whom she had now given his final *congé*.

Popiel took her home and, as they reached Lexham Gardens, they saw Muldowney patrolling the pavement. Christine and Popiel greeted him amiably, and they stood chatting with him for a little while. Then Muldowney blurted out that he wanted to talk to Christine privately. She shook her head, and said that anything he had to say could be said in front of Popiel. Muldowney insisted, his face twitching.

'I'm sorry, Dennis,' Christine said firmly, 'but this persecution really must stop. You are embarrassing me by your peculiar behaviour. I have done my best to repay the great debt of gratitude I owe you, but now I have had enough of being hounded by you. I don't think we should meet again. Do I make myself clear?'

Muldowney's eyes rolled in his head like those of a bolting horse.

'You had better go now,' said Popiel.

'Right, I will,' and with that Muldowney stumped off into the darkness. 'I'm afraid I haven't seen the last of him,' said Christine. 'He really is an obstinate and terrifying little man.'

Christine made two more journeys to Australia, with a break of three weeks between voyages, before being taken on by the Union-Castle Company. In 1952, it was still considered more amusing to travel to and from South Africa by mail boat than to go by plane. The passengers had their own way of enjoying the sea-voyage, and the stewards and stewardesses liked this run because of the rich pickings – South Africans tipped generously – and because of the pleasant climatic conditions.

Determined to break with Muldowney, Christine sailed as a stewardess in the 20,000-ton RMMV luxury liner *Winchester Castle* from Southampton to South Africa on 30 April 1952.

The hierarchy of stewards and stewardesses aboard these vessels was as strict as that which had once obtained in the servants' hall. The Second Steward was responsible for the work and welfare of the stewardesses. They usually slept two to a cabin, and took their meals either in the Children's Square, or in the Tourist Saloon before the passengers.

Stewardesses worked hard, and their hours were long. Starting at 6 a.m. when they prepared early morning tea, they worked through Captain's Rounds at 11 a.m. Their afternoons were normally free, the disadvantage being that they had no deck of their own for exercise. It was customary for most ships to allow their stewardesses to make use of the poop deck, which was out-of-bounds to passengers.

The stewardesses' work included some of the duties of a personal maid. They had to be available when the passengers were changing for dinner; they turned down beds or bunks, tidied the cabins and replenished bowls of fruit and jugs of iced water. They were expected to be on hand in any emergency. Most of the stewardesses were of a high calibre, and a number of them were SRNs. There was no shore leave for the crew until the ship reached its destination.

Before Christine was half-way to Capetown, she had decided on her course of action. Although she disliked the idea of being unkind to Muldowney, she knew that she must, at all costs, rid herself of this incubus, whose possessiveness, jealousy and insensate rages were making her life in London impossible. She readily admitted that, in her efforts to show her gratitude to Muldowney for his many kindnesses on that first voyage in *Rauhine*, she had indeed created a rod for her own back, for she realized now that the steward's pathological obsession about herself was rapidly becoming a real threat to her safety.

She knew that as long as Muldowney was able to contact her, to follow her, to see her, she would be unable to shake him off. Having decided that the only way to rid herself of him for good was to go abroad, to go somewhere he would be unable to find her, Christine wrote and informed Andrew of her future plans. She was aware that he would be relieved by her decision, for he too was beginning to be heartily sick of her protégé.

The ship docked on 13 June 1952, and Christine travelled up to London with a lighter heart, arriving at the Shellbourne Hotel, Lexham Gardens, her usual domicile in London, to find a letter from Andrew from Bonn, saying he thoroughly approved of her decision to leave England for a while, and that he would come and join her at Liège where she could rest, relax and map out a further plan of campaign.

Christine felt as if a great weight had been lifted off her shoulders. She had made arrangements to leave immediately for Liège. Unfortunately, the flight was cancelled, so she made a booking for the following day, and sent a telegram to Andrew explaining the delay.

Hardly had she unpacked her suitcase before Muldowney was scratching, in his usual fashion, at the door of her room. She greeted him pleasantly, but coolly, and went on unpacking while he watched her, pale-faced and silent. With a sinking heart she recognized the signs of mounting tension in him; tension that would certainly erupt into a violent scene. Hoping to calm him, she chatted about the voyage and asked him how the new job he had taken as kitchen porter at the Reform Club was working out. He said he had taken on this particular work so as to be available when she came back to London from her travels. Christine said she did not think she would be going to sea again for some time.

Suddenly, Muldowney was upon her, white and shaking, accusing her of lying to him, of plotting to forsake him, of trying to drive him out of his mind. He raved on about her relationship with Andrew and with a score of other men. He quoted promises she was supposed to have made to him, and finally he demanded the return of the letters he had written to her.

Christine let him rave on. She had seen him in this state before, and knew that he was temporarily uncontrollable. She was furiously angry, but she was also frightened. She prayed that someone would call her to the telephone or that one of her friends would call in informally as they usually did. But nobody appeared, and Muldowney, shaking and twitching, raved on, threatening to kill her, and then himself. Christine shrugged her shoulders, and this started him off again. Finally, when he was so hoarse that he could only whisper, she said calmly that she had an appointment at the Polish Hearth, and asked him whether he would care to accompany her. The normality of her tone of voice jolted him back to reality and to sanity. He apologized for his outburst, and said he could not accompany her as he had to be back on duty at the Reform Club. He then escorted her downstairs.

It was with a sense of grave foreboding that Christine boarded a bus that would take her part of the way to the Polish Hearth in Exhibition Road, where she had an appointment with friends for coffee. She was badly shaken by her scene with Muldowney, and when her friends asked her, jokingly, what had become of her 'shadow', she replied curtly that he had taken a new job which would, she hoped, keep him busy. She then added a rider to the effect that it was strange that there could be so much violence in so puny a frame.

Monday 15 June dawned fine and sunny. In her drab, high-ceilinged room, whose former fine proportions had been halved by a hardboard partition, Christine began sorting out her possessions. She intended putting her uniform in mothballs in one of her trunks, which a kindly Polish management allowed her to store in the basement of the hotel.

She was excited at the thought of seeing Andrew the next day in Liège, and she was looking forward to discussing her future plans with Ludwig Popiel, with whom she was dining that night.[1]

She spent the rest of the day putting her affairs in order. Then she washed her hair, because she wanted to start her new life with a different hairstyle. Andrew recalls that she often changed her coiffure. Sometimes it was bouffant, sometimes long and sometimes short. Occasionally, she wore it piled up on her head, or in a bubble of curls.

Having done a little shopping, Christine went to the Polish Hearth and on to dine with Popiel in a little Polish restaurant called Marynka, just off the Brompton Road. They had a pleasantly relaxed meal during which Christine explained to Popiel that she was going abroad mainly because Muldowney had become such a problem. She said she had recently had two unpleasant encounters with him, and that she hoped he would not waylay her on her way home. When they left the restaurant, Popiel offered to escort her back to the hotel; but she assured him that she was all right. Popiel reluctantly left her at the tube station, and went on his way. Christine got back to the hotel at 10.30 p.m. She had a chat with the Polish hotel porter, Joseph Kojecki, and asked him whether the basement was still unlocked as she wanted to finish storing her uniforms. He gallantly offered his assistance, and went down to make sure that the basement was still open.

Christine left her room with such a large pile of uniforms in her arms that she could just see over the top of it. She walked across the tiled half-landing to the top of the staircase, which was steep and narrow; she had to adjust her load carefully to preserve her balance on the way down. At the foot of the stairs Muldowney was waiting for her. He asked her whether she really intended leaving England. She said she did. He then asked her again to return his letters. She said she had burned them. He asked her how long she proposed staying away. She answered that she thought she would probably be gone for about two years.

Suddenly he lunged at her, plunging a long-bladed knife deep into her breast. Christine cried out, 'Get him off me, get him away.' While an appalled hotel guest was phoning for the police and for an ambulance, the porter, on his knees, was cradling Christine and trying to support her head. By the time medical help had arrived, she was dead.

Muldowney did not try to run away. He stood there, staring at Christine's body, and repeating over and over again, 'I killed her because I loved her.' When the police arrived, he was seen to try to pour 'a white substance' into his mouth. This proved to be powdered aspirin, and was taken away from him. The police took him into custody and next day he was driven to West London Police Court in a police car, handcuffed to Detective-Inspector Woolner.

Chief-Inspector George Jennings told the magistrate, Mr E. R. Guest: 'At 12.45 a.m. today, I saw Muldowney in the front ground floor lounge at the Shellbourne Hotel, Lexham Gardens, Kensington. I said to him, "At 12.15 a.m. I saw the dead body of Christine Granville at the foot of the stairs in the hall here. From enquiries I have made I have reason to believe that you murdered her by stabbing her with this knife."' Inspector Jennings then held up a dagger-shaped knife with a wooden handle. The Inspector then said that Muldowney replied, 'I killed her. Let's go away from here and get it over quickly.'

Muldowney stood stiffly to attention in the dock as the magistrate asked, 'Do you wish me to consider the question of legal aid for you or not?' Muldowney replied curtly, 'No.'

After a brief hearing he was remanded in custody until 1 July. Meanwhile, in the absence of Andrew, who had been named in Christine's papers as her next-of-kin, the police, while waiting for him to fly in, contacted the head of the Skarbek family, Colonel Andrew Skarbek.

His eldest son John said, 'I dashed up from the farm I was managing in Buckinghamshire to join my father and younger brother Andrew, who was a medical student at the time. We went to a police-station in Kensington where a grim-faced inspector asked us innumerable questions. We then had the terrible experience of seeing our cousin lying in the mortuary there under a white sheet. When we came out we were surrounded by press photographers and journalists all anxious to get a story.'

Count Skarbek gave identification of Christine at the inquest on 19 June, when Doctor F. E. Camps, the pathologist, said she had died of shock and haemorrhage due to a stab wound in the chest. The hearing lasted three minutes and the inquest was adjourned to allow criminal proceedings to take their course.

Andrew flew in in a state of total shock, and the funeral arrangements got under way. Rumours were rife as to why

Christine had been murdered.[2] It was said variously that the former British secret agent had been the victim of a Communist plot; of reprisals by the Nazis, or that she had been done to death as an act of vengeance by French traitors. The Chief of MI5, Sir Percy Sillitoe, sifted through the various reports and dismissed them out of hand. There was no reason to doubt that Christine had died at the hands of a jealous and violent psychopath.

On Thursday 11 September, 1952 Dennis George Muldowney walked into the dock at the Old Bailey. He stood there with his hands plunged deep into the pockets of his seedy raincoat and gazed indifferently around the court-room, which was packed with the family and friends of the woman he had killed.

The clerk rose and said, 'You are charged upon indictment with the murder of Christine Granville on 15th June of this year. Are you guilty or not guilty?'

'Guilty as charged,' shouted Muldowney.

Mr Justice Donovan intervened. 'Do you intend to adhere to that plea, because, if you do, there is only one thing left for me to do, and that is to pass sentence?'

'Quite. I would like you to do that as soon as possible.'

'Are you still determined not to be defended?' asked the Judge.

'Quite determined,' replied Muldowney.

The Clerk of the Court then addressed the man in the dock. 'Have you anything to say why the Court should not give you judgement of death according to the Law?'

'I have nothing whatever to say.'

As the Judge concluded the sentence and placed the black cap on his head, he said solemnly, 'May the Lord have mercy on your soul.'

'He will,' said Muldowney, 'He will.'

When the prisoner had left the dock on his way to the death cell, Mr Roger Frisby, who represented the relatives and friends of Christine Granville, said that a most distressing feature of the case had been the wide publicity given to certain statements made by Muldowney to the police. Mr Frisby said that he had been instructed to point out that there was not a particle of truth in Muldowney's statements. Mrs Granville, he said, came of an old, proud and respected family in her own country. As the world knew, she was a very gallant lady who had rendered services to her adopted country which that country would never forget; and counsel hoped that his remarks would help to ensure that in the future her memory would be as untarnished as her life had been. Mr Christmas Humphreys, on behalf of the Director of Public Prosecutions, said he desired to concur with these observations.

On 29 September, the Home Secretary announced that there were no grounds for recommending a reprieve in the case of Dennis George Muldowney. To the last, Muldowney showed utter contempt for his warders and for all those who approached him. He refused to get up in the morning, and had to be forcibly dressed. He would take no exercise and complained that the food sent in to him was of poor quality. He refused the games and recreations offered to distract him. Nor would he accept the ministrations of a priest. He wrote to nobody and received no visitors. He left no last requests of any kind, though he had been fond of his son, who was now aged nine, and was living but a short distance from Pentonville prison.[3]

On Tuesday 30 September, 1952, Dennis George Muldowney left his cell to go to the gallows. On the way he made only one remark: 'To kill is the final possession.'

Earlier that year, on 21 June at 11 a.m., a concourse of silent people had gathered outside the tiny chapel of St Mary in the Roman Catholic Cemetery of Kensal Green. They had come to pay tribute to Christine Granville. The manner of her dying had deeply shocked her friends and colleagues into a tardy realization of how little they had known or worried about her welfare in the post-war years. Only Andrew and her close and dear friends such as Francis Cammaerts, John Roper and Patrick Howarth, who knew how little honour had been paid to Christine in her lifetime, were saddened by the ironical sight of the representatives of so many august and military bodies who, having ignored her needs when she was alive, were now gathered solemnly to pay homage round her dead body.

The light oak coffin was covered with a white and red flag. Upon it was a crimson cushion on which lay Christine's medals and other insignia – her Parachute Badge, badges from the French Pioneers of the Resistance, and from the Polish Resistance Movement. Here, too, were the only two personal possessions she prized above all others because they had come with her from Poland. These were her medallion of the Black Virgin of Czestochowa and her signet ring.

Quantities of wreaths, sheaves of flowers and little humble posies were banked outside the chapel; some of them had been sent or brought by people who, although they had not known her personally, had wished to come to the cemetery in person to salute her gallantry. Such a one was a Mrs Lily Holliday from Wembley, who said, 'I have no courage, but I have come to pay my respects to a woman who had it in the extreme.'

Among the two hundred mourners was the tall figure of Francis Cammaerts. Twelve members of the FANY Special Forces Section came to stand at the graveside of their comrade. Leaning on a stick was an old friend and colleague of Christine who, when she was well over fifty, became one of the leaders of the Polish Underground Movement. Under one of the close-fitting sleeves of her dress, Countess Teresa Lubienska bore the infamous brand mark of Auschwitz Concentration Camp.[4]

Poland was represented by General Stanislaus Kopanski, Britain by Major General Gubbins, and France by a contingent of survivors from the Vercors massacre.

After a brief religious ceremony in the chapel, the pallbearers, among them Andrew Kennedy, Colonel Skarbek and Andrew Skarbek, carried the coffin to its final destination. The French maquisards dropped red and white carnations into the grave of their 'Miss Pauline', and a feeling of deep oppression descended on those present as Polish earth was sprinkled on the grave from a small sack so that Christine could sleep in peace beneath her native soil. Then it was all over. For the first time since they had met, Andrew had at last to abandon Christine.

Bosham, 25 March 1975

AUTHOR'S AFTERWORD
Spotlight on Secrets and Lies

When this book was first published in 1975, many of Christine's friends and colleagues in SOE were still alive. Her lover, partner and best friend, Andrew Kennedy (Andrzej Kowerski), had spent three months working with me in Bosham, dictating the tapes which formed its factual basis. Upon publication it was well received, and the small flame I had ignited to keep Christine's work in the public memory burned steadily. During the intervening years, Christine, her heroism and terrible death, continued to amaze and intrigue those who read of her exploits.

Andrew and I kept in touch. He used to meet me when I came to London, which was fairly often. It seems he was still working undercover for the British Government in Germany, where he ran automobile agencies. Although he never discussed his working life with me he told me how much he missed Christine, his alter ego, and that he looked forward to being reunited with her.

I also stayed in touch with Vera Atkins, who had semi-retired to Winchelsea. Selwyn Jepson and I remained friends and he often talked about Christine. Each year on 16 June I made a pious pilgrimage to the Vercors, to attend the ceremony of remembrance. Among the dwindling band of SOE agents present would be the tall figure of Francis Cammaerts, whose life Christine had saved.

Once it became known that my researches might become the basis for a film, a tide of new information about Christine alerted me to the fact that there were lacunae in my book that would need further digging and verification. Andrew had died in 1988 and Patrick Howarth in 2004. Cammaerts was now elderly and frail, though still fierce in his desire to protect her memory.

One of Christine's contemporaries, Madam X, a Polish lady who was working as a translator with the Poles in Kenya in 1947, met Christine at the time she was accompanied by Michael Dunford, who from all accounts was deeply attached to her. Madam X seems to have had a curious relationship with Christine. On the one hand she welcomed her as an intelligent newcomer and a compatriot. On the other hand she, like many Poles, was upset that the aristocrat Krystyna Skarbek should have worked as an accredited SOE agent under a British code-name. Madam X recalled:

Christine did not live with Dunford, but in an hotel, where I visited her. She was not in the least domesticated and disliked all housework. The first time I called on her I found her in a small room. It was as immaculate as she was, but bare of ornaments, with the exception of a small, shining stiletto knife on the mantelpiece. I asked Christine the history of this curious ornament. 'I hate guns', she said, 'so noisy. This weapon is swift and deadly, and I have made good use of it on many occasions.'

Madam X's summing-up of Christine was interesting:

'She was not beautiful in the usual sense of the word, but she was fascinating and mysterious.'

'Why mysterious?' I asked.

'Because she had a strange habit of just melting away in the middle of a party or conversation. She had fantastic legs, and her only concession to fashion was her colourful collection of scarves. She loved small children, and communicated with them as she did with animals.

The fact is she wasn't happy in Nairobi. I think that it held too many memories of George Gizycki. She pined for action, for danger, for the ancient parapets of Europe, and for Andrew. Also she had pressing financial problems, she was always down to her last fifty pounds. She was grateful to Dunford for all he had done for her but she wanted out, and so she returned to London.'

In 1947 Christine was in Cairo worrying about her future, which looked extremely bleak. She had no wish, and indeed no desire, to become a secretary. All she wanted was to resume her life of action and adventure, and, examining the humble prospects on offer, she became sad and discouraged. As always, she had a wide circle of friends, and one day she met up with Edward Howe, the Kemsley Newspapers' correspondent, who was on a visit to Cairo from his base in Istanbul. Howe was well aware of Christine's background and work for SOE, so when she asked him if he knew of anyone who might have a wartime background and could help her find the right niche for her particular talents, he gave her the address of his friend Ian Fleming. He felt sure he would be interested in her – as a fascinating personality certainly, and maybe as a correspondent somewhere or the other.

Fleming was interested and arranged to meet Christine for the first time, in a restaurant in Charlotte Street, London. After this meeting he wrote to Edward Howe, 'I see exactly what you mean about Christine, she literally shines with all the qualities and splendours of a fictitious character. How rarely one finds such types.' It was an auspicious meal.

At that time Ian Fleming was one of London's most eligible and sought-after bachelors. Tall, debonair, highly intelligent and head of the prosperous foreign news service for all Kemsley Newspapers, he was every woman's dream lover. Unfortunately for his female admirers he did not respond to their flirtatious advances, for he suffered from a deep-seated form of boredom which could only be kept at bay by constant diversion and action. He came from a distinguished and wealthy family, of Scottish descent on the paternal side. His mother, Evelyn Beatrice St Croix Rose, had cosmopolitan forbears, one of whom she claimed was John of Gaunt, Duke of Lancaster, an ancestor of whom she was extremely proud, making sure that her sons, especially Ian, were aware of their ancient lineage.

Fleming's father, Major Valentine Fleming, died in action in the Second World War. He was awarded a posthumous DSO. His widow made him into a role model for his sons Ian, Peter, Michael and Richard. At the time of his father's death, Ian was barely nine years old, and greatly influenced by his mother to follow in his father's heroic footsteps.

Ian was always something of a rebel, and did not seem to fit into any conventional pattern, much to the dismay of his devoted and domineering mother, who tried to be both parents to her boys. He was pushed into a series of careers but none interested him until, in 1931, he joined Reuters News Agency, a job which suited him and was to provide him with an intimate knowledge of journalism, and in particular of newsgathering.

In 1939, on the eve of the Second World War, the Rear Admiral John Godfrey, Director of Intelligence of the Royal Navy, recruited Fleming, then aged thirty-one, as a personal assistant – first as a lieutenant, then as a commander. The Admiral's faith in his PA was fully justified by Fleming's auda-cious and adroit handling of many important and vital missions.

After the war Fleming became foreign manager for Kemsley Newspapers. He built his house, Goldeneye, in Jamaica and, in a somewhat lackadaisical manner, courted socialite Anne, Lady Rothermere, whom he was eventually to marry. At the same time he became deeply involved with Christine Granville.

Due to the fact that Christine was obsessively secretive, their affair was not common knowledge, and their meetings were conducted away from London and from prying eyes. Only one of Christine's Polish women friends, Olga Bialoguski, was aware that Christine was having a new love affair but even she was never told any details. Nor, it seems, did Fleming confide in anyone. Their meetings became infrequent as Christine had started a new career as a stewardess, on ocean liners plying the Australia and South Africa routes.

It may well be that with Fleming's help Christine resumed her espionage work. All her friends were aware that she disliked all forms of domestic work, preferring to live in hotels, or serviced accommodation, rather than having to attend to such trivial details as bed-making or polishing furniture. In view of these facts, it seems strange that Christine became a humble stewardess, whose work was mainly domestic. What is much more likely is that working as a stewardess she had access to the captain, his officers, the crew, and to what was taking place politically in the ports of call visited by the liners.

While the couple had much in common, they gradually drifted apart, mainly, one suspects, because Anne Rothermere was expecting Fleming's baby. He married her and, insofar as one knows, remained silent about his liaison with the Polish countess. However, whatever his private feelings about the life and death of Christine, it is my view that he did not forget her.

Aged forty-four, Fleming wrote *Casino Royale*, the first novel to feature Commander James Bond, in whom he created the greatest British espionage icon of the late twentieth century. *Casino Royale* also featured a fascinating and unusual heroine, a beautiful double agent called Vesper Lynd, with whom Bond fell passionately in love. Introducing Vesper to Bond as his new assistant, Mathis says: 'She is as serious as you could wish and as cold as an icicle. She speaks French like a native, and knows her job backwards.'

Bond's first description of Vesper could be a portrait of Christine: 'Her hair was very black, it was cut square and low on the nape of her neck, framing her face to the clear and beautiful line of her jaw . . . her skin was lightly tanned . . . her bare arms and hands had a quality of repose.' At their first dinner together, Bond says he could not 'drink the health of her new frock without knowing her Christian name.' To this she replies 'Vesper Lynd.' She then explains that according to her parents she was born on a very stormy evening and apparently they wanted to remember it.

In fact, Countess Krystyna Skarbek *was* born on a stormy night, and her father, Count Jerzy Skarbek, had given his baby daughter the nickname 'Vesperale' or, as he explained, 'like the evening star'.

One of the many biographies of Fleming – Donald McCormick's – majors on his affair with Christine. I cannot confirm that Fleming used Christine as the model for Vesper Lynd but there is real passion in Fleming's novel and his account of Vesper's beauty and character adds up to a fair description of Christine. He writes: 'He found her companionship easy and unexacting. There was something enigmatic about her that was a constant stimulus. She gave little of her real personality away, and he felt however long they were together, there would always be a private room that he could not invade. She was thoughtful and full of consideration, without being slavish, and without compromising her arrogant spirit . . . She would surrender herself without ever allowing herself to be possessed.'

Renewing my links with SOE led me to another aspect of Christine's life of which I had been ignorant. I recently attended an SOE 'get together' at the Tangmere Military Aviation Museum. We were received in a large tent already filled with the children and grandchildren of SOE agents who had come from all over the world. Among those attending were the heroic Nancy Wake, and Violette Szabo's daughter, Tania. I was seated with an elderly SOE agent. He told me he had known Christine Granville at the time she was in training at Beaulieu. I knew, of course, that SOE agents had been trained in safe houses, on estates all over the United Kingdom, and that one of them was at Beaulieu.

Later, I met Margaret Rowles, public relations officer for Beaulieu, who told me that an SOE exhibition, The Secret Army Museum, was due to open in March 2005 and that I should meet John Smith, the project organizer. So, in November 2004 on a grey and chilly day, I set out for Beaulieu. There is something feudal about the New Forest. Time has stood still here, tall trees guard the secrets of the forest, and in the open spaces wild ponies are free to roam at will.

My interest in the vast estate concerned its secrets, most of which are still unknown to the public at large. In the quadrangle within the medieval ruins of Beaulieu Abbey, in a recess in the ancient cloister wall known as the 'Bookcase', is a large, modern, circular plaque which reads:

REMEMBER BEFORE GOD
THOSE MEN AND WOMEN OF
THE EUROPEAN RESISTANCE
MOVEMENT WHO WERE SECRETLY
TRAINED IN BEAULIEU TO FIGHT
THEIR LONELY BATTLE AGAINST HITLER'S
GERMANY, AND WHO, BEFORE ENTERING NAZI TERRITORY,
HERE FOUND SOME MEASURE OF THE PEACE FOR WHICH
THEY FOUGHT

These words commemorate over three thousand men and women of at least fifteen European nationalities, and a number of Canadians and Americans who during the Second World War had been trained as secret agents of various sorts, at what was officially known as the 'Finishing School'.

This school was a complex of eleven country houses in the Beaulieu area that had been requisitioned by SOE. During the second half of 1940, SOE had created a number of establishments countrywide for training agents of various nationalities in a tough syllabus of commando techniques and skills such as sabotage, subversion and codes. The idea for these establishments was supposed to have originated with Guy Burgess, at that time an official of the Foreign Office and a member of Section D. He was one of the sponsors in the recruitment of Kim Philby into his section. Both were assiduously spying for the Russians. Beaulieu was one of the estates chosen, mainly because it was deep in the woods and had ready-made accommodation in the shape of a number of large, private houses in prime positions, hidden away in big gardens. Christine would have been housed in Boarmans.

Having taken a ten-day agent training course at The Rings, Philby took up his appointment at the 'Finishing School', as tutor in propaganda warfare. One of his pupils was to be Christine Granville.

Edward, Lord Montagu of Beaulieu, became my guide and escort on my visit that day. 'Secrecy was the name of the game,' he told me. 'Students undergoing training at the various houses never knew the names of the houses in which they lived. I was at Eton at the time, I came home for the holidays and of course I knew something was up, but I never found out what it was, and I never saw a single agent. My young sisters entertained resident staff who naturally remained silent as to what they were really doing.'

There were some sixteen officers on the teaching staff of what became the Beaulieu finishing school. There was also staff of around six 'residential adjutant house-masters', who supervised some of the field exercises. Most of these men spoke several languages and were able to instruct their students in their varied skills. The curriculum included such subjects as silent killing, arson, train-wrecking and burglary – a one-time burglar was hired to teach the students his special skills. Also on the syllabus was house-breaking, forgery and 'black' propaganda.

Some of the best-known agents were trained at Beaulieu. In the French section were Peter Churchill, Ben Cowburn and Robert Heslop. Sixty-five famous women agents, including Christine, were trained at Beaulieu. Among them were Pearl Witherington and Odette Hallowes.

This document, Appendix 'A': 'Qualifications of proposed Operational Candidate for Hungary', illuminates some of Christine's activities at Beaulieu:

1. TRAINING

By the end of March CHRISTINE will have been
trained in the following subjects:

(a) W/T, the set with which she is most familiar being a
     'B' set.

(b) Parachute jumping.

(c) Use of elementary explosives.

(d) SIS course.

(e) Preparation of reception committees.

(f) Simple personal disguises.

In addition, arrangements have been made for her to be
trained in the use of S-phones at BARI.

Though Christine did not finally go on this particular mission, the document does give an indication of the breadth of practical skills instilled in operatives. W/T, wireless telegraph, was used in the field for communication back to base. Reception committees for freshly parachuted agents had to be minutely well prepared with much local knowledge. Yet the dangers were not only on foreign fields occupied by Germans and collaborators. The SIS course referred to was a broad introduction to the Special Intelligence Service, a separate (and, it must be said, often rival) department. SIS, or MI6 as it was also called, dealt with external security. It resented the formation of SOE and offered only technical back-up, initially providing signals and cipher services, radio sets and fake documents, all paraphernalia that they thought they could track and, therefore, control.

One of my most fruitful visits was to the National Archives (formerly the Public Record Office) housed in a magnificent modern building at Kew. For years the documents accumulated in this vast complex have been mainly unavailable, tantalizing historians and writers seeking the truth about individuals involved in espionage work during the Second World War. It was, therefore, with a frisson of anticipation that, after a number of security checks, I took my seat at a little desk and opened 'Christine Granville's Personal File'.

Vera Atkins had told me in confidence that immediately after VE Day, Winston Churchill ordered that SOE be disbanded and its records destroyed. SOE was eventually disbanded on 1 January 1946. In an unsigned leaflet produced by the PRO (now the National Archives) in July 1998 upon the release of more papers, it is revealed that at least 87 per cent of SOE files were deliberately destroyed between 1945 and 1950, some by SOE and some by the SIS. A mysterious fire at SOE headquarters in 1946 saw the loss of most of the files from the Polish Section, but other files were saved from the flames, and Vera admitted to having herself destroyed a number of records. So what we are left with is a very partial picture.

It is quite evident that Christine was a very complex character and not 'easy to handle' unless engaged on a dangerous mission which she undertook with brio and courage. She seems to have relished the disguising of her true identity under a series of code names. As Madame Marchand, Christine travelled on a hazardous mission to Poland under the guise of gathering information for British newspapers. As Christine Mary Granville, she prepared herself to undertake a dangerous mission known as 'Operation Folkestone', which was eventually aborted. During her work in France with Francis Cammaerts, she was known and much loved as Pauline Armand.

The file contains numerous documents about the chaotic state of her finances and, although she lived a seemingly frugal life, she must have had some expensive tastes. On one occasion she incurred the wrath and sarcasm of a minor official when, in November 1944, she sent in an expense account for £240.7s.0d, a small fortune in those days. 'I have now had an opportunity to consider your memo', the official states. 'The claim for clothing lost by enemy action . . . is out of all proportion to any claim for such losses, which cannot be allowed as a charge on public funds, insomuch as the items included therein are on a luxury scale both as to quality and to quantity.'

This carping reprimand is issued to a woman so scrupulous about money that she refused the gift of a house in London from one of her admirers. This same exhausted agent returning from a perilous mission in France, wearing a body-belt heavy with sovereigns, walked the streets during the night rather than spend one penny of money that did not belong to her. One memorandum signed by Christine refers to her request that an aunt living in France, a cousin and her ex-husband George Gizycki, then domiciled in Montreal, Canada, should be sent funds drawn from any pay standing to her credit.

In 1945 Christine was demobilized. She relinquished her commission in the WAAF. On 11 May 1945 she was given a gratuity of £100. An ungrateful British Government then forgot all about her, and there was no help from Poland, nor any gesture from her former country to honour one of its most heroic women.

Later in 1945, Christine, marooned in Cairo, was worried about obtaining more of the type of dangerous work she loved. A letter from a colleague asking for help dashed her hopes.

My Dear C,
    I'm very much afraid that the prospects of employment for you in an operational capacity, either now or in the near future, have become exceedingly remote . . . Knowing your dislike of office work I do not suppose that any form of secretarial work would be of interest to you, and this rather limits the possibility of finding something for you to do. Andrew will be returning to this country, probably on the next convoy, and we are making efforts to secure employment for him in Germany. We are taking all necessary steps so that you and Andrew can acquire British nationality as soon as the regulations allow this, probably at the conclusion of the war.

There are a number of letters from official sources, praising Christine's outstanding courage, one signed by H. R. Alexander,

Supreme Allied Commander, recommending that Christine
Granville be awarded the CBE. Because she was a foreign
national, she was disqualified from gaining such an award, but
after naturalization was awarded the OBE.

There is only one letter written by hand when Christine was
in Cairo, which is addressed to Perks. (In the late summer of
1945, the Polish section, headed initially by Bickham Sweet-
Escott, came into being. Later Captain (Colonel) H. B. 'Perks'
Perkins took over.) Dated the 25th of the third month of 1945,
the letter is evidence of her anxiety as to her future.

Her handwriting is large, graceful and distinguished (according
to a graphologist, it bears the hallmark of the well-educated, convent-trained pupil). Her English, though fluent, is not perfect. It
is in many ways a pathetic and inexplicably humble epistle.
Having apologized for her spelling, Christine explains to 'Perks':

> I have already put in an application for a work with RAF,
> but I am afraid that it's too late. If I need it – will you write
> and tell them that I am honest and clean Polish girl? . . .
>   I should like to keep in touch with you, and for God's
> sake do not strike my name from the outfit, if it still
> exists. Please remember that I am too pleased to go and
> do anything for it. Maybe you find out that I could be
> usefull [sic] getting people out from camps and prisons
> in Germany just before they get shot. I should love to do
> it and I like to jump out of a plane even every day.

As always Christine is anxious about her brother and Andrew
and includes a plea to 'Perks': 'and please look after Andrew
and don't let him do anything too stupid.' She is also worried
about the fate of one of her old friends, A. G. G. de Chastelain,
DSO, whom she had met in the early days. De Chastelain was
'our man in Bucharest', an oil engineer, and an exceptional
human being. He was a friend and admirer of both Christine
and her husband Gizycki. In her letter to 'Perks' she writes:
'Will you please see that de Chastelain gets this letter that I am

P.S. SORRY FOR THE SPELLING!   - 1 -   Cairo 25. III. 45

Forks kochany.

Thank you very much for your very nice letter. I was expecting something like that since our Polish scheme fell through - but you always put things in a kindest way. I am very grateful to you for the three month pay you are offering to me. I should like to stay here in Cairo for at least three thru month and, in the meantime look around for another job. If I do not succeed - then I will again ask for your help. I have already put in an application for a work with R.A.F. but I am afraid that it's too late. if I need it - will you write and tell them that I am honest and clean polish girl? I have got two other things in mind en it may be one will come off. Anyway I should like to kep in touch with you and for God's sake do not strike my name from the firm till it exist. - remember that I am always too pleased to go and do anything for it.

Christine's letter to Captain (Colonel) H. B. 'Perks' Perkins in 1945 (NATIONAL ARCHIVES)

sending him. He may needs [*sic*] it if it is true he was into troubles
[*sic*]. There are people here who could give him some evidence
that may be helpful to him.'

I had always wondered about the dark cloud of suspicion that
had enveloped Christine and her partner Andrew during their
stay in Cairo. With the help of friends who gave me some valuable new information, I discovered a few more of the pieces
missing from my psychological jigsaw puzzle. At that time, she
had been working for two years for SOE, and had no intention
of taking orders from the new Polish government-in-exile in
London. In order to punish her for refusing to work under
them, they may have been responsible for spreading the
rumours that were calculated to destroy her credibility and that
of Andrew. The word was that the pair were double-agents.

Documents recently released by the government show that
Jakob Alek, the Polish station chief in Cairo, was responsible for
the accusation that Christine was in contact with the Germans
and the Vichy French. He was unable to give any proof of their
'treachery', but SOE believed him, and Christine and Andrew
were cast out.

Colonel Peter Wilkinson, the newly-appointed SOE head
in Cairo, summoned the pair and informed them that their services were no longer needed, but possibly because he himself
did not believe that they were traitors, he did not remove their
names from the payroll. For two years Christine and Andrew
kicked their heels in Cairo, and it was not until the new SOE
chief, Patrick Howarth, took Christine back into the fold that
she began training for possible missions. In July 1944, Christine
was parachuted into France to begin that most spectacular part
of her achievements.

Andrew Kennedy never married. He continued to live and
work in Munich until his death in 1988, aged 78. In his will he
expressed the wish that his ashes should be interred in
Christine's grave.

Once again, I stood with a silent crowd of mourners in the Kensal Green cemetery. Christine's grave, which at her own funeral had been covered with her medals and other insignia, her medallion of the Black Virgin of Czestochowa, and her signet ring, the only piece of jewellery she ever wore, was now covered with flowers.

Members of both Andrew's and Christine's families were present, as were those surviving of her colleagues from SOE. Francis Cammaerts, faithful to the last, watched as the urn containing Andrew's ashes was carefully placed in the grave. There was a brief religious service, and then it was all over. Andrew and his beloved Christine were now united for all eternity.

Madeleine Masson
Bosham, 1 March 2005

AFTERWORD

Written as a Foreword to the 1975 edition of Christine

by Francis Cammaerts

It is impossible to read a book about someone you have known well without imagining the reactions of the subject to the book and to its treatment. I believe that friends of Christine would agree that her reaction to this, and to any book about her would have been an outburst of mocking laughter; 'a book about me, how ridiculous, what is all the fuss about?' She would certainly have claimed that there were many other people more interesting and more important who would be delighted to have books written about them, so why pick on her? She did not want to be known, or admired as a person who had done many brave things during the war, she wanted to be known and appreciated for herself, and, as Madeleine Masson says, 'she was a very private person'. Why and when are we justified in invading that privacy? Does the passage of twenty-three years justify such an invasion?

I believe we must have some doubts on this score and this must often be the dilemma of a biographer. In spite of these doubts I have agreed, after talking to the many friends concerned, to cooperate with Mme Masson in providing information for this book and to write this foreword. I have agreed because I was convinced that, sooner or later, this book would be written and because I was equally convinced that the author's sincerity and objectivity, her willingness to try to find

the truth to write, were beyond question. Having read the script
I am sure that I was right in this assumption. As far as anyone
can discover the truth about someone so private, so tragically
uprooted and so much the victim of circumstances then this
study has arrived at a fair and balanced picture.

I must also wonder who will read this book and why they will
read it. Again there can be little doubt about the answer. It will
be read because it is part of that massive volume of literature
about the Second World War. It is curious that in this country, in
most of Europe and perhaps to a slightly lesser extent in the
United States, there appears to be an insatiable curiosity about
human behaviour during the tragic years of 1939–1945. After
the First World War the appearance in the middle 1920s of
Erich Maria Remarque's *All Quiet on the Western Front* seems to
have put an end to the flow of 'war books'. Certainly the real-
ism of that book put an end to the unbalanced emphasis on
heroics. Yet in spite of the success of *Catch-22*, which might
have been expected to perform a similar function in the later
1960s, there seems to be no end to the willingness to absorb
books on this subject. Books about escapes, about the Battle of
Britain and about Special Operations still have a powerful
appeal thirty years later. This appeal is clearly not just to the
ageing sentimentalist or the nostalgic ex-serviceman but is
clearly equally strong in Secondary schools and among students.

Last year I was invited to a Reunion in memory of the dead
of the Plateau of the Vercors which was held at Vassieux and is
mentioned by Madeleine Masson in this book. Three thousand of us belonging to three generations had an open air
barbecue after the official ceremonies. Here were the survivors,
their children and their grandchildren. I had the opportunity, in
a relaxed and unhurried atmosphere, to talk to many young
men and women aged fifteen to twenty-five years. I was anxious to find out whether they were not completely fed up with
continuous talk and preoccupation with events as remote in
time to them as the Boer War had been to me at their age.

The answers I received were in many forms and expressed

very differently but all carried the same clear message. 'We want to know all about that time, we want to get at the truth, we envy you. You knew the difference between right and wrong, life was straightforward to you, the path to action was clear.' Is this perhaps the answer to their curiosity? There have been other wars since 1945, other human tragedies, famine, floods and earthquakes, times when issues were simple and human choice unambiguous, but these were remote and not associated with their culture and their families.

I suppose that it is equally true that young African writers in the 1970s tend to be over-concerned with the period of their struggle for independence, that there is a real need to identify with a time when issues were clear and the decision on action was straightforward. However understandable this may be the danger of glamourizing war and wrapping it up in a glossy cover remains great.

I have no doubt that, since this book will be read by many because of its association with the war, Christine would have felt as I do that to focus attention on an individual or on individuals creates an inevitable distortion of the truth. Living and struggling from day to day within a community where total interdependence was the essence of everyday life, the singling out of individuals cannot give a picture of reality. Individual agents either in France or in Poland were dependent for every meal and every night's rest on people whose small children, aged parents, property and livelihood were continually put at risk by our presence. Their contribution involved a much greater sacrifice than ours.

However this is a portrait and, if you paint a portrait you cannot paint the whole of the environment. Mme Masson has been drawn to the story of one of the multitude living between the Atlantic and the Ural Mountains whose life, culture, language, religion and family ties were totally destroyed by the events of the war and its aftermath. It is indeed the story of a 'displaced person', that hideous phrase which buried behind its banality so many lost lives. It is also the story of someone who, in the face of the loss of all those things which normally make life acceptable, was able to retain a sense of humour, courage to achieve the impossible, kind and generous human contacts.

The spread of little bits of knowledge about psychology in the post-Freudian century has increased man's tendency to fit people into stereotypes and to attempt to explain their conduct and their patterns of behaviour. Madeleine Masson has certainly not attempted to do so here but no doubt many readers will attempt it. It would be a pity if this book were taken for anything else than it is – a sincere search for a person. In that search much that is interesting and admirable has been discovered, much more still remains hidden and unknown. This has been an admirable task, honestly and perceptively accomplished and written with compassion and sympathy. I can only hope that it will be read with as much understanding as it has been written.

ACKNOWLEDGEMENTS

This book could not have been written without the vital and valuable tapes and close co-operation given to me by Andrew Kennedy and Francis Cammaerts.

I am also deeply indebted to Colonel E. G. Boxshall, Professor M. R. D. Foot, Selwyn Jepson and the Skarbek family in England for their kindness, patience and encouragement over a long period, and to Roger Machell.

I also extend thanks to the many people whose assistance was invaluable in the compilation of this work: Julian Amery, MP, John Anstey, Mrs Irene Atayan, Miss Vera Atkins, Admiral J. Bartosik, Madame Edmund Bauthier, Claude Benedick, Paul Betts, Francis Brooks-Richards, Maurice Buckmaster, Stanley Christopher, Mervyn Cowie, Aidan Crawley, Mrs Nina Crawshaw, Colonel Sir William and Lady Deakin, David Driscoll, Michael Dunford, Mrs Antonina Edwards, Xan Fielding, Major-General Sir Colin Gubbins, Havard Gunn, Mrs Odette Hallowes, Bruno de Hamil, Donald Hamilton-Hill, Tadeusz Horko, Patrick Howarth, Mrs Angela von Kolichen, Michael L., Joseph La-Picirella, George Lotroicq, Mrs Heather McConnell, Neil Marten, George Millar, Catriona Moncrieff, Mrs E. C. W. Myers, Mrs S. Y. Parkinson, FANY, Madame Sylviane Rey, Mrs Betty Rigg, John Roper, Lord St Oswald, Dr Andrew Skarbek, John Skarbek, Col. S. Skarbek, Dr Celina Sokolow, Miss Madeau Stewart, Peter Storrs, Mrs Annette Street, Bickham Sweet-Escott, Mrs Eve Sykes, Henry Threlfall, Lt. Col. D. Trafford-Roberts, Prof. Richard Truscoe, Mrs Sam Westmacott, Sir Peter Wilkinson, Mrs Elizabeth Young, Adam Zamoyski and Tadeusz Zawaszki.

My thanks also go to: The Jewish Board of Deputies, The British Museum, The Canadian High Commission in London, The Comité d'Histoire de la 2ème Guerre Mondiale, Monsieur A. Vincent-Beaume in Valence, and M. Henri Michel in Paris, 'Le Dauphiné Libéré', Monsieur L. Bonnaure, Secrétaire Géneral, The Guildhall Library, N. K. Finlayson of the Home Office, and the Nationality Division of the Home Office,

Imperial War Museum, the Secretary and staff of the London Library, Metropolitan Police Office, New Scotland Yard, HM Stationery Office for permission to quote from *SOE*, by Professor M. R. D. Foot, National Library of Ottawa, Canada, (Miss Patricia Jenkins), *Radio Times* Hulton Picture Library, Southampton Library, *Sunday Express*, Sidney Smith of Union-Castle Mail Steamship Co., and West Sussex County Library – in particular, Miss Shirley Stone.

And, finally, I would like to thank the members of my home front: my husband, John, for special operations concerned with a Xerox machine; my son, Merrick, for fetching and carrying heavy books and manuscripts; my secretary, Joan Hunt, for her unflagging interest in the book and cheerful willingness to help, despite having to re-type innumerable drafts; and Miss Louise Frances Taber for having looked after the domestic side of my life so I could work in peace.

The manuscript of this book has been submitted to the Foreign and Commonwealth Office for reasons of security, and has been passed by them.

ACKNOWLEDGEMENTS FOR THE
AUTHOR'S AFTERWORD

I am deeply indebted to the many people who helped me to find new material for the final chapter of this edition. My literary agent, Mike Wallington, was tireless as a go-between, gathering information when age and infirmity made it difficult for me to do vital legwork. Warm thanks to Diana Blamires for setting the ball rolling. Michael 'Tim' Buckmaster brought SOE back into my life and, so doing, produced a valuable fount of knowledge.

Madam X gave generously her souvenirs of Christine in East Africa. Edward, Lord Montagu escorted me round Beaulieu, and his team (Margaret Rowles, Susan Tomkins and John Smith) were more than helpful. Count Andrew Skarbek, Christine's cousin, Douglas Hayler of Chichester Library, and Carole & David Harrison gave me important leads. Marcus Binney gifted me his excellent book, *The Women Who Lived for Danger*. Cyril Cunningham allowed me to quote from his invaluable work on SOE at Beaulieu. The staff at the National Archives (formerly The Public Record Office) acted diligently on my behalf – especially Howard Davies, Stephen Harwood and Paul Johnson. Mieczyslawa Wazacz generously allowed me to make use of research which resulted in her wonderful documentary, *No Ordinary Countess*. Countess Jolanta Mycielska offered the beautiful photo of Christine. John Purvis lent me his father's memoirs, *A Farmer & A Temporary Soldier*, by Paula Stiles. Thanks to Lennie Goodings and Vanessa Neuling, my editors for the new edition at Virago, for a most professional job. And last but not least, my grateful thanks go to Patrick Horstead who patiently translated my scribbled handwriting onto my computer.

NOTES

INTRODUCTION

1 Lt Col F. C. A. Cammaerts, DSO, 'Roger' – head of the 'Jockey' circuit in South East France.
2 The unfortunate Radziminski was to crop up again in Christine's life. He loved her to distraction, but was never anything more to her than one of her 'lame dogs'.
3 Colonel Guy Tamplin died of a heart attack in his office in Cairo. His widow later married Dick Crawshaw.
4 A later interview with Patrick Howarth gives the explanation to this mystery, and has been incorporated into Chapter 6.
5 1 August 1946.
6 Sir Frederick William Dampier Deakin, DSO 1943, MA, Warden of St Antony's College, Oxford. Born 1913. Served war of 1939–45 with Queen's Own Oxfordshire Hussars, 1939–41. Seconded to Special Operations, War Office 1941. Led first British Military Mission to Tito, May, 1943. In 1943 he married 'Pussi', Livia Stela, daughter of Livin Nasta of Bucharest.
7 This was El Effendi Durani, the son of the ex-King of Afghanistan, whose dynasty after many hundreds of years was ousted by Amanullah.

CHAPTER ONE

1 Letter from Zdzislaw Bau.
2 Ibid.
3 Letter from Mrs Antonina Edwards, first cousin to Christine. Her father was Josef Goldfeder, brother of Stephanie. Mrs Edwards lives in the USA.
4 Stanley Christopher has a reproduction of the famous painting by Lesser of the 'Habdank' episode.

5 'In the Polish Commonwealth the country population was divided into the *szlachta*, or freemen, who fought the battles of the country and in whom was vested the entire political power, and the *chlopi*, or peasants, who were serfs, and cultivated the estates of the *szlachta*. These formed about a tenth of the population of the country and were all legally of equal rank, though differences of property created great social and even political distinctions between them. Some possessed mere patches of land and lived a life little different to that of the peasants. Others having completely lost their estates became attached, sometimes even as servants in the households of their more prosperous neighbours. The great land-owners or magnates by gathering round them hordes of gently-born, landless dependants were able to support private armies and thus to exercise a proponderating influence on the affairs of the country.' – Miscellaneous Notes in a summary of Polish History by G. R. Noyes in 1930 edition of *Pan Tadensz* by Adam Mickiewicz (Everyman's Library).

6 Christine was to meet Colonel Bobinski later in Cairo, where he commanded the Carpathian Lancers.

7 Labunie was an estate belonging to the Tarnowski family, later owned by the Szeptycki family.

CHAPTER TWO

1 *Jews, God and History* by Max I. Dimont (W. H. Allen, London).

2 In 1655 the Swedes invaded the Polish Commonwealth. Russia, fearing the rise of Swedish power, signed an armistice with Poland, the terms of which provided, among other things, for a joint campaign against Sweden. From the outset the new war took a disastrous turn for Poland; Warsaw fell to the Swedes, then Cracow surrendered. From his exile in Silesia John Casimir issued a summons for resistance. The prevailing feeling of hatred towards the enemy was roused still further when the Swedes besieged the monastery of the Pauline monks in Czestochowa. From the military point of view the siege was a complete failure and the widespread indignation it aroused was eventually to bring unhappy consequences to the invader.

3 The following appears in the General Catalogue of Printed Books in the British Library, and in the Catalog of the Library of Congress: Gizycki (Georg) (*Biali i Czarni*) *Die Weissen und die Schwarzen* Erlebuisse in Franzosisch-West-Afrika. Mit 16 Anbilden, nach Aufnahmen der Verfassers p.p. 413. Essener Verlagsanstalt: Essen 1936.

4 *The Teschen* (Cieszyn) *Question*. The erstwhile Austrian Duchy of
Teschen had already been the subject of strife between Poland and
Czechoslovakia for some time. Czech troops had occupied the western half of the disputed territory on 22 January 1919, and thus created
a *fait accompli* which could not be set aside even by an agreement
made between Beneš and Dmoski on 1 February, though this agreement envisaged a referendum. The Supreme Council's decree of
27 September 1919, dealing with the proposed plebiscite, was equally
ineffective, since the Inter-Allied Commission under Count
Manneville appointed in February 1920 recognized that a referendum was impracticable, and direct Polish–Czech negotiations ended
in failure. On 28 July 1920, the Inter-Allied Commission, in accordance with the directives of Spa, made an award which gave Poland
only the districts to the east of the little river Olsa, with about 142,000
German and Polish inhabitants. The larger and more valuable portion
of Teschen, with its mines and foundries and the town of Teschen
itself, was assigned to Czechoslovakia. In the Beskids mountains
twenty-seven border villages with about 30,000 inhabitants were
ceded to Poland. The territorial claims which Poland continued to
make delayed the final fixing of the frontier until 16 September 1924,
and were to cast a shadow over Polish–Czech relations in the future.

   The reason why a just division of the disputed Teschen area of
Silesia was so difficult was that the centre of the region was inhabited
by Slovaks, people who spoke a Polish dialect, but were distinguished from the Poles of Galicia by their Evangelical religion and
Germano-Austrian culture. Slovaks formed the majority of the
140,000 Polish speakers who were left on the Czech side of the new
frontier.

5 Mr Kowerski was appointed to represent all the landowners who had
spirit distilleries on their estates.

CHAPTER THREE

1 *Out of Africa* by Karen Blixen. First published 1937, Jonathan Cape,
London.

2 From *A History of Modern Poland* by Hans Roos (Eyre &
Spottiswoode, London).

3 *British Guarantees for Poland:*
A statement in the House of Commons by the Prime Minister (Mr
Neville Chamberlain) on 31 March 1939 included the following: '. . . in
the event of any action which clearly threatened Polish independence,

and which the Polish Government accordingly considered it vital to resist with their national force, His Majesty's Government would feel themselves bound at once to lend the Polish Government all support in their power. They have given the Polish Government an assurance to this effect.'

On 6 April 1939, after a visit to London by Mr Josef Beck, Polish Minister of Foreign Affairs, a joint Polish–British communiqué was issued in which Poland committed herself to give all help to Great Britain in time of emergency.

General Ironside, Chief of the British Imperial General Staff, conferred in Warsaw between 17 and 21 July with the Polish Commander-in-Chief, Marshal Rydz-Smigly, and Mr Beck. On 25 August 1939 a treaty of mutual assistance and co-operation in case of war was signed by the United Kingdom and Poland.

4 'In the spring of 1939 Colonel Gubbins (later head of SOE) working with Holland paid a number of secret visits to the Baltic States, Poland and the Danubian countries, examining the terrain with an eye to suitable areas for diversionary action.' From *Poland, SOE and the Allies*, by J. Garlinski (George Allen & Unwin, London).

5 From *Great Britain and European Resistance*, by F. W. D. Deakin.

6 Florian Sokolov, London correspondent of the Warsaw Press, and also attached to the BBC. His beautiful sister Sophie was to become one of Christine's closest friends in Palestine.

7 *Approach March* by Julian Amery (Hutchinson). While a 19-year-old undergraduate, Julian Amery covered the Spanish Civil War as a newspaper correspondent. After diplomatic service in Belgrade and the Balkans, he joined the RAF, transferred to the Army and as a SOE officer was parachuted into Albania for two years, and was later Winston Churchill's personal representative with Chiang Kai-Shek. MP from 1950, he held several Ministerial posts under Conservative governments, including Minister of Aviation and Minister of State, Foreign Office.

8 Sir Robert Vansittart was permanent Under Secretary for State. George Taylor worked for SOE almost from its inception.

9 The Polish equivalent of the Victoria Cross.

10 After the accident Kowerski was released from the Army; as a Reserve Officer, he petitioned the Polish Commander-in-Chief, Rydz-Smigly, and was transferred from the Horse Artillery to the Motorized Artillery under the command of Colonel Kopanski, who later commanded the Polish Brigade in the desert. Andrew was called

for retraining in 1938 during the Czechoslovakian tragedy, and then back to the Army two months before the war began in 1939. Half the regiment was then attached to the famous 'Black Brigade', the only motorized unit in Poland.

11 'Resistance in Eastern Europe' by H. Seton-Watson, from *Special Operations*, edited by Patrick Howarth (Routledge & Kegan Paul).

12 'The Underground Factory: Poland in 1939–45', by Adam Zamoyski. From *History Today*, December 1975.

13 Poland was to have the shame of having the most infamous concentration camps built on her land. All these camps, no matter what they were called, were built as labour camps for prisoners and as extermination centres.

14 Famous Polish salt mines.

15 Through their affiliation with the trades unions the Polish Socialist Party had rapidly become highly organized in Hungary, and while all Polish political parties flamed back into life after the initial shock of invasion, the Socialist Party was particularly active.

16 See Chapter Five note 3.

17 *The Phantom Caravan* by Sir Owen O'Malley, KCMG (John Murray, London).

18 Eddie was arrested that same day but, through his influential family connections, was deported to Yugoslavia.

19 Andrew and Ludwig Popiel had chanced on a thieves' pub on the Danube where they were nearly lynched until it was discovered that they were not Germans but Poles occupied in helping people to escape. They took Andrew and his cousin to their hearts, and promised help in any emergency.

20 By this time the Nazi Governor Frank had taken over the administration of Poland and was busy suppressing Polish cultural life and conducting a policy of extermination. Worst of all was the fate of three and a half million Polish Jews who, having been forcibly concentrated in ghettoes, were condemned to death by Himmler. No more than 100,000 escaped the gas chambers and crematoriums of the death factories such as Oswiecim (Auschwitz), Treblinka and Belzec.

Moreover, the Germans transferred Jews from all over occupied Europe to Poland, where altogether about five million met their death. Before the final liquidation, 19 April 1942, of the Warsaw ghetto – the largest of them all – a handful of Jews of both sexes, armed with nothing but their fists, and a few machine guns and rifles smuggled in by the Polish Underground Movement, for ten days fought their oppressors, killing 300 Germans and wounding l,000. A few Jews managed to escape through the sewers, but 26,000 were massacred, while around 14,000 survivors were deported.

21 Radziminski was a plucky man. On leaving Budapest, he went to France where the Polish Government in exile was regrouping its forces. He did much the same kind of work Andrew was doing in Budapest. He helped people to escape from the Occupied Zone to the Free Zone and then got them conveyed from Marseilles via the Pyrenees to Portugal and on to England.

When it was time for him to escape himself, he got a false Portuguese passport, reserved a sleeper, bribed the conductor and got through all the frontiers. Unfortunately, there was a train crash in Spain and when Radziminski was rescued it was discovered that he could speak neither Portuguese nor Spanish. He was sent to a camp in Miranda for escapees, and abominably treated by the Spaniards. Pretending to fall in with a German plan to return prisoners to Poland to work, he jumped with immense courage from the train, but was never heard of again.

22 Information provided by Stanley Christopher.

CHAPTER FOUR

1 Andrzejewska – the feminine of Andrzej (Andrew) in Polish.
2 'The first Polish land forces ready for action were the Highland Brigade, which was sent to Norway in April 1940, and fought at Narvik. The Brigade earned the praise of the French Commander, General Béthouart, and of the British Command. They were ordered to abandon Narvik and return to France owing to the gravity of the situation there. On arrival they immediately covered a retreat of the BEF in the region of Rennes.

'Of the other Polish troops in France, the First Grenadiers Division relieved a French division on the Metz sector in front of the Maginot Line. The French General Pretel stated that if the French High Command had possessed ten divisions as good as this Polish one, the defeat of the French armies might have been averted.

'General Duch, the Officer Commanding, received orders from General Sikorski to retreat to the coast, but the French asked him to stay and cover their retreat. This he did, and thus saved part of the French army at great cost to his own forces. Then the division carried out a hazardous retreat along the Western slopes of the Vosges in order to join up with the Second Division of Chasseurs which was fighting at Besançon. This division also covered a French retreat, and having suffered considerable losses finally crossed over into Switzerland. They arrived in such excellent order that the Swiss military authorities paid them the tribute of not disarming them immediately.

'The Motorized Armoured Brigade was rapidly armed and on 10th June thrown into battle on the Marne front. This Brigade retreated in perfect order with its colours to Hungary. It took the colours to France, saved them after the battles there, and carried them victoriously to Scotland.

'The Polish Army also supplied nine anti-tank batteries which were incorporated into French divisions. These were almost completely destroyed in consequence of the tasks entrusted to them by the French command.' – From *Poland's Part in the War* by F. C. Anstruther (Polish Library, 1943).

3   In November 1940, Franz Stangl, former Commandant of Treblinka extermination camp, was ordered to report to Berlin for briefing. He was sent to Tiergartenstrasse 4, seed bed of the most hideous secret operations of the Third Reich. This was where the 'mercy killings' of the mentally and physically handicapped were organized like a military campaign.

CHAPTER FIVE

1   It later transpired that the good Hungarian doctor had put in so strong a report on Christine's health that even the Gestapo were not anxious to incur the wrath of her aunt and of her relation, the Regent Horthy. The doctor had said that, in his view, if Christine were sent to prison she would die very soon. And that if the Gestapo tried to take her over the border, she would be unable to stand the journey and would die in transit. Both Andrew and Christine suspected that the doctor purposely emphasized the severity of Christine's illness, and always longed to express their gratitude to him for his gallant gesture.

2   'The "Green Frontier" twisted round every conquered country of Europe, "the underground way", leading both to safety and to danger. At first when Poland fell it passed into Hungary. But as country after country fell, it became closed and was taken over by the Germans and the Russians and those who crossed did so at their peril. It was then that the long frontiers became "Green", and people no longer went

openly but slipped through secretly, bent always on service, so that many took the road back again after delivering and receiving messages. They stole through like the wolves and the deer. Every rock, the trees, the folds of snow sheltered them.' From *A Fringe of Blue*, the autobiography of Joice NanKivell Loch (John Murray, London).

3 A. G. G. de Chastelain, DSO, OBE, was an exceptional human being. He was 'our man' in Bucharest, where he lived for some years. He was an oil engineer, and became a close friend and admirer of George Gizycki, of whom he said that, besides being the most difficult man he had ever known, he was also the most efficient and capable individual he had ever worked with. De Chastelain was in charge of the I. Section, British Embassy, Turkey.

4 Sir Owen was also consulted, and it was through his good offices later on that George Gizycki, who was doing undercover work for the British military authorities in Abyssinia, was moved to Budapest, issued with a British passport and appointed Sir Owen's Military Attaché's clerk.

5 Aidan Merivale Crawley, MBE Journalist. Asst. Air Attaché, Ankara, Belgrade (resident Sofia), May 1940–May 1941. Joined RAF Egypt; shot down 1941, prisoner till 1945. MP Labour 1945–51; Conservative 1962–67. Parliamentary Under Secretary of State for Air 1950–51. Editor-in-chief Ind. Television News 1955–56, Chairman London Weekend Television 1967–71. President from 1971. He was married to writer Virginia Cowles and died in 1993.

6 Aidan Crawley later confirmed that the microfilms had been sent to the Air Ministry. They were passed on to Churchill, who then warned Stalin of what the Germans were piling up on the Russian border. Andrew has always felt that some kind of official letter could have recorded the fact that their microfilms were certainly the first of the early warnings about the impending attack on Russia by Germany to reach the British Prime Minister.

CHAPTER SIX

1 Julian Amery, op. cit.

2 It seems that there were ten Turkish pounds to a British pound.

3 Khamsin, an oppressive hot wind from the south or south-east.

4 'Ah, you are most fortunate, ladies and gentlemen. You'll be shot of this filth by tomorrow, while I stay and get up to my neck in it.'

5 'I'll give you the best room at the ordinary price, just for the pleasure of having English people in the hotel.'

6   Sophie Raczkowski, whose name was later changed to Raziel, met Christine through her brother Florian Sokolov, the writer and journalist. Christine had helped Florian with secretarial work when he was living in Hampstead. Dr Celina Sokolov said, 'Christine was a great friend of my late sister Sophie. She often visited our family home and knew my late father, who was very fond of her.'

7   *Near East* by Cecil Beaton (Batsford, London).

8   Major-General Wladyslaw Bobinski, DSO, MC, and Virtuti Militari. Commanded the Motorized Brigade in Italy. Died February 1975.

9   Wilkinson, Sir Peter, KCMG, DSO, OBE. Ambassador to Vienna 1970–71 Active service in Poland (despatches), France, Italy and Balkans. Cross of Valour (Poland) 1940, Order of White Lion (IV Class) (Czechoslovakia) 1945.

10 When the author discussed this incident with Sir Peter Wilkinson, he said that he remembered feeling very sorry for Christine and Andrew. They were a most attractive pair, who had carried out several very hazardous missions and had every reason to expect the continued support of the British authorities.

But he had received explicit instructions from London that, at the urgent request of the Polish authorities, Christine's and Andrew's current activities were to be wound up with the least possible delay.

Sir Peter explained that when the Polish Government established themselves in London after the Fall of France, it had been agreed, for reasons of practical security as well as of State, that all communications with Occupied Poland should be channelled only through the Polish authorities in London. The Polish authorities were, therefore, entirely within their rights to request withdrawal of any support from Christine's and Andrew's friends in Poland.

11 The Musketeers organization was incorporated into the Polish Home Army by order of General Sikorski, Polish Commander-in-Chief. Its main task was to collect intelligence material and to convey it to the Commander of the Home Army. Under the leadership of Stanislaw Witkowski ('Tensczynski') the group was very active. Against the strict orders of the Home Army, it sought direct contact with British Intelligence and to engage in certain political activities. This incurred the suspicion of both the Polish Staff in London and the Deuxième Bureau. Witkowski is believed to have been shot dead in 1942 by German police.

12 George 'Jerzy' Gizycki continued his writing career in Canada by becoming first a contributor to, and later an editor of the Polish-

Canadian newspaper *Zwiazkowiec*. According to Mr Benedyct Heydenhorn, ex-editor of *Zwiazkowiec*, George Gizycki died c. 1973 in Mexico.

13 Letter from Mrs Irene Atayan to the author.

14 When France fell, the Carpathian Brigade under General Kopanski was in Syria. General Mittelhauser wished it to follow the example of the French troops in laying down their arms. This General Kopanski refused to do, and the Brigade, with all its equipment, made its way to Palestine. It then went to Egypt and from there, by sea, to Tobruk. There, with an Australian and a Czech battalion, it defended the fort for seven months, made numerous sorties and inflicted heavy losses on the enemy, while having relatively light casualties of its own. The Brigade played a prominent part in the assault of Gazala, taking a large number of prisoners and war *matériel*.

15 After the war he changed his name to Truscoe, and went to live in New Zealand. He became a professor at the Victoria University of Wellington.

16

PLAY BACK A LIFETIME
A previously unpublished poem
by Patrick Howarth

So I first met the Countess Gizycka, née Skarbek, known as
    Christine Granville,
stretching in cat-like delight with the Gezira sun,
dull dark-brown jacket, dull light-brown skirt, brilliant brown mobile
    arresting eyes,
resisting with sudden passion a proposal of office employment;
'*J'ai tant d'endurance physique mais pas intellectuelle.*'
Well, she had made illicit crossings of some dozen frontiers,
usually on skis, at times in the boot of an Ambassador's car.
Living as they mostly do in a militarily indefensible plain,
Poles, since the outwitting of the pachyderm Czartoryskis
by resilient rulers of rapacious eighteenth century powers,
have found their epic theme in return from exile.
Marsz, marsz Dabrowski. The legions marched again under Piludski
    and Haller;
the great pianist gave the pedant American president his thirteenth
    point;
and Freedom shrieked . . . as Kosciuszko fell.

So now to the Perthshire glens, to Khanaquin under the Zagros
    mountains,
to Cyrenaica enrolled in their Carpathian Brigade
Poles in their tens of thousands had come to fight their way back to
    their homeland,
their accolade to be despatched to the *armja krajowa*,
the underground force that was gathering strength in Poland.
The links with this force were devious, various, fashioned by dedi-
    cated men,
who yet were pawns in the intrigue which, like a cancer, claw through
    government in exile,
whose ministers have portfolios but no departments.
So with two secret Polish networks, duplicating each other's func-
    tions,
I learnt to live as a man with a wife and a mistress
who have a tacit agreement to deny the other exists.
Besides these there were the freelance groups, with Christine at the
    heart of one:
from the freelances, it was hinted, I should be wise to withdraw in
    safety.
In the secret agents' world a hint can be finally damning:
Christine and her associate Andrew were thoroughly damned by faint
    hints.
So I steered at first an orthodox course through the secret shoals and
    currents
learning daily from the ancient Polish lore in my missions through
    Asia Minor . . .

17   The 'Baltic Baron'.

CHAPTER SEVEN

1   *SOE in France* by M. R. D. Foot (HM Stationery Office, 1966).
2   This phrase occurs in *The Four Just Men* by Edgar Wallace (Tallis
    Press, London, 1905).
3   'The original F Section, the main British body organizing French sub-
    version, was launched by Leslie Humphreys in the summer of 1940
    when he returned from France; he had been Section D's Paris repre-
    sentative, and came out by warship from the Gironde, in
    circumstances of some turmoil, on 20 June. In December he moved
    over to work on clandestine lines, and F passed to a civilian head, H.
    R. Marriott, long Courtauld's representative in Paris. A year later,

Marriott handed over to Major Maurice Buckmaster, formerly a Ford manager in Asnières, who remained in charge till the end . . .' From M. R. D. Foot, op. cit.

4   SOE's first offices consisted of three dreary, dingy rooms in St Ermin's in Westminster. It was soon evident that new premises were needed and these were found at 64 Baker Street. The new organization moved in at the end of October 1940. By the middle of November, the house was bursting at the seams, and SOE took over the lease of five neighbouring buildings.

5   At the same time reference was made to Scotland Yard's Criminal Record Office. Maurice Buckmaster has a chapter in his book *Specially Employed* on the selection and types of agents who worked for SOE. In the early days it was assumed that only persons with a criminal background would be able to pit their wits against the German Abwehr, the Gestapo and the French *Milice*. Jepson never subscribed to this theory: 'The only loyalty – and loyalty of a supreme nature was what we had to have – that a crook knows is loyalty to himself and sometimes, passingly as a necessity, to his fellow crooks. It would have been recruiting double-agents to use such people.'

6   To be in uniform also went a long way towards satisfying the curiosity of friends and relations who might want to know what the girl was up to. Sometime later the WAAF bent its rules to the extent of granting 'honorary' commissions to the women whom Jepson recruited from their ranks. A further value in this procedure was the possibility that in the event of capture a legitimate claim to be a 'commissioned officer' in a known women's service might perhaps ensure better treatment than a civilian saboteur would receive.

7   Jozef Garlinski, op. cit.

8   Jozef Garlinski, op. cit.

9   Now Betty Rigg. In a letter to the author she said: 'Everyone at the Club felt it was a privilege to have Christine there and to do anything to make that awful waiting more bearable.'

10   Francis Brooks-Richards, CMG, DSC and Bar. HM Diplomatic Service.

11   See his book, *No Cloak, No Dagger* (Jarrold, 1960).

12   *Specially Employed* by M. J. Buckmaster (Batchworth Press, 1952).

13   Sir Douglas Dodds-Parker. Employed on special duties 1940, served in London, Cairo, East Africa, North Africa, Italy and France. Colonel 1944 (despatches, French Légion d'Honneur, Croix de Guerre).

14 SOE Gaullist Section.

15 M. R. D. Foot, op. cit.

16 'Throughout its life the FANY as Staff Officers, secretaries, coders, W/T operators, escorting officers, packers and drivers took an active part in the launching of SOE operations to Tunisia, Corsica, Sicily, Sardinia, Italy and Southern France.' *F.A.N.Y. Invicta* by Irene Ward, DBE, MP (Hutchinson, London).

17 Irene Ward, ibid.

18 *Old Men Forget* by Alfred Duff Cooper (Hart-Davis, London).

19 *Trumpets from the Steep* by Diana Duff Cooper (Hart-Davis, London).

20 A Jewish tailor, a refugee from Vienna, acted as adviser to SOE on Continental garments. He copied typical clothes of every occupied country in his workshops. Hitler's fury would have been even more intense had he known that many of SOE's most successful agents outwitted both the Abwehr and the Gestapo and carried out their dangerous missions dressed in clothes bought by the Jewish tailor from his friends when he visited his synagogue.

21 *Secret Agents, Spies and Saboteurs* by Janusz Piekaliewicz (David and Charles).

22 John Anstey – letter to the author. Brig. John Anstey, CBE, TD, DL, North Africa, France (despatches). Légion d'Honneur, Croix de Guerre (France), Legion of Merit (USA).

23 John Roper memorandum.

CHAPTER EIGHT

1 Colonel F. C. A. Cammaerts ('Roger'), DSO, Légion d'Honneur, Croix de Guerre.

2 Captain Harry Rée, DSO, MBE, H. A. Ree, Professor of Education at the University of York until 1974, served as an SOE agent in the region of Besançon, and was responsible for the planned sabotage of the Peugeot factory. He died in 1991.

3 Francis Cammaerts says this 'story' was basically true, as he *did* buy sheep and cattle for the Wragby farm from time to time.

4 *SOE Assignment* by Donald Hamilton-Hill (William Kimber, London).

5 'Lise': Odette Sansom, later Odette Churchill, then Mrs Geoffrey Hallowes. GC, MBE, Légion d'Honneur. She died in 1995.

6 'Arnaud': Adolphe Rabinovitch, MC. A brave and honourable man. Later caught by the Gestapo. Being Jewish he was sent to the extermination camp at Rawicz in Poland and terribly tortured. He was killed in March 1944.

7   Abwehr: the successor of the old Military Intelligence Service of the German War Ministry; from 1939 it was known as the Security Offices. Amtsgruppe Abwehr. It was organized in five departments and sub-departments. Bleicher belonged to the branch which employed foreign agents. Its task was to penetrate the ranks of foreign secret services. Hugo Bleicher was a man of formidable intelligence, and his memoirs make interesting reading.

8   M. R. D. Foot op. cit.

9   Ibid.

10 A letter-box is somebody with whom one could leave a message or a letter to be collected later by another person giving the right pass-word. There were letter-boxes in all manner of shops. Anyone acting as a letter-box was exposed, if caught, to the brutality of the enemy.

11 Maurice Buckmaster, op. cit.

12 Pearl Witherington, a trained British courier, was one of the few women to take over and run an active Maquis – of some two thousand men in Berry – which she did with the brio and dash that had charac-terized her gallant ancestor Richard Witherington, who, at the Battle of Chevy Chase, 'when both his knees were hewn in two yet he kneeled and fought on his knee.' She later married Henri Cornioley. She was given the MBE, but returned it saying she had done nothing 'civil'. Rail cuts were one of the specialities of her Wrestler circuit.

13 In the summer of 1944 Madame Lefort died in the gas chambers of Ravensbruck.

14 'Dans la nuit un parachutage eut lieu sur le terrain de Vassieux (Taille-Crayon). Ce fut la mission Paquebot, comprenant le capitaine d'aviation Tournissa (Paquebot) et une femme agent de liaison, Christine Granville (Miss Pauline), et quatre sous-lieutenants. L'un d'eux, le sous-lieutenant Francis Billon, s'étant fracturé la cuisse droite lors de sa réception, fut transporté a l'hôpital de maquis à St Martin-en-Vercors.' From *Témoignages sur le Vercors* by Joseph La-Picirella (Imprimerie Rivet, Lyons), who was present on this occasion.

15 The people of the Vercors were justifiably proud of their Resistance hospital which was hidden in a children's convalescent home. It had 700 beds, an operating theatre and a special training school for nurses cum stretcher-bearers.

16 Sylviane Rey in a letter to the author.

17 This was one of three major movements in the south of France. Libération, Combat and Francs-Tireurs.

18 Francis Cammaerts in a letter to the author. He also said 'Descours

and Zeller, like me, were not regular Vercors "maquisards". They had the same kind of supportive role that I had.'

19 Translated by the author from *La Vie des Français sous l'Occupation* by Henri Amouroux (Fayard).

20 Henri Amouroux, ibid.

21 The correct fabrication of false identity papers was of vital importance, for they would inevitably be scrutinized by the police or by the Germans: if they did not pass muster, the life of whoever was bearing them could well be jeopardized. Agents arriving from England and impersonating a fictitious French civilian had to feel complete confidence that their papers were 'bona-fide'. Constant checks took place on trains, in hotels, in restaurants and in the streets. The French police were fairly tolerant and did not inspect all documents too closely; but the Germans were meticulous and difficult. Supporters of the Resistance in the Prefectures and in Government departments were helpful in supplying blank papers, and in advising what official stamps they ought to carry.

22 The Resistance depended greatly on 'safe-houses' owned by families who were prepared to take the risk of receiving, feeding and lodging a member of the underground. The risks were tremendous and persisted even after the departure of the 'guest'. The punishment for sheltering a member of the Resistance was generally imprisonment or deportation; or the whole family would be punished by burning down their house.

Brothels and convents were considered fairly safe. Those seeking 'safe-houses' looked for dwellings with large gardens, where there were spare rooms with access to the garden. An isolated house without prying neighbours was ideal.

Access to ration-cards was vital for working a cutout – a kind of fail-safe device in the Resistance. It was a way of establishing contact between two agents, which, if properly worked, made it difficult for the enemy service to intercept.

23 Note from 'Roger': 'The South Drôme was the mountainous area south of Vercors – that is south of the railway and Drôme river. Crest, Dieulefit, Bourdeau, Serres, Montélimar, Pierrelatte etc. were some of the places I worked in from May to October, 1943. The South Drôme was under the command of Alain, a French officer of SOE parachuted in to help me in May 1943.'

24 'Lying on the sun': the phrase recurs and is possibly a direct translation from the Polish.

25 The aircraft carried out mass drops of *matériel*, including mortars, machine guns and field artillery. The containers were distributed to many camps; but the situation in the Vercors was becoming critical.

26 J. La-Picirella, op. cit.

CHAPTER NINE

1 J. La-Picirella, op. cit.

2 In March 1944, General de Gaulle decreed the formation of 'Les Forces Françaises de l'Intérieur', the army of the new France to be. 'Local clandestine activities,' he said later, 'had to take on at the right moment the character of a national effort; had to become consistent enough to play a part in Allied strategy; and lastly, had to lead the Army of Shadows to fuse with the rest into a single French Army.' (*Mémoires* II 312 tr.) It was understood that the FFI would be used as an auxiliary force to attack the Germans at the moment of the invasion of Western Europe.

3 Letter from Henry Threlfall, Commander of France 139, to which Christine was briefly attached in Italy.

4 F Section – SOE Independent French Section.

5 Barcelonette (pop. approx. 2,500), a little town – subprefecture of the department of the Basses-Alpes. Many foreigners had built luxurious villas and holiday homes on the banks of the River Ubaye. Some of these houses enjoyed superb views of the peaks of Mont Tinibras and the Col de Larche, scene of one of Christine's most important missions.

6 ANVIL (DRAGOON) The landing on the Riviera at many points between Toulon and Nice of the Americans and French took place on 15 August, 1944. There was strong naval and air support.

7 'Stores were packed either in rubber or fibre packages or panniers or in metal containers. Packages travelled inside the aircraft and were looked after by the dispatcher who bundled them out into space just before or after the agents, who were his prime responsibility . . . Something over twenty thousand packages and panniers were dropped into France for SOE during the war, and nearly one hundred thousand containers were dropped as well. There were two sorts of containers: the C-type, a single cylinder nearly six feet long, containing three cylindrical canisters, and the H-type: five cylindrical cells held together by a pair of metal rods while they dropped. The H-type was the invention of an ingenious Pole.' From *SOE in France* by M. R. D. Foot (page 80).

8 M. R. D. Foot, op. cit.

9 J. La-Piricella, op. cit.

10 Francis Cammaerts to the author.

11 *Hide and Seek* by Xan Fielding (Secker and Warburg, London). In fact, Francis Cammaerts says that, at this point, he had been in France for only eighteen months.

12 Fielding, ibid.

13 'The Oriental Legion' was composed of units of Tartars, Georgians, Armenians and Bashkirs. They were a tough and uncouth group who spoke neither French nor German.

14 This incident was corroborated by Christine's guide Gilbert Tavernier ('Tatar'), who worked with her after the Digne incident.

15 'Tatar' was the guide hired by Gilbert Galetti to escort Christine on her terrifying expedition. 'Tatar' later said that her climb to the Col was a triumph of mind over matter, and that when she came back her legs were bloody and swollen.

16 Gilbert Galetti was Chef de La Résistance, a larger than life character, and a great friend of 'Roger' and Christine.

17 Xan Fielding, op. cit.

18 'Mongols' – 'The Oriental Legion'.

19 German Security Forces.

20 Xan Fielding, op. cit.

21 During the testing time when Christine was going to and fro between Seyne and Digne she rode a bicycle, walked throughout one night and was also driven by Monsieur Turrel's son.

22 John Roper, CMG, MC. Joined the Scots Guards at the outbreak of war. Served in the Guards Armoured Division until autumn 1943, when he went to Cairo and was seconded to SOE. HM Ambassador to Luxembourg, 1970–1975.

23 John Roper says that late that same evening, Christine went back to Seyne and picked him up. 'We did not speak at all in the car but it was evident to me that we were engaged in laying a false trail. Eventually, we slowed down at a cross-road, got an all-clear signal from a man standing by a hedge, and a few hundred yards further on we walked cautiously to the barn where "Roger's" wireless operators were and where we found the three men.' (It will be noted that there seems to be some slight divergence of opinion as to the exact sequence of events when the three men left the prison with Max to drive to the barn. Francis Cammaerts, Xan Fielding and John Roper each have a different memory of when Christine first appeared to lead them to safety.)

24 Information from John Roper.

25 Xan Fielding, op. cit.

CHAPTER TEN

1 Donald Hamilton-Hill went to Greece as Second-in-Command of Colonel Ronnie Todd's Commando Force, which liberated Athens and Salonika.

2 Memorandum from F. Cammaerts to the author.

3 Francis Cammaerts was to name one of his daughters after Christine.

4 Major Peter J. F. Storrs, a member in 1940 of the British diplomatic mission to N. Norway, was awarded the Norwegian Military Medal and acted during 1941–42 as liaison with the Norwegian Brigade. From 1942–45 he was in the Free French Section of SOE in London and Algiers and was later in the Political Division, Control Commission in Germany. After the war he served in France, USA, Cyprus, London, Canada and Turkey in the Foreign, Commonwealth and Colonial Services.

5 A. M. Brooks, DSO, MC. One of F Section's best men, and head of Pimento Circuit.

6 Nothing would have induced her to use the currency in her money-belt.

7 Lieutenant Colonel H. M. Threlfall, OBE By profession a Unilever executive with service in France and Germany before the war. Commissioned into the Intelligence Corps. Transferred to SOE in 1941 as an expert on the German Army. Having been Instructing Officer in the SOE finishing school at Beaulieu, served in the German and Scandinavian Sections of SOE in 1942 and 1943. After very distinguished service in Italy, Lt. Col. Threlfall returned to the UK, and was demobilized in November 1945.

8 F. W. Deakin, op. cit.

9 Crucial summit meeting between Churchill, Stalin and Roosevelt.

10 Memorandum to the author from John Roper.

11 Harrods have no record of Mrs Christine Granville's brief term of employment.

12 Michael Dunford in a memorandum to the author.

13 Mervyn Cowie, born in Kenya and educated in England, was responsible for instituting National Game Parks in Kenya. He was appointed first Director of Kenya National Parks, and from 1946 to 1966 he developed and administered these vast areas. An authority on wild life, he wrote many books on the subject and was Financial Director of the Flying Doctors of East Africa. He died in 1996.

14 Michael Dunford was appointed by the East Africa High Commission to study and report on ways to develop tourism in East

Africa. His report was accepted and he was appointed the first General Manager of the East Africa Tourist Travel Association which he established along the lines of his own recommendation. Mervyn Cowie later referred to him as 'the architect of Kenya's tourism'.

15   It may not have been entirely irrelevant that there were many thousand Poles in Kenya at the time.

CHAPTER ELEVEN

1   Ludwig Popiel was described in the press as 'a builder and decorator in a small way'. In fact, Andrew's cousin was a man of matchless courage. A Major in the Carpathian Lancers, he holds not only the MC for capturing a German machine gun nest when armed only with a handful of bricks, but was also *twice* awarded the Virtuti Militari, the Polish equivalent of the VC.

2   It was just about the same time that the ill-fated Drummond family had been murdered in their caravan near Manosque. Sir Jack had been involved in underground work in France. Suspicion had been cast on the Dominici family whose role in this case remains ambiguous. Strangely, they and their farm were well-known to 'Roger'. 'They had worked with us,' he said. 'One of our parachute grounds was just above their farm, and they supplied us with food. The Dominici family helped us a lot and I spent a night in their farmhouse.'

3   His ex-wife had remarried when the boy was a baby, and he had no idea of his real father's identity.

4   Teresa Lubienska was stabbed to death on the Piccadilly Line platform at Gloucester Road Station on Friday 24 May 1957, at 10.20 p.m. The reason for her death remains a mystery.

BIBLIOGRAPHY

Amouroux, H.: *La Vie des Français sous l'Occupation*, Fayard 1961.

Aron, Robert: *Histoire de la Libération*, Fayard 1959.

Astier de la Vigerie, Emmanuel d': *Seven Times Seven Days* (tr. Hare, Humphrey), Macgibbon & Kee 1958.

Avon, Earl of: *The Eden Memoirs – The Reckoning*, Cassell 1965.

Bechmann-Lescot: *Le Vercors*, L'Armée Française, July 1948.

Benouville, G.: *Sacrifice au Matin*, 1946.

Bertrand: *Faux papiers*, Nathan.

Binney, Marcus: *The Women Who Lived For Danger: Women Agents of SOE in the Second World War*, Hodder & Stoughton 1988.

Bleicher, Hugo: *Colonel Henri's Story*, (ed. Borchers, E., and ed. and tr. Colvin, Ian), Kimber 1954.

Blocq-Mascart, M.: *Chroniques de la Résistance*, Correa 1945.

Braddon, Russell: *Nancy Wake*, Cassell 1956.

Bright Astley, Joan: *The Inner Circle*, Hutchinson 1971.

Bryce, Ivar: *You Only Live Once – Memories of Ian Fleming*, Weidenfeld & Nicolson, 1975, revised edition 1984.

Buckmaster, Maurice: *Specially Employed*, Batchworth Press 1952.

—— *They Fought Alone*, Odhams 1958.

Butler, Ewan: *Amateur Agent*, Harrap 1963.

Calvocoressi, Peter, and Wint, Guy: *Total War*, Pelican 1974.

Cambridge History of Poland, Vol. 1, Cambridge University Press 1950.

Churchill, Peter: *Of their Own Choice*, Hodder 1952.

—— *The Spirit in the Cage*, Hodder 1954.

—— *Duel of Wits*, Hodder 1957.

—— *By Moonlight*, Hale 1958.

Churchill, Winston S.: *The Second World War*, Cassell 1948–53.

Collier, Richard: *Ten Thousand Eyes*, Collins Fontana 1966.

Colvin, I.: *Vansittart in Office*, Gollancz 1965.

Concentration Camps: *Le système concentrationnaire allemand*, Revue d'Histoire de la 2ème guerre mondiale.

Cowburn, Benjamin: *No Cloak, No Dagger*, Jarrolds 1960.

Crossman, R.: *Psychological Warfare*, Journal RUSI 1952.

Cunningham, Cyril: *Beaulieu – The Finishing School For Secret Agents 1941–45*, Leo Cooper, an imprint of Pen & Sword Books Ltd, 1998.

Dalloz, P.: *Rapports sur Vercors*.

Dansette, Adrien: *Histoire de la libération de Paris*, Fayard 1946.

Davidson, Basil: *Partisan Pictures*, Bedford Books Ltd.

Dimont, Max I.: *Jews, God and History*, W. H. Allen 1964.

Duff Cooper, A. (Lord Norwich): *Old Men Forget*, Hart-Davis 1953.

Duff Cooper, Lady Diana: *Trumpets from the Steep*, Hart-Davis 1960.

Durandet, Christian: *Les Maquis de Provence*, Editions France-Empire 1974.

Ellis, Major L. F. (and others): *Victory in the West, 1944–5*, Vol. 1, HMSO.

Encyclopaedia of Dates and Events: Ed. L. C. Pascoe. English University Press 1974.

Farran, Roy: *Winged Dagger*, Collins 1948.

Farson, Daniel: *Riddle of the Woman Pimpernel, Observer Magazine*, 20 Oct 1974.

Fielding, Xan: *Hide and Seek*, Secker & Warburg 1954.

Fleming, Ian: *Casino Royale*, Jonathan Cape, 1953.

Foot, M. R. D.: *SOE in France*, HMSO 1966.

Frenay, Henri: *La Nuit Finira*, Robert Laffont 1973.

Garlinski, Jozef: *Poles, SOE and the Allies*, Allen & Unwin 1969.

Gaulle, Charles de: *Mémoires de Guerre*, Plon pocket edition.

Gillois, André: *Histoire Secrète des Français à Londres de 1940 à 1944*, Libraire Jules Tallandier 1973.

Ginter, Maria: *Life in Both Hands*, Hodder & Stoughton 1964.

Granet, M.: *Dessin Général des Maquis*, Revue d'Histoire 1950.

Gubbins, Sir C. McV.: *Resistance Movements in the War*, Journal RUSI 1948.

Hackett, J. W.: *The Employment of Special Forces*, Journal RUSI 1953.

Hamilton-Hill, Donald: *SOE Assignment*, Kimber 1973.

Howarth, Patrick (editor): *Special Operations*, Routledge & Kegan Paul 1955

Institute (Royal) of International Affairs: *Chronology of the Second World War*, 1947

Irving, David (editor): *Breach of Security*, Kimber 1968.

La-Picirella, Joseph: *Témoignages sur le Vercors*.

—— *Mon Journal du Vercors*.

Lemoine, C.: *Vercors, Citadelle de la Résistance*, Nathan 1945.

Marshall, Bruce: *The White Rabbit*, Evans Brothers Ltd. 1952.

Masterman, Sir J. C.: *The Double Cross System*, Sphere 1973.

McCormick, Donald: *The Life of Ian Fleming*, Peter Owen, 1993.

Michel, Henri: *Histoire de la Résistance*, Presses Universitaires de France 1950.

—— *Les Mouvements Clandestins*, Presses Universitaires 1958.

—— *Maquis et maquis*, Revue d'Histoire No. 49.

—— *Bibliographie sur le maquis* and *La Guerre de l'Ombre*, Revue d'Histoire.

Mickiewicz, Adam: *Pan Tadeusz*, Dent 1930.

Millar, George: *Maquis*, Heinemann 1945.

—— *Horned Pigeon*, Heinemann 1947.

Minney, R. J.: *Carve Her Name with Pride*, Newnes 1956.

Moorehead, Alan: *A Late Education*, Hamish Hamilton 1970.

Mornet, J.: *Dans le maquis de Haute Savoie*, Gardet 1946.

Noguères, Henry: *Histoire de la Résistance en France*, Robert Laffont 1972.

O'Malley, Sir Owen: *The Phantom Caravan*, John Murray 1954.

Parkes, James: *History of the Jewish People*, Weidenfeld & Nicolson 1962.

Passy (Col. A. Dewavrin): *10 Duke Street*, Ed. Raoul Solan 1948.

Pergamon Press: *European Resistance Movements, 1939–1945*, 1st symposium (published 1960), 2nd symposium (published 1964).

Piquet-Wicks, Eric: *Four in the Shadows*, Jarrolds 1957.

Piekaliewicz, Janusz: *Secret Agents, Spies and Saboteurs*, David & Charles 1974.

Polish Scientific Publishers: *History of Poland*, Warsaw 1968.

Raczynski, Count Edward, *In Allied London*, Weidenfeld & Nicolson 1962.

Remy (Gilbert Renault-Roulier): *The Silent Company*, Barker 1948.

—— *Courage and Fear*, Barker 1950.

—— *Portrait of a Spy*, Barker 1955.

—— *Ten Steps to Hope*, Barker 1960.

Remy and Livry-Level, Philippe: *The Gates Burst Open* (tr. Search, Pamela), Arco 1955.

Rivet, L.: *Abwehr et Gestapo*, Revue d'Histoire No. 1.

Roos, Hans: *A History of Modern Poland*, tr. from the German by J. R. Foster, Eyre & Spottiswoode 1966.

Rude, F.: *Le dialogue Vercor-Algers*, Revue d'Histoire No. 49.

Ryan, Cornelius: *The Longest Day*, Gollancz 1960.

St Exupéry, A. de: *Letters to a Hostage*, Heinemann 1950.

Schallenberg, Dr E. W.: *Frederick Chopin*, Continental Book Co., Stockholm.

Singer, Kurt: Spy *Omnibus*, W. H. Allen.

Sweet-Escott, Bickham: *Baker Street Irregular*, Methuen 1965.

Tanant, Pierre: *Vercors, Haut-lieu de France*, Arthaud 1948.

Taylor, A. J. P.: *The Origins of the Second World War*, Hamish Hamilton 1961.

Thomson, David: *Europe since Napoleon*, Pelican Books 1966.

Tickell, Jeremy: *Odette*, Chapman & Hall 1949.

Turek, Victor: *Polish Language Press in Canada*, Polish Research Institute in Canada, 1962.

Vomecourt, Philippe de: *Who Lived to see the Day. France in Arms 1940–1945*, Hutchinson 1961.

'Vercors' (Jean Bruller): *Le Silence de la Mer*, Albin Michel 1951.

Walker, Alan (editor): *Frederic Chopin*, Barry & Rockliff 1966.

Wallace, Edgar: *The Four Just Men*, Tallis Press 1905.

Walters, Anne Marie: *Moon Drop to Gascony*, Macmillan 1946.

War Crime Trials, Pub. William Hodge 1949.

Ward, Irene: *FANY Invicta*, Hutchinson 1955.

Wierzynski, Casimir: *The Life and Death of Chopin*, Cassell 1951.

Wighton, Charles: *The Real World of Spies*, Collins Fontana 1965.

Wilmot, Chester: *The Struggle for Europe*, Collins 1952.

Winterbotham, F. W.: *The Ultra Secret*, Weidenfeld & Nicolson 1974.

Woodward, Sir Llewellyn: *British Foreign Policy in the Second World War*, HMSO 1972.

Zamoyski, Adam: *The Underground Factory: Poland in 1939–45*. Article in *History Today*, 1974.

INDEX

Abwehr, 174, 294, 295, 296
Abyssinia, 290
Acre, 134
Addis Ababa, 34
Africa, 26, 34, 38–9, 239, 241; *see also* East Africa; French West Africa; North Africa; South Africa
Albania, 61, 144, 145
Alek, Jakob, 274
Aleppo, 134–5
Alexander, Field Marshal Earl, 271–2
Algeria, 159, 161, 163
Algiers, 159–60, 161–5, 168; Sidi Ferruch, 163–4, 222; SOE base, 187, 198–200, 202, 205, 210, 212, 215, 223
Alpes-Maritimes, 186
Aly Khan, 147
Amanullah Khan, 135
America, *see* United States of America
Amery, Julian, 42, 121, 286
Ankara, 61, 121, 147
Anstey, Colonel John, 168, 200
Antek, 99–101
anti-tank weapons, 62, 99, 187
Apt, 209
Ardèche, 186, 221, 223
Arisaig, 140

'Armand, Pauline', *see* Granville, Christine
Armée Secrète, 180
Armia Krajowa, *see* Home Army
Armstrong, General, 145
Atayan, Irene, 137
Athens, 65, 236, 250
Atkins, Vera, xx, xxi, 153, 261, 270
Atlas mountains, 164
Auschwitz, 259, 287
Australia, 217, 242–4, 246–7, 251
Austria, 39, 79
Avignon, 224

BBC, 200, 217
Bailey, Bill, 130, 133
Balkan Airforce, 230
Balkan Institute, 140
Balkans, 141, 144
Baltic Institute, 140
Banbury, Captain, 219
Barcelonette, 199, 298
Bari, 148, 217, 225, 226, 229, 232–3
Barret, Serge, 220
Bartosik, Admiral Josef, xviii
Battle of Britain, 112
Beaulieu, 266–9
Beaumont-Nesbitt, Major-General F. G., 149
Beck, Josef, 286
Beirut, 124–6, 134

Belfast, 171
Belgian Congo, 239
Belgium, 217
Belgrade, 61, 88, 108–9, 111, 112
Bene_, Eduard, 285
Bengal Lancers, 135
Benghazi, 146
Bennes, Captain Robert ('Bob'), 200
Bennett, John, 109, 110
Berlin, xxiii, 227
Besançon, 289, 295
Beskids mountains, 285
Béthouart, General, 288
Bialoguski, Olga, 264
bigos, 12
Billon, Lieutenant, 178
Black Brigade, 44–5, 287
Bleicher, Hugo, *see* Henri, Colonel
Blixen, Karen, 36, 38
Bobinski, Colonel Wladyslaw, 13, 130
Bomber Command, 227–8
Bonn, 236, 253
Bonnier de la Chapelle, Fernand, 162
Bosphorus, 118, 124
Bourne-Patterson, Major, 153
Brand, Tita, 171
Brema, Marie, 171
Briançon, 212
Bridge, Ann (Lady O'Malley), 65, 78, 104
Brindisi, 228, 229, 231
Britain, *see* England
British Council, 234
British Guarantees for Poland, 285–6
British Intelligence, 148, 159
Brooks, Tony, 223
Brooks-Richards, Francis, 159, 163, 215, 223

Bucharest, 290
Buckmaster, Major Maurice, 153, 160, 176, 197, 294
Budapest, 51, 53, 59, 62, 66–9, 78–80, 87, 109; Christine arrives, 42–3; accommodation, 45–7, 85; British Embassy, 64–5, 93, 97, 101, 105; Second Bureau prison, 89, 91–5; Christine and Andrew's departure from, 101–6, 108; George Gizycki posted to, 290
Bulgaria, 59, 112–13, 116–17, 119
Burgess, Guy, 267
bustards, 136

Cairo, 85, 118, 138, 147, 245; Christine and Andrew's life in, 128–30, 133, 274; SOE organization in, 140–1; Rustem Building, xxii, 132; Gezira Sporting Club, 136, 139, 141, 143; Zamalek, 142–3; SOE, 160; Christine returns to, 233, 242; post-war, 263, 271
Cambridge University, 171
camels, 136
Cammaerts, Emile, 171
Cammaerts, Francis ('Roger'), xix–xx; collaboration with Christine, 160, 178–9, 187–8, 194, 197, 200, 205, 207, 221–2; requests assistant, 167, 176–7; background, 171–3; arrival in France, 173; suspicious of network, 173–4; establishes new network, 175–6; security-consciousness, 175; territory, 175–6, 186; troubled by fate of 'Alice', 177; activities in France, 187, 197–201, 204–5, 209–10; friendship with Paul Herault,

188–9; friendship with the Reys, 189–91; and battle for Vercors, 201–2, 204, 223; arrested and freed by Christine, 210–18, 299; final days in France, 219–24; and Christine's last days, 244, 249; and Christine's death, 258–9, 275; at Vercors commemorations, xxv, 261, 277

Camps, Doctor F. E., 256

Canada, 121, 271, 291

Cannes, 174

Carpathian Brigade, 138, 286, 292

Carpathian Lancers, 130, 139, 301

Carpathian mountains, 69, 73, 80

Casablanca, 161

Casimir the Great, King, 19

Catawe Pasha, Madeleine and Ashlan, 147

Catherine the Great, Empress, 20

Catholic Church, 226

Catroux, General, 134

Cavalaire, 198

Cavendish-Bentinck, Bill, 234

CFLN (Comité Français de Libération Nationale), 181

Chabeuil, 201

Chamberlain, Neville, 150, 285

Chavant, Eugène ('Clément'), 180, 185

Chetniks, 143

Chiang Kai-Shek, 286

children, 137, 262

Chinese guerrillas, 149

Chopin, Frederic, xxviii, 6–7

Christmas, Polish, 11

Christopher, Stanley, xviii–xix, 72, 244

Churchill, Captain Peter ('Michel'), 171, 173–4, 268

Churchill, Winston, 41–2, 76–7, 78, 230, 286, 290; and formation of SOE, 149–50; at Teheran, 167; orders SOE records destroyed, 270

Cicha Dolina, 53

Citroen, André, 4

Clark, General Mark W., 162

Col de Larche, 208–9, 220

Coleman, Captain, 153

Communists, 94

Compiègne, 173

concentration camps, 88, 94, 287

conscientious objectors, 171–2, 173

Conseil National de la Résistance, 162–3

Cooper, Duff, 165

Cooper, Lady Diana, 165

Copenhagen, 140

Cornioley, Henri, 296

Corsica, 164, 223, 295

Cossacks, 15, 20

Costa de Beauregard, Commandant, 186

Cowburn, Major Ben, 160, 268

Cowie, Mervyn, 239, 300

Cowles, Virginia, 240

Cracow (Krakow), 108, 284; dragon, 5; University, 28, 49

Crawley, Aidan, 112, 117–19, 238, 240

Crawshaw, Nina, xxi–xxii, xxiv

Crest, 189, 196, 204

cricket, 127

Cyprus, 241

Czech, Wladek (ski-teacher), 29, 31–2

Czechoslovakia, 39, 40, 66, 226, 285

Czestochowa, 284; Black Virgin of, xxxi, 24, 259, 275

Dakar, 161
Dalton, Hugh, 149–50
Danube, River, 48, 64, 65, 67, 68, 79, 287
Danzig, 40
Darlan, Admiral, 162
Daujat, Monsieur, 177
Davis, General, 145
D-Day, 167, 184, 200
de Chastelain, A. G. G., 61, 110, 121, 133, 272, 290
de Gaulle, General, 153, 161–2, 180, 181, 200, 298
de Guélis, Jacques, 163
de Montcheuil, Father, 203
Deakin, F. W. D., xxv–xxvii, 40
Deakin, Pussi, xxv–xxvi, 137, 245
Delegatura Rzadu, 158
Delestraint, General, 181
Denmark, 227
Dentz, General, 134
Descours, Colonel ('Bayard'), 180, 186, 200, 296
Die, 191
Digne, xix, 177, 189, 208, 210, 223, 233, 245; 'Roger' imprisoned in, 211–12, 216–18
Dobski, Julian, 245
Dodds-Parker, Douglas, 163, 168, 223
dogs, 64, 115, 116, 128, 207
Dolan, Captain Charles, 171, 173
dollars, 77, 78
Donovan, Mr Justice, 257
Drôme, 177, 179, 189, 194, 198, 205, 297
Dub, 49
Duch, General, 288
Dunford, Michael, 234, 239, 241, 262, 263, 300–1
Dunkirk, 79, 109, 152
dwor (Polish manor-house), 8–9

East Africa, 33, 34, 38–9, 41, 241
East African Tourist Association, 240
East Prussia, 40
Ede, Chuter, 238
Eden, Sir Anthony, 149
Edgar, Captain, 199
Egypt, 190
Eisenhower, General Dwight D., 167
El Alamein, 161
England, 41, 43, 49, 50, 78, 81, 147
English Channel, 151, 167
Euphrates, River, 134

FANY (First Aid and Nursing Yeomanry), 156–7, 159, 160, 164, 259, 295
Far East, 217
Farge, Yves, 180, 202
Farouk, King, 147
FFI (Forces Françaises de l'Intérieur), 185, 196, 198, 200, 298
Fielding, Major Xan ('Armand de Pont Levé'), 205–6, 209–11, 216, 217–18, 299
Finland, 42, 110
First World War, 11, 14, 18, 27, 82, 195
Fischer, Doctor ('Ferrier'), 203, 204
Fleming, Ian, 263–6
Fleming, Major Valentine, 264
Floiras, Auguste ('Albert'), 177, 204
Foot, M. R. D., xiv, 148
Force 139, 226, 230
Foreign Office, 42, 65, 149, 234, 236
France, 27, 236, 243; alliance with Poland, 39, 40, 49, 62; Polish

Government in exile in, 42, 43; fall of, 63, 70, 78, 86, 149, 155, 291, 292; SOE operations in, 151–2, 155, 295; Liberation, 155, 163, 198, 207; Christine's missions to, 157, 160, 165–8, 177–8; Allied landings in, 159–60, 197, 199, 209; Occupation, 162, 182; cultural education in, 188

Free French, 153, 161, 163

Fréjus, 198

French Resistance (Maquis), xvii, 152, 162–3, 164, 173, 179, 221, 297; organization, 180–6, 195; Axis troops desert to, 197, 207–9; revenge killings, 213, 214–15; hospital, 296

French West Africa, 26, 162

Ffrench, Mrs, 225

Frisby, Roger, 257

Galetti, Gilbert, 208

Galicia, 285

Ganimède, Captain, 203, 204

Gap, 188, 189, 219–20

Gard, 221

Gauze, Major, 142

Gazala, 292

Gdynia, 140

Geneva, 238

Geneva Convention, 156–7

George Medal, 234

Getlich, Charles, 23–4

Getlich, Christine, see Granville, Christine

Geyer, Capitaine ('Thivollet'), 180, 186

Giraud, General Henri, 161–2

Gizycki, Christine, see Granville, Christine

Gizycki, George (Jerzy), 33, 263, 271, 272, 290, 291–2; marriage, xxiii–xxiv, 25–7, 39; in Africa, 34–9, 41; bravery, 42; joins clandestine organization, 110, 120; and Christine's affair, 110, 119, 133–4; reunions with Christine, 120–1, 133–4; death, 292

Gleiwitz, 40

Godfrey, Rear Admiral John, 264

Goebbels, Joseph, 60

Goldfeder, Bronislaw, 4

Goldfeder, Josef, 4

Goldfeder, Roza, 4, 9

Goldfeder family, 3–4, 18, 19, 21–2, 25

Goorals, 22–3

Granowski, Captain, 228

Granville, Christine (Christine Skarbek; Christine Getlich; Christine Gizycki; 'Pauline Armand'): birth, 8; nickname, 8, 266; childhood, 9–12; commitment to Poland, 10, 12, 41, 188; Jewishness, 10, 19; affinity for nature, 10–11; affinity for horses, 12–13; first meeting with Andrew, 13; education, 17–20; elected Beauty Queen, 19; and father's death, 21–2; employment and illness, 22, 98; skiing expeditions, 22–3, 25, 27; marriage with Charles Getlich, 23–4; visits Czestochowa, 24; unsuccessful romance, 24–5; marriage with George Gizycki, xxiii–xxiv, 25–7, 39; dabbles in journalism, 26–7; second meeting with Andrew, 33; in Africa, 34–9, 41; returns to England, 41–2; affinity for Britain, 41–2, 142, 238;

Granville, Christine – *cont.*
    travels to Budapest, 42–3; meets
    Andrew in Budapest, 44–5,
    48–9; affair with Andrew, 50–1,
    61–2, 85–6, 110, 119, 133–4; first
    journey into Poland, 51–7;
    clandestine activities in
    Hungary, 59, 62–8, 78–81, 85–6;
    affinity with dogs, 64, 115, 116,
    128, 207; admirers, 64, 135, 138,
    166, 206, 225, 232, 271; second
    journey to Poland, 70, 71–5; and
    mother's fate, 72, 188, 244;
    relationship with Ledochowski,
    74–5; emotional life, 74, 129;
    third journey to Poland, 76–8;
    fourth journey to Poland, 87–8;
    arrested and imprisoned in
    Budapest, 90–1, 95–9; departure
    from Hungary, 99–108; takes
    name of Granville, 104; reunion
    in Belgrade, 108–9; dislike of
    music, xxviii, 111; journey to
    Istanbul, 110–19; reunions with
    George, 120–1, 133–4;
    suspected by Deuxième
    Bureau, 122–3, 130–1, 139, 274;
    journey through Middle East,
    122–8; reception in Beirut,
    125–6; apprehensions, 129;
    dismissed by Wilkinson, 132–4;
    mission to Syria, 134–6; love of
    children, 137, 262; sexuality,
    138, 158; friendship with
    Howarth, 140–5; takes
    parachute course, 146; social
    life, 147; and Andrew's affair,
    148, 232; works for British
    Intelligence, 148; joins SOE,
    148, 155, 157–61; life in Algiers,
    159–60, 164–5; and firearms,
    xxviii, 159, 168, 262; cycling,

    159, 212, 299; collaboration with
    'Roger', 160, 178–9, 187–8, 194,
    197, 200, 205, 207, 221–2;
    preparations for mission to
    France, 165–8; friendship with
    John Roper, 166, 224–5;
    fatalism, 166; flies to France,
    168, 177–8; friendship with Paul
    Herault, 188–9; friendship with
    the Reys, 189–91; evades
    capture, 197, 208; and battle for
    Vercors, 201–2, 204, 223;
    described by Fielding, 206;
    moves to Italy, 206, 225, 229;
    influences Russians to desert,
    207–9; subverts Col de Larche
    garrison, 208–9, 220; rescues
    'Roger' at Digne, 212–18; final
    days in France, 219–24; returns
    to London, 224; financial
    probity, 224, 271; religion, 224;
    reunion with Andrew, 229–30;
    aborted mission to Poland,
    231–2; changed relationship
    with Andrew, 232–3, 234, 241;
    awarded medals and honours,
    234–5, 239, 272; relationship
    with Dunford, 234, 239, 241;
    seeks employment after war,
    234, 236–8, 242, 263, 271–2;
    relinquishes commission, 234,
    271; refuses bequest, 237, 271;
    depression, 237; British
    citizenship, 238, 240; returns to
    Africa, 239; business plan,
    242–4, 247–8; Polish friends,
    244–5; suffers accident, 245;
    works as stewardess, 246, 251–2,
    265; relationship with
    Muldowney, 246–55; death, 255;
    funeral 258–60; relationship
    with Ian Fleming, 263–6;

training at Beaulieu, 268–9; love of code names, 270
Greece, 144, 219, 250
'Green Frontier', 102, 289–90
Grenoble, 175, 180, 181, 204
Grodzicki, Jan, *see* Ledochowski, Count Wladyslaw
Gubbins, Colonel (General) Colin McVean, 141, 151, 172, 259, 286
Guest, E. R., 256
Gunn, Havard ('Bambus'), xxix–xxx, 166, 217, 221
Guyotville, 163

Habdank, xxxi, 5, 283
Hadassah Hospital, 144
Haifa, 127, 144
Halifax, Lord, 149
Hallowes, Odette ('Lise'), xiv, xv, 173–4, 268
Hambro, Sir Charles, 151
Hamburg, 236
Hamilton, Norman, 242, 248
Hamilton-Hill, Donald, 172, 219
Hancza, Colonel, 225–6
Harker, Paul, 232, 236
Harrods, 237, 300
Henri, Colonel (Hugo Bleicher), 174, 296
Henry II, Emperor, 5
Herault, Paul, 188–9
Heslop, Robert, 268
Himmler, Heinrich, 287
Hissam, Prince, 135–6
Hitler, Adolf, 39–40, 61, 78, 87, 162, 295
Holland, Colonel, 40
Holland, Major John, 151
Holliday, Lily, 259
Home Army (Armia Krajowa), 55–6, 70, 133, 158, 226, 227
Horko, Tadeusz, xxi, 27

Horthy, Regent, 98, 289
Howarth, Patrick, 160, 165, 234, 244, 248; takes over SOE in Cairo, 140–5, 274; death, 262; at Christine's funeral, 258; poem on Christine, 292–3
Howe, Edward, 263
Howe, Ted, 142
Hudson, Bill, 143
Huet, Colonel ('Hervieux'), 180, 186
Humphreys, Christmas, 258
Humphreys, Leslie, 293
Hungary, 58, 70, 81, 112, 117, 121, 226; Poles in, 43, 45, 289; under Germans, 59, 79; as escape route, 88, 95, 109, 143; frontier, 107; Britain breaks off relations with, 122; weather, 128; anti-aircraft defences, 231
Hyde Park Corner, 245

identity papers, 166, 297
India House, 237
Inter-Services Research Bureau, 150
Irish, 103, 104
Ironside, General, 286
Iscandria (Alexandretta), 124
Isère, 175, 179
Israel, 128
Istanbul, 60–1, 110, 114, 117–19, 263
Italy, 43, 61, 71, 110, 144, 197; Andrew in, 159, 225–6; SOE operations in, 164, 295; Christine moves to, 206, 225, 229; base for operations into Poland, 228, 231–2

January Rising, 13–14
Japan, 149

Jaski, Doctor, 144
Jazlowiec, 18
Jazwinski, Major, 228
Jennings, Chief Inspector George, 256
Jepson, Captain (Major) Selwyn, xiv, 153–7, 172, 261, 294
Jerusalem, xxiii, 127, 133, 141
Jews, xiii, 19–21, 55, 72, 182, 226, 287–8; imprisoned in Budapest, 89, 94; tailor advising SOE, 295
John Casimir, 284
Joint Technical Board, 150
Jouneau, George ('Commandant Georges'), 184
Jouve, Doctor Paul, 177, 212

Kennedy, Andrew (Andrew Kowerski), xx, xxvii–xxxii, 27, 261; first meeting with Christine, 13; affinity for horses, 13, 16; birth, 15; childhood, 15–16; education and military service, 28; caught in avalanche, 28–33; second meeting with Christine, 33; clandestine activities in Hungary, 44–7, 58–9, 62–70, 78–86; meets Christine in Budapest, 44–5, 48–9; arrested, 46, 59, 80, 87–8; loss of his leg, 49–50; affair with Christine, 50–1, 61–2, 85–6, 110, 119, 133–4; and Christine's trips to Poland, 52–3, 54, 57, 57, 76, 87; admired by Kate O'Malley, 65, 97; and Christine's relationship with Ledochowski, 75–6; collaborates with Colonel Schell, 81–5; arrested and imprisoned in Budapest, 89–99; departure from Hungary, 99–108; takes name of Kennedy, 104; reunion in Belgrade, 108–9; journey to Istanbul, 110–19; meeting with George, 119–20; suspected by Deuxième Bureau, 122–3, 130–1, 139, 274; journey through Middle East, 122–8; reception in Beirut, 125–6; apprehensions, 129; dismissed by Wilkinson, 132–4; mission to Syria, 134–6; welcomed by General Kopanski, 138–9; friendship with Howarth, 140–5; takes parachute course, 144–6; leg operation, 144–5; social life, 147; joins parachutists' school, 147–8; affair in London, 148, 232; moved to Italy, 159, 225–6; gives Christine cycling and shooting lessons, 159; receives letters from Christine, 165; audience with Pope, 225–6; reunion with Christine, 229–30; aborted mission to Poland, 231–2; changed relationship with Christine, 232–3, 234, 241; makes life in Germany, 236, 271, 274; car crash, 241; business plan, 242–4, 247–8; and Christine's last days, 248–9, 253; and Christine's death, 256, 259–60; death, 262, 274
Kensal Green, xxxi, 258, 275
Kenya, 34, 239–41, 242, 262, 301
Kenya Tourist Travel Association, 240
Kenya-Uganda railway, 36, 37
Kenyan Civil Aviation, 240
Klauber, Major I. C., 229
Kojecki, Joseph, 255

Konopka, Baron Adam, 45–8, 51
Kopanski, General Stanislaus,
    138–9, 259, 286, 292
Koszyce, 52, 53, 74, 76, 77
Kowerska, Maria, 14–16
Kowerski, Andrew, *see* Kennedy,
    Andrew
Kowerski, George, 29–32
Kowerski, Stanislas, 14–16, 27
Kowerski estate, 28–9
Kowerski family, 13–14, 27
Kozak, L., xxxi
Kritzer, Major, 228
Kryzanowska, Justyna, 6
Krzeptowski (mountain guide), 32
Kuibishev, 141

La Britière, 191
La Chapelle-en-Vercors, 193, 202
La-Picirella, Joseph, 191, 196
Labunie estate, 13, 15, 27, 284
Laski, Father, 86
Latiano, 228, 229
Lebanon, 124, 134
Ledochowski, Count Wladyslaw
    ('Jan Grodzicki'), 73–8, 87, 147
Lefort, Cecily Marie ('Alice'),
    176–7
Lenti, 106
letter boxes, 175, 177, 296
Lezzard, Captain Julian, 205
Liaison France-America, 221
Liège, 253, 254
Litvinov, Maksim Maksimovich,
    138
Lobkowitz, Prince Eddie, 66–8,
    147
London, 105, 165; Gizyckis live
    in, 42; Polish Government in
    exile in, 133, 140, 158, 188, 227,
    230, 274, 291; Andrew's affair in,
    148, 232; post-war, 237, 240, 243

Lubienska, Countess Teresa, 259,
    301
Lubomirski, Prince Marcin, 86
Lwow (Lemberg), 21, 50, 83
Lyons, 177, 180, 186, 187, 221,
    222, 224

McCormick, Donald, 266
Maciag, Captain, 143
Macmillan, Harold, 165
Madam X, 262–3
Maginot Line, 71
Maitland Wilson, General Sir
    Henry, 134
Mallaby, Dick, 144
Manneville, Count, 285
Maquis, *see* French Resistance
Marriott, H. R., 293
Marsac, Commandant, 174
Marseilles, 186, 198
Martin, Doctor, 180
Marusarz, Janek, 51, 53–4, 57, 87
Mauthausen concentration camp,
    86
'mercy killings', 87, 289
Meyer, Doctor, 144
MI5, 154, 257
MI6, 269
Michael L., 59–61, 144
Michalek (patriot), 58, 69
Michalof, 242–4, 247
microfilms, 110–12, 118, 121, 131,
    132, 138, 290
Middle East, 69, 85, 110, 124, 129,
    134, 136, 234, 236, 241
Mihailovitch, General, 143
Mikolajczyk, Prime Minister, 230
Mikus (artist), 84
Mitchell, Sir Philip, 239
Mitford, Captain, 135
Mittelhauser, General, 292
Mlodziesyn estate, 3, 8

MO4, 132
Mombasa, 34–6
Monnetier-l'Allemand, 205
Monopoli, 225, 229, 231, 234
Mont Cenis tunnel, 196
Montagu of Beaulieu, Edward, Lord, 268
Montauphin, 189
Montélimar, 177, 200
Montgomery, Field Marshal Bernard, 213
Morel, G., 153
Morocco, 161, 162
Morrell, Bill, 110
Moscow, 230
Moulin, Jean, 181
Muldowney, Dennis George, 246–58
Munich, 274
Munkacs, 82
Munn, J. W., 163
'Musketeers', 56, 70, 86, 88, 109, 111, 118, 133, 142, 291
Muzlumian, Koko, 135

Nairne, Jacqueline, 176
Nairobi, 36–8, 239, 241, 263
Napoleon Bonaparte, 7, 20, 49
Narvik, 288
Nazis, 21, 69, 149, 172, 226
New Zealand, 246, 292
Nice, 217, 221
No. I Military Mission to Poland, 40
Noon, Mrs, 37
Normandy landings, 45, 186, 199
North Africa, 161, 162, 201, 228
Nowy Sacz, 73

Old Bailey, 257
O'Malley, Kate, 65, 78, 89, 102, 103, 104, 109
O'Malley, Lady, see Bridge, Ann

O'Malley, Sir Owen, 65–6, 78, 102–5, 107, 121, 148, 290
Operation Overlord, 167
Oran, 161
'Oriental' Legion ('Mongols'), 207, 210, 299
OSS, 163
Ostuni, 148, 225, 228, 229
Oxford University, 29, 135, 140

Paddington, 238
'Pale of Settlement', 20
Palestine, 78, 126, 128, 292
Palfi, Count Pali, 68
parachute operations, 144–6, 148, 158–9, 161, 164, 190, 191–2, 215
Paris, 56, 76, 165, 173, 219, 224
Patch, General, 221
Pentonville prison, 258
Perkins, Captain (Colonel) H. B., 158, 226, 272, 273
Pétain, Marshal Philippe, 153, 188, 195
petrol, 184, 190
Philby, Kim, 267
pilots, 80, 85, 112, 119
Pius XII, Pope, 225–6
Polish, 14, 232
Polish Army, 69, 78, 86, 118, 131, 132
Polish Deuxième Bureau, 122–3, 130–1, 139, 291
Polish IVth Department (Quartermastership), 56
Polish Government in exile: in France, 42, 43; in London, 133, 140, 158, 188, 227, 230, 274, 291
Polish Hearth, 254
Polish Resistance, 55, 143; see also Home Army
Polish School for Parachutists, 148, 225

Polish 7th Bureau, 227
Polish Sixth Bureau, 143, 158, 228, 229, 231
Polish Socialist Party, 59, 287
Polish Underground Movement, 87, 109, 111, 227, 288; Press, 56
polo, 135
Pomorze, 40
Popiel, Ludwig, 63, 99, 130, 251, 254–5, 301
Porter (friend), 128–9
Pretel, General, 288
Prince Albert Victor's Own Regiment, 135
Pripet marshes, 27
prisoners of war, 65, 87, 112, 118, 121
Proust, Marcel, 188
Provence, 160, 194
Przewlocki, Sophie, 14
Pupin, Aimé, 180
Puslowska, Countess, 248

RAF, 159, 172, 229, 239, 272, 273
Rabinovitch, Adolphe ('Arnaud'), 173, 295
Raczkiewicz, President, 42
Raczkowski, Sophie, 128, 144, 291
Radziminski (unfortunate suitor), xxi, 64, 71, 283, 288
Ramat David, 144, 146
Rauhine (ship), 246, 252
Ravensbruck, 296
Red Cross, 132, 204, 209–10
Rée, Harry, 171–2
Reform Club, xii, 253–4
Renoir, Claude, 209–11
Rey, Jean, 189–91
Rey, Sylviane, 189–91, 204, 222
Reynaud, Pierre ('Alain'), 177
Rhône Valley, 175, 180, 187, 197, 221

Romans, 181
Rome, 225
Rommel, General Erwin, 141
Roosevelt, Franklin D., 167
Roper, John, 212, 215, 217, 219, 250, 299; returns to London, 224–5, 244; friendship with Christine, 166, 224–5; in Italy, 229; aborted mission to Poland, 232; joins Foreign Office, 236; at Christine's funeral, 258
Rothermere, Ann, Lady, 264–5
Route Napoléon, 198, 205
Rowles, Margaret, 266
Rumania, 42, 43
Russia, 15, 20, 27, 71, 122, 140; German invasion, 111–12, 121, 132, 138
Russian Revolution, 104, 110
Ruthenians, 82
Rydz-Smigly, Marshal, 286

Sacré-Coeur Convent, 17, 18
Saillans, 189
St Aignan, 202
St Croix Rose, Evelyn Beatrice, 264
St Etienne, 221
St Jorioz, 173
St Julien-en-Vercors, 187, 202
St Martin-en-Vercors, 178, 193, 196, 202
St Nazaire-le-Désert, 205
St Nizier, 179, 201
St Tropez, 217, 223
Sale, Betty, 159
Samuel, Doctor, 180
Sardinia, 164, 295
Savournon, 205
Schell, Colonel Zoltan, 81–2, 84–5
Schenk, Albert, 213–15, 217
Selborne, Lord, 230

Sereni, Captain Antoine ('Casimir'), 204
Service de Travail Obligatoire (STO), 182
Seyne-les-Alpes, 205–7, 209–12, 215, 217, 299
Shaw Savill Line, 246
Shellbourne Hotel, xxxi, 253, 256
Sicily, 164, 295
Sikorski, General Ladislas, 42, 76–7, 288, 291
Silesia, 230, 284
Sillitoe, Sir Percy, 257
Simon, André, 153
Simplon railway route, 197
Sinn Fein, 149
Sisteron, 219
Skarbek, Alexander, 7
Skarbek, Colonel Andrew, xviii, 7, 256, 259
Skarbek, Charles, 9
Skarbek, Christine (Krystyna), see Granville, Christine
Skarbek, Count Frederic, 6
Skarbek, Frederic Florian, 6
Skarbek, Helena, 9
Skarbek, Count Jerzy, 3–5, 6, 10–12, 13, 17; Christine's birth and nickname, 8, 266; financial difficulties and move to Warsaw, 18; illness and death, 21–2
Skarbek, John, xviii, 21, 256
Skarbek, Countess Ludwika, 6
Skarbek, Martin, 9
Skarbek, Count Stanislas, 7
Skarbek, Countess Stephanie (née Goldfeder), 3, 7, 10–11; financial difficulties and move to Warsaw, 18; husband's illness and death, 21–2; remains in Warsaw, 54–5, 72; Christine's concern for, 72, 188, 244

Skarbek family, 5–7, 25
Skinner's Horse, 135
Slovakia, 52, 53, 66, 72, 74, 77
Smith, John, 267
SOE, (Special Operations Executive), xiv–xvi, 61, 109, 132, 140–2; Christine joins, 148; history, 148–59; women in, xv, 150, 156–7, 168, 294; F Section, 153–4, 156–7, 160, 163, 198, 223, 293; Baker Street headquarters, 153, 225; recruitment, 155–7; operations into Poland, 158–9, 226–9, 230; 'Massingham' operation, 160, 163–4, 201; pseudonyms, 161; scientific support, 166; Special Training Schools, 171, 172; and 'Roger', 186, 198–201; maps, 197; treatment of Christine, 236, 242; Beaulieu training school, 266–9; disbanded and records destroyed, 270
Sofia, 61, 111, 112, 115
Sokolov, Florian, 286, 291
Sokolov, Nahoum, 128
Sorenson, Commandant ('Chasuble'), 209–11, 216, 218, 219, 234
Sosnokowski, General, 227
South Africa, 37, 39, 251, 265
Spain, 288
Spanish Civil War, 286
SPOC (Special Projects Operational Centre), 200
Stalin, Joseph, 167, 230, 290
Stangl, Franz, 289
stewardesses, 251–2
storks, 124
Storrs, Peter, 222, 300
Suez Canal, 128
supply drops, 191–4, 201, 231, 298

Sweet-Escott, Bickham, 158, 272
Syria, 78, 122, 124, 126, 134, 136, 292
Szabo, Violette, xv, 266
Szczerbinski, M., 119
szlachta (gentry), 8, 14, 284

Tain l'Hermitage, 180
Tamplin, Colonel Guy, xxii, 130–1, 133, 139, 141–2, 144
Tangmere, 171, 266
tanks, 62, 200, 220
Tarnowski, Andrew, 32, 108, 130
Tarnowski, Sophie and Chouquette, xxii
Tatar, General, 225
'Tatar' (guide), 208, 299
Tatra mountains, 42, 52–4, 73
Tavernier, Gilbert, 207
Taylor, George, 42, 142
Teheran Summit Conference, 167, 234
Teschen (Cieszyn), xxi, 27, 285
Teutonic Knights, 5
Threlfall, Colonel H. M., 226, 229, 231, 232, 300
Tigris, River, 134
Tito, Josip Broz, Marshal, 143
Tobruk, 147
Tokyo, 122
Tommy (O'Malley's PA), 103–8
Toulon, xxv, 162
Tournissa, Captain ('Paquebot'), 178, 193, 196
Treblinka, 287, 289
Truszkowski, Major Richard, 141
Trzebnica estate, 8
Tunisia, 295
Turkey, 20, 60, 110, 113–14, 116–17, 124, 126, 134
Turrel, Monsieur, 205–6, 212, 215

Ubaye, 198
Ukraine, 26, 110, 136
Ulmann, Doctor, 203, 204
Union-Castle Line, xi, 251
United States of America, 26, 67, 79, 137

Valence, 181, 191–2
Vansittart, Sir Robert, 42, 286
Vassieux, xxiv, 178, 191–3, 196, 202, 277
Vatican, 86
Vaucluse, 221
Vercors, 175, 178, 196, 198, 207, 233, 259; topography, 179–80; Resistance in, 181, 184–5; liberated, 186; under attack, 191–3; battle for, 201–4; commemorations, xxiv–xxv, 243, 261, 277; Resistance hospital, 296
Verdillac, General, 134
Victoria, Queen, 136
Villers-de-Lans, 196
Vistula, River, 230, 231
Vitold, Grand Duke of Lithuania, 19
Voigt, Freddy, 42
von Weise, General, 207
Vosges mountains, 288

WAAF, 229, 234, 239, 271, 294
Waem, Max, 214–17
Wake, Nancy, 266
Walewska, Maria, 7
War Cabinet, 149
Warsaw, 18, 21, 26, 27; wartime, 54–7, 72; British soldiers in, 87, 109; Underground, 109, 227; Military Mission, 141; rising, 228, 230–2; British Embassy, 234; falls to Swedes, 284; ghetto, 287–8

White Eagle Club, xxix, 248–9
Wieliczka, 58
Wigan, 247
Wilkinson, Captain P. A., 158
Wilkinson, Major (Colonel) Peter, 132–4, 139, 141, 274, 291
Willetts, H. T., 158–9
Wilson, Field Marshal Sir Henry, 200
Winchester Castle (ship), ix, 251
Witherington, Pearl, 176–90, 268, 296
Witkowski, Stanislaw, 56–7, 133, 291
Woolmer, Detective-Inspector, 255
Wragby, 173

Young, James, 140
Yugoslavia, 59, 102, 107–8, 117, 145, 287; German invasion, 121; civil war, 143; anti-aircraft defences, 251

Zakopane, xix, 22, 25, 29, 248; Andrew meets Christine and George, 33, 44, 120; as entry point to Poland, 42, 51–2, 57
zal (Polish national melancholy), 10
Zamosc, 17, 27
Zamoyjska, Countess, 29
Zamoyski, John, 27
Zeller, General ('Joseph'), 180, 185, 198–9, 201–2, 297